canyon ranch cooking

canyon ranch cooking

BRINGING THE SPA HOME

JEANNE JONES

HarperCollins*Publishers*

All photographs by Tom Eckerle

except pages vii, 25, 88, 89, 154, 155, 167, 202, 203, 235, 259, 267, 281, 287, 366, 367, 400, 401 by Dana Gallagher

The author is grateful to Calvin Klein Home, in New York City, and Seeds, in Great Barrington, Massachusetts, for their help.

Canyon Ranch is a registered trademark of Canyon Ranch, Inc.
Website: www.canyonranch.com
Telephone: 800-742-9000

HarperCollins books may be purchased for educational, business, or sales promotional use. For information please write: Special Markets Department, HarperCollins Publishers, Inc., 10 East 53rd Street, New York, NY 10022.

FIRST EDITION

Designed by Ph.D

Library of Congress Cataloging-in-Publication Data

Jones, Jeanne.
 Canyon Ranch cooking : bringing the spa home / Jeanne Jones. — 1st ed.
  p. cm.
  Includes index.
  ISBN 0-06-018718-2
  1. Cookery. 2. Low-fat diet—Recipes. 3. Salt-free diet—Recipes. 4. Canyon Ranch. I. Title.
 TX714.J6497 1998
 641.5'638—dc21   97-24125

98 99 00 01 02 ❖/RRD 10 9 8 7 6 5 4 3

To Enid and Mel Zuckerman, *Canyon Ranch Founders*,
whose vision and dedication have positively changed the lives
of thousands of people

contents

preface

I first met Enid and Mel Zuckerman, the owners of the Canyon Ranch Fitness Resorts, almost twenty years ago when they invited me to Tucson to see the property in the foothills of the Catalina Mountains where they wanted to build a world-class fitness resort. They asked me if I would be their food consultant and design the menus for the resort if their dream came true. Their vision, determination, and hard work made it happen. The ranch has become one of the most popular and most highly regarded spas in the world. Their success led to still bigger dreams, and the resort in Tucson now shares the spotlight with the Canyon Ranch in the Berkshires, in Lenox, Massachusetts.

I feel very fortunate to have been able to share in the Zuckermans' dream. For many years my job has been to keep the Canyon Ranch cuisine on the cutting edge of food fashion while holding to our commitment to use only the highest-quality ingredients in our nutritionally balanced and calorie-controlled menus. As I travel around the world I am always in search of innovative food preparation and presentation ideas that we can adapt to meet our criterion. As new trends develop in international cuisine you will always find them reflected in our menus.

Designing the many different types of menus we offer at Canyon Ranch and developing the necessary recipes is a never-ending challenge. It is also an ongoing culinary adventure that is both fun and rewarding for me, our chefs, and our nutrition professionals.

This book is not just a collection of recipes. It is more like a Canyon Ranch cooking course, complete with all of the tips and techniques we use to develop our recipes. Whether you are a past guest, or someone who has never been to one of the resorts, this book can teach you how to design your own Canyon Ranch menus and create new and imaginative dishes based on your own favorites as well as using our recipes.

Also included are a variety of international and ethnic menus and a wide assortment of presentation ideas that you can use for entertaining. In fact, you have all of the information necessary to help you in planning menus for your own Canyon Ranch weekend at home.

As Mel Zuckerman often says, "Wellness is not a destination. It's a journey." The purpose of this book is to empower you to either start, or continue, on your own journey to a healthier and happier culinary lifestyle.

KATHLEEN JOHNSON, M.S., R.D., Program Director Nutrition Services, Canyon Ranch, Tucson
KATHIE SWIFT, M.S., R.D., Director Nutrition Services, Canyon Ranch, in the Berkshires
MARILYN MAJCHRZAK, M.S., R.D., Food Development Manager, Canyon Ranch, Tucson

nutrition made easy

TIPS FROM CANYON RANCH

In our food-oriented, health-conscious society, you can't open a magazine without learning about the latest unbeatable diet, shocking new research findings, or the ultimate food fad. Nutrition tips often sound contradictory, and the "facts" about various foods seem to change over time. It is confusing, but don't despair.

The Canyon Ranch nutrition philosophy offers a simple, consistent, and practical approach for eating healthier every day. The guiding principles are balance, moderation, and mindfulness. Our meals are high in fiber, abundant in fruits and vegetables, and low in fat, but there's plenty of room for personal preferences as well. Good nutrition consists of a wide variety of foods served in moderate portions.

tips and techniques for canyon ranch cooking

HOW TO ENHANCE FLAVOR AND IMPROVE TEXTURE WITH MINIMUM FAT

We taste only four things with the taste buds on our tongues: sweet, salt, sour, and bitter. Every other "taste" is actually smell. In other words, flavor is olfactory, or achieved by our sense of smell as well as our sense of taste. That is why many people say they can't "taste" when they have a cold. The truth is that they can still taste just fine, but they can't smell. With the worst cold imaginable you can still determine whether something is sweet, salty, sour, or bitter, but you can't tell whether it's chocolate, vanilla, or strawberry if you can't see it, because you can't smell it!

30: Slice fatty fish, such as salmon and mackerel, paper-thin and cook without any added fat either under the broiler or in a hot, non-stick skillet for about 1 minute or until opaque. The fish releases its own fat and has a wonderful texture.

31: Use tofu (soybean curd) as a flavor carrier and to extend volume in sauces and salad dressings. Good examples in this book are the Tofu Mayonnaise and Thousand Island Dressing.

32: Marinate tofu cubes in stock, salad dressing, or fruit juice and add to soups and salads. Tofu is a true culinary chameleon. It completely absorbs the taste of any marinade.

33: Use tofu to make egg- and dairy-free custards and to thicken sauces. This is essential in vegan cooking where dairy products cannot be used.

34: Bake tofu or cook it in a pan which has been sprayed with non-stick cooking spray, rather than cooking it in oil, for a firm texture with less fat.

35: Smoke fruits, vegetables, grains, fish, poultry, and meat to enhance flavor. This can be accomplished either by adding aromatic wood chips to a barbecue or putting the chips in a pan under a steamer basket and then placing the food to be smoked in the basket. Cover the basket and allow the food to smoke until the desired flavor is achieved.

36: Grill over aromatic wood such as hickory, mesquite, or applewood or add herbs and spices such as rosemary, cloves, and cinnamon sticks to the fire to enhance the flavor of what's to be grilled.

37: Cook en papillote (either parchment paper or foil) to seal in moisture.

38: Use phyllo dough to seal in moisture and spray phyllo with a non-stick cooking spray rather than brushing it with melted butter.

39: Marinate fish and poultry in buttermilk or yogurt to tenderize and add richer flavor.

appetizers

Appetizers are sometimes described as just more easily spelled hors d'oeuvres. They are both usually finger food, one or two bites in size, and customarily served before the meal with cocktails. They can be served hot or cold and can range all the way from truly fancy canapés to a selection of crudités — vegetables with dips—or bowls of nuts.

This particular category of food can play havoc with daily calorie and fat goals. In fact, it is often possible to take in more calories before a meal, without ever realizing it, than in the meal itself. For this reason, this is a short chapter because we don't serve many appetizer-type dishes at Canyon Ranch. Instead, we encourage our guests to visit the salad bar and create their own appetizers by selecting small portions of their favorite items.

That said, many of the recipes in this brief chapter can easily be increased in size and served as salad or even as a light entree.

blue corn blinis

These lavender-colored little pancakes are sure to be a conversation piece at any party. They make wonderful Southwestern appetizers spread with a small amount of light sour cream seasoned with a hint of cumin and then topped with about a quarter teaspoonful of good caviar or smoked salmon. Surprise your guests at your next party with these colorful Canyon Ranch hors d'oeuvres.

½ cup plus 1 tablespoon unbleached all-purpose flour

½ cup plus 1 tablespoon blue cornmeal

1 package (1 tablespoon) active dry yeast (check date on package before using)

2 egg yolks

1½ cups non-fat milk, warmed

4 egg whites, beaten stiff, but not dry

2 tablespoons corn oil margarine, melted

1. Combine the flour, cornmeal, and yeast in a bowl and mix well. Add the egg yolks and milk and again mix well. Fold in the egg whites and melted margarine.

2. To cook, heat a griddle or heavy skillet over medium heat. Oil the surface and wipe dry. For each blini, spoon 1 tablespoon of batter onto the hot surface and cook until bubbles form and break. Turn over and lightly brown on the other side.

MAKES 6 CUPS BATTER, ABOUT 90 BLINIS

blinis
Classic blinis (BLEE-nees) are small, yeast-raised buckwheat pancakes. They originated in Russia and are usually served with sour cream and caviar or smoked salmon.

32

• EACH BLINI CONTAINS APPROXIMATELY:

CALORIES: **12** FAT: **negligible** CHOLESTEROL: **5 mg** SODIUM: **8 mg** CARBOHYDRATES: **2 g** PROTEIN: **negligible**

caponata

Caponata is a Sicilian dish that can be served as an appetizer, salad, side dish, or relish. It is most often served at room temperature, but it can also be served hot and it is an excellent vegetarian topping for pasta.

1 tablespoon extra-virgin olive oil

1/2 cup minced onion

1 medium eggplant, unpeeled and cut into 1-inch cubes

1 cup tomato sauce

1 teaspoon anchovy paste

1 teaspoon salt

2 tablespoons capers, drained and rinsed

3 tablespoons red wine vinegar

1 cup water

1/2 teaspoon dried basil, crushed

1 tablespoon sugar

1. Heat the oil in a skillet. Add the onion and cook, covered, over medium-low heat until soft and translucent, about 10 minutes. Remove the onion from the pan and set aside.
2. In the same skillet over medium-high heat, cook the eggplant, stirring frequently, for 10 minutes. Return the onion to the pan and add all the remaining ingredients. Reduce the heat to low and simmer, uncovered, for 30 minutes.
3. Let cool to room temperature and store, covered, in the refrigerator.

MAKES 3 CUPS, OR 12 (1/4-CUP) SERVINGS

• EACH SERVING CONTAINS APPROXIMATELY:

CALORIES: **33** | FAT: **1 g** | CHOLESTEROL: **0** | SODIUM: **340 mg** | CARBOHYDRATES: **5 g** | PROTEIN: **negligible**

tofu guacamole

This recipe incorporates the avocado of traditional guacamole with other green vegetables plus tofu in order to lower the fat content of the dip.

$^1/_2$ cup packed finely sliced
   spinach leaves

$^1/_3$ cup frozen peas

2 tablespoons light silken tofu

1$^1/_2$ tablespoons fresh lemon juice

pinch salt

pinch ground cumin

pinch cayenne pepper

pinch chili powder

dash Tabasco sauce

6 tablespoons mashed avocado

3 tablespoons minced tomato

2 tablespoons hot salsa, or to taste

3 tablespoons minced white onions

1 tablespoon chopped cilantro

2 teaspoons chopped scallions

1. Steam the spinach until wilted. Remove from the heat, let cool, then squeeze with your hands to remove excess water.
2. Briefly steam the peas. Rinse under cold water.
3. Combine the spinach, peas, tofu, lemon juice, seasonings, and avocado in a food processor and puree.
4. Spoon the mixture into a bowl. Add all the remaining ingredients and mix to combine.

MAKES 1$^1/_2$ CUPS, OR 12 (2-TABLESPOON) SERVINGS

35

tofu

Tofu ranks high in nutritional characteristics. Not only is it a source of high-quality protein, it's loaded with iron, B vitamins, and potassium. If curdled with calcium salts it will also contain impressive amounts of calcium. Yet tofu is fairly low in calories and saturated fat, contains no cholesterol, and is very low in sodium. All soy products, like tofu, are rich in phytoestrogens, plant hormones believed to reduce the risk of breast and prostate cancer, and to minimize the mood swings and hot flashes associated with menopause. Tofu is available in firm, regular, and soft consistencies. Silken tofu has a satin-smooth, creamy texture, while other types of tofu tend to be a bit grainy. Tofu has a bland, slightly nutty flavor that gives it a chameleonlike capability to take on the flavor of the food with which it is cooked. After opening, tofu will keep for several days if stored in the refrigerator, covered with water that is changed daily. Tofu can be frozen up to 3 months, but freezing will change its texture, making it slightly chewy.

• EACH SERVING CONTAINS APPROXIMATELY.

CALORIES: 30 | FAT: 2 g | CHOLESTEROL: 0 | SODIUM: 237 mg | CARBOHYDRATES: 3 g | PROTEIN: 1 g

canyon ranch guacamole

We have served this asparagus guacamole at Canyon Ranch since the day we opened and it has always been extremely popular with our guests. Because it is so unusual it was an immediate favorite with the press whenever articles were written about our Southwestern cuisine. Serve it with fat-free baked tortilla chips for your next fiesta.

2 cups (12 ounces) chopped lightly steamed asparagus (If you're using frozen asparagus spears, it is not necessary to steam them. Just thaw them to room temperature.)

2 1/4 teaspoons fresh lemon juice

3 tablespoons chopped onion

1 large tomato, chopped

3/4 teaspoon salt, optional

1/2 teaspoon chili powder

1/4 teaspoon ground cumin

1/4 teaspoon freshly ground black pepper

1 garlic clove, pressed or minced

dash tabasco sauce

1/3 cup light sour cream

1. Combine all the ingredients in a blender and blend until smooth.

2. Transfer the guacamole to a bowl. Cover tightly and refrigerate several hours or overnight before serving.

MAKES 3 CUPS, OR 12 (1/4-CUP) SERVINGS

36

• EACH SERVING CONTAINS APPROXIMATELY:

CALORIES: **11** | FAT: **negligible** | CHOLESTEROL: **0** | SODIUM: **147 mg** | CARBOHYDRATES: **2 g** | PROTEIN: **negligible**

hummus with roasted red pepper sauce

Hummus is a thick Middle Eastern sauce made with mashed chickpeas, lemon juice, garlic, and either olive or sesame oil. Other ingredients are often added to the basic hummus mixture for variety. This lower-fat hummus is particularly delicious served with the roasted red pepper sauce.

HUMMUS:

1 medium onion, minced

1 garlic clove, minced

1¼ cups canned chickpeas, drained and rinsed

¼ cup fresh lemon juice

2 teaspoons rice vinegar

2 teaspoons sodium-reduced soy sauce

2 teaspoons tahini

2 tablespoons thinly sliced scallions

2 tablespoons chopped parsley

ROASTED RED PEPPER SAUCE:

1 tomato, cored and seeded

1 red bell pepper, cut in half and seeded

½ jalapeño pepper, cut in half and seeded

pinch coriander

pinch cumin

pinch chili powder

pinch white pepper

pinch fructose

⅛ teaspoon extra-virgin olive oil

2 whole-wheat pita breads

1. Preheat the oven to 375°F.

2. To make the hummus, spray a small skillet with a non-stick cooking spray and place over medium heat. Add the onion and garlic and cook, stirring frequently, until soft, about 10 minutes.

3. Place all the remaining hummus ingredients in a food processor and blend until smooth.

4. To make the roasted red pepper sauce, lightly spray a baking sheet with non-stick cooking spray. Place the tomato, bell pepper, and jalapeño on the sprayed baking sheet. Bake in the preheated oven until the vegetables are soft, about 15 minutes.

5. Transfer the vegetables to the food processor, add the remaining sauce ingredients, and process until combined.

6. To serve, place ½ cup of hummus on a plate. Top with 2 tablespoons of the red pepper sauce. Serve with ½ whole-wheat pita bread.

MAKES 4 SERVINGS

hummus
In Middle Eastern countries when tahini, a thick paste made of ground sesame seeds, is added to the hummus, they call it hummus bi tahina. Both types of hummus are always found in Middle Eastern markets in jars and cans, and usually fresh as well.

38

• EACH SERVING CONTAINS APPROXIMATELY:

CALORIES: **195** | FAT: **3 g** | CHOLESTEROL: **0** | SODIUM: **417 mg** | CARBOHYDRATES: **37 g** | PROTEIN: **8 g**

celery root dijon

This recipe can also be made with raw celery root, but I prefer it lightly steamed and then chilled because I think it has better texture. For a pretty appetizer or salad presentation, line small plates with radicchio leaves, spoon the celery root mixture into the center of the leaves, and garnish with sprigs of fresh tarragon. If fresh tarragon is not available, then use another fresh herb both in the recipe and for garnish. Even fresh parsley is better in this recipe than any dried herb. For an even more colorful presentation sprinkle the top of each serving with diced tomato. This mixture can also be served as a dip or used as a vegetarian sandwich filling.

1 small celery root (1½ pounds), peeled and grated

1 teaspoon fresh lemon juice

2 tablespoons dijon mustard

2 tablespoons water

1 tablespoon white wine vinegar

⅛ teaspoon freshly ground black pepper

1 tablespoon chopped fresh tarragon leaves

1 tablespoon finely chopped drained capers

celery root

Celery root is really not celery root at all, but the root of the celeriac plant. It is a rather unattractive, bulbous brown root; it tastes like a combination of celery and parsley. Delicious eaten raw or cooked, it contains small amounts of calcium, iron, and vitamin B. Available from September through May, celery root can range in size from that of an apple to a small melon.

39

1. Steam the celery root over boiling water for 2 minutes. Rinse in cold water, drain thoroughly, and set aside.
2. Combine the lemon juice, mustard, water, vinegar, pepper, tarragon, and capers in a bowl and mix well. Add the drained celery root to the mustard mixture and mix well.
3. Cover tightly and refrigerate for at least 2 hours before serving.

MAKES 2 CUPS, OR 4 (½-CUP) SERVINGS

• EACH SERVING CONTAINS APPROXIMATELY:

CALORIES: 15 | FAT: negligible | CHOLESTEROL: 0 | SODIUM: 140 mg | CARBOHYDRATES: 3 g | PROTEIN: negligible

cucumber raita

Raita is a spicy yogurt condiment from India that is served with much hotter and spicier dishes to refresh the palate. Usually made with thinly sliced or diced cucumber, as it is here, it can also be made with other vegetables, or even fruits. Try serving it with Lentil Dhal (see page 300) or Tandoori Chicken (see page 257) and Curried Basmati Rice (see page 314).

½ teaspoon extra-virgin olive oil

1 garlic clove, pressed or minced

2 cups peeled and finely diced cucumbers

1¼ cups non-fat plain yogurt

1 tablespoon chopped cilantro

pinch cumin

pinch salt

pinch freshly ground black pepper

dash tabasco sauce

½ teaspoon honey

½ teaspoon rice wine vinegar

1. Spray a small skillet with non-stick cooking spray. Add the olive oil and place it over medium-low heat. Add the garlic and cook just until it starts to sizzle. Remove from the heat and set aside.

2. Fold the cucumbers into the yogurt. Add all the remaining ingredients, including the garlic, and mix well.

3. Store, tightly covered, in the refrigerator.

MAKES ABOUT 3 CUPS, OR 12 (¼-CUP) SERVINGS

40

• EACH SERVING CONTAINS APPROXIMATELY:

CALORIES: **18** | FAT: **negligible** | CHOLESTEROL: **negligible** | SODIUM: **30 mg** | CARBOHYDRATES: **3 g** | PROTEIN: **2 g**

eggplant caviar

This simple but intensely flavorful appetizer is the creation of James Boyce, the talented executive chef at Loew's Coronado Bay Resort on San Diego Bay. I first tasted it in his kitchen and I immediately asked him for the recipe so that we could adapt it for the Canyon Ranch menus and include it in our salad bars. It is good spread on crusty bread or used as a dip for chips and vegetables. It even makes a great sauce for fish, poultry, or meat. On top of all that, it is both easy and inexpensive to make.

1 medium eggplant (1½ pounds)

8 kalamata or 15 niçoise olives, pitted

2 tablespoons chopped chives

2 small garlic cloves, halved

¼ teaspoon salt

¼ teaspoon freshly ground
   black pepper

1 tablespoon extra-virgin olive oil

kalamata and niçoise olives
Greek kalamata olives are medium-sized and a deep, almost black-purple color. They are always marinated in wine vinegar and sometimes packed in olive oil. French niçoise olives are extremely small and dark brown in color. They are brine-cured before being packed in olive oil. These are the two most popular imported olives used in this country. In this recipe I like to use kalamatas because they are available pitted and niçoise olives are not.

1. Preheat the oven to 400°F.

2. Cut the eggplant in half lengthwise and place it, cut side up, on a baking sheet. Spray the cut surfaces with a non-stick vegetable cooking spray. Bake the eggplant for 40 minutes, or until it can be pierced easily with a fork. Remove from the oven and let cool until safe to handle.

3. Peel the eggplant and discard the skin. Place the peeled eggplant in a colander or a large strainer and press out any excess liquid.

4. Put the pressed eggplant in a blender or food processor. Add all the remaining ingredients and blend to the desired consistency.

MAKES 1½ CUPS, OR 12 (2-TABLESPOON) SERVINGS

41

• **EACH SERVING CONTAINS APPROXIMATELY:**

CALORIES: 24 | FAT: 1 g | CHOLESTEROL: 0 | SODIUM: 72 mg | CARBOHYDRATES: 3 g | PROTEIN: negligible

roasted eggplant couscous salad

This is both a pretty and extremely nutritious appetizer. It is practically fat-free, the combination of couscous and beans provides a complete plant protein, and the vegetables and orange juice add valuable vitamins and minerals.

42

EGGPLANT SALAD:

1 small eggplant (1 pound)

6 garlic cloves, peeled

$^{1}/_{2}$ cup canned diced green chiles

pinch ground cumin

pinch paprika

pinch freshly ground black pepper

pinch salt

$^{1}/_{4}$ cup frozen orange juice concentrate, undiluted

2 tablespoons chopped cilantro leaves

1$^{1}/_{2}$ cups water

$^{3}/_{4}$ cup dry couscous (5 ounces)

3 cups baby greens

6 tablespoons fresh orange juice

6 tablespoons cooked kidney beans

6 tablespoons cooked garbanzo beans

1. Preheat the oven to 375°F.

2. Spray a baking sheet lightly with non-stick vegetable cooking spray. Place the eggplant on the baking sheet and roast for about 1 hour, or until it is very soft. Halfway through the baking time place the garlic on the baking sheet with the eggplant. Remove the baking sheet from the oven and let cool until the eggplant can be safely handled.

3. Peel the eggplant and cut it into thin strips. Mince the garlic.

4. Combine the eggplant and garlic with the remaining ingredients for eggplant salad.

5. Bring the water to a boil in a small saucepan. Add the couscous, mix well, cover, and remove from the heat. Let stand for at least 5 minutes, or until all the liquid has been absorbed.

6. To serve, place $^{1}/_{2}$ cup of the greens on each of 6 plates. Drizzle the greens with 1 tablespoon of orange juice.

7. Spray the inside of a small, 3-inch bowl or ramekin with non-stick cooking spray. Pack $^{1}/_{4}$ cup of the eggplant salad into the bowl. Top it with $^{1}/_{4}$ cup of the couscous, pressing down firmly. Invert the bowl on the greens on each plate, then carefully remove the bowl.

8. Sprinkle the greens on each plate with 1 tablespoon each of kidney and garbanzo beans.

MAKES 6 SERVINGS

• **EACH SERVING CONTAINS APPROXIMATELY:**

CALORIES: **140** | FAT: **negligible** | CHOLESTEROL: **0** | SODIUM: **63 mg** | CARBOHYDRATES: **29 g** | PROTEIN: **6 g**

garbanzo nuts

These easy-to-make garbanzo nuts are a popular substitute for high-fat nuts at parties and a nutritious solution for both brown bag lunches and after-school snacks. In fact, they are so simple to prepare that even young children can do it with just a little supervision. And, of course, if the kids make them they are much more likely to want to eat them!

32 ounces canned garbanzo beans, drained

onion and/or garlic powder to taste

garbanzo beans

Garbanzo beans also go by the names chickpeas and ceci. They are a pale goldish beige in color, almost round, firm-textured, and have a mild, nutlike flavor. They are most often used in African, Asian, Middle Eastern, and Italian cuisines.

1. Preheat the oven to 350°F.

2. Spread the drained beans in a single layer on a non-stick baking sheet. Sprinkle them lightly with onion or garlic powder, or a combination of both. Bake for 50 to 60 minutes, stirring occasionally, or until the beans are browned and crisp.

3. Store in a tightly covered container.

MAKES ABOUT 3 CUPS, OR 12 (1/4-CUP) SERVINGS

44

• EACH SERVING CONTAINS APPROXIMATELY:

CALORIES: **227** | FAT: **4 g** | CHOLESTEROL: **0** | SODIUM: **18 mg** | CARBOHYDRATES: **46 g** | PROTEIN: **15 g**

israeli cabbage rolls in citrus sauce

This recipe was given to me by a friend in Tel Aviv who uses ground beef. However, I prefer ground turkey breast with the citrus, and I use frozen orange juice concentrate rather than fresh orange juice. Using uncooked rice in this recipe gives these rolls their crunchy texture. For an appetizer-size portion allow one roll, and four for an entree.

1 head cabbage

12 ounces ground turkey breast

3/4 cup uncooked white rice

1/4 cup chopped parsley

2 tablespoons chopped basil leaves

3/4 teaspoon salt

3/4 teaspoon freshly ground black pepper

1 teaspoon sugar

8 garlic cloves, thinly sliced

2 tablespoons chopped mint leaves

CITRUS SAUCE:

1/4 cup thawed frozen orange juice concentrate

2 tablespoons fresh lemon juice

1/4 cup water

orange slices or strips of peel for garnish, optional

1. Cut the center core out of the cabbage, then hold it under running water, allowing the leaves to separate before removing them. Remove the leaves whole, if possible, being careful not to tear them. Arrange the leaves in a steamer basket and steam until they are pliable, 2 to 3 minutes.

2. Combine the ground turkey, rice, parsley, basil, salt, pepper, and sugar in a bowl and mix well. Place 2 tablespoons of the mixture in the center of each of 16 steamed cabbage leaves and fold the leaf around it. Squeeze each cabbage roll in the palm of your hand to get rid of any excess liquid.

3. Spray a large skillet with non-stick cooking spray. Arrange the cabbage rolls in the skillet and sprinkle the garlic and mint over the top. Cook over medium heat until the cabbage rolls start to brown. Pour in enough hot water to cover the rolls and bring to a boil. Reduce the heat to low and simmer, uncovered, for 1 hour.

4. Combine the orange juice concentrate and lemon juice with the 1/4 cup of water and mix well. Pour the juice mixture over the cabbage rolls and allow to simmer for 5 more minutes.

5. To serve, garnish with orange slices or strips of peel.

MAKES 16 CABBAGE ROLLS

45

• EACH CABBAGE ROLL CONTAINS APPROXIMATELY:

| CALORIES: 72 | FAT: negligible | CHOLESTEROL: 13 mg | SODIUM: 119 mg | CARBOHYDRATES: 10 g | PROTEIN: 6 g |

caramelized onion patties

When Marcel Desaulniers, the chef-owner of the Trellis restaurant in Williamsburg, Virginia was a visiting chef at Canyon Ranch in Tucson he worked with John Luzader, our executive chef, to create these delightfully different vegetarian burgers. You can serve larger portions as an entree if you prefer.

$1/4$ cup arborio rice

2 tablespoons buckwheat

$1^1/2$ cups vegetable stock
(see page 56)

$1/2$ cup peeled and diced
russet potato

$1/4$ teaspoon salt

$1/4$ teaspoon freshly ground
black pepper

$1/4$ teaspoon finely chopped fresh
rosemary

$1/4$ cup diced onion (1 ounce)

2 tablespoons diced carrot
($1/2$ ounce)

2 tablespoons diced celery
($1/2$ ounce)

2 large onions ($1^1/2$ pounds),
thinly sliced

4 large shallots (8 ounces),
thinly sliced

$1^1/2$ tablespoons extra-virgin
olive oil

$1/2$ pear (2 ounces), peeled and
diced ($1/2$ cup)

1. Combine the rice, buckwheat, and $1/2$ cup of the stock in a small saucepan and bring to a boil. Cook over medium heat, stirring frequently, until the liquid is almost completely absorbed. Add the potato, salt, pepper, rosemary, and $1/4$ cup of the remaining stock. Continue cooking and stirring until almost dry again. Continue to add the remaining stock, $1/4$ cup at a time, until it has all been absorbed and the mixture is mushy. This will take about 20 minutes. Set aside.

2. Spray a large skillet with non-stick cooking spray and place it over medium heat. When it is hot enough for drops of water to dance on the surface, add the diced onion, carrot, and celery. Cook, stirring constantly, for 2 minutes. Remove from the skillet and set aside.

3. Add the sliced onions and shallots to the same skillet. Cook, covered, over low heat, stirring occasionally, until soft and translucent, about 15 to 20 minutes. Remove the lid and continue cooking and stirring until the mixture caramelizes, or turns a deep shade of brown, about 20 minutes.

4. Combine the rice mixture, cooked carrot mixture, and the caramelized onion mixture in a large bowl. Add the olive oil and pear, and mash together to mix thoroughly. Form the mixture into 16 patties, $1/4$ cup each.

5. Cook the patties on a hot grill or skillet that has been sprayed with non-stick cooking spray, for about 3 minutes per side, or until browned on both sides.

MAKES 8 SERVINGS

46

caramelizing

Caramelize is a term used for heating sugar until it liquefies and turns a dark golden brown in color. It is also used to describe cooking onions, shallots, leeks, and garlic until they are soft and turn the same dark golden brown in color. This can be done in the oven or on top of the stove, as it is in the recipe for Caramelized Onion Patties. Keeping caramelized onion–type vegetables in the refrigerator is a good idea because they can be added to many dishes for flavor without adding fat.

• **EACH 2-PATTY SERVING CONTAINS APPROXIMATELY:**

CALORIES: 112 | FAT: 3 g | CHOLESTEROL: 0 | SODIUM: 538 mg | CARBOHYDRATES: 18 g | PROTEIN: 3 g

roasted portobello mushrooms on balsamic vinaigrette

This marvelous mushroom appetizer can be served with just grilled vegetables, such as asparagus and red onions. However, to reduce the percentage of calories from fat in this dish, at Canyon Ranch we also add polenta or pasta and serve it as an entree.

BALSAMIC VINAIGRETTE:

4 small plum tomatoes, peeled (see page 58) **and diced (1 cup)**

1/2 teaspoon salt

1/4 cup tightly packed fresh basil leaves

2 tablespoons balsamic vinegar

1 teaspoon extra-virgin olive oil

MUSHROOMS:

4 large portobello mushrooms (12 ounces)

1/4 cup extra-virgin olive oil

4 garlic cloves, pressed or minced

1 1/2 teaspoons chopped fresh thyme leaves, or 1/2 teaspoon dried thyme, crushed

1 teaspoon freshly ground black pepper

grilled vegetables for garnish, optional

sprigs fresh thyme for garnish, optional

1. Combine the diced tomatoes and salt in a colander and mix well. Let them drain for 1 hour or as long as possible. Combine the drained tomatoes, basil leaves, and vinegar in a blender or food processor and blend until pureed, adding the olive oil at the end to incorporate it into the mixture.

2. Preheat the oven to 350°F.

3. Carefully clean the mushrooms with a mushroom brush or a damp cloth or paper towel. (Do not submerge the mushrooms in water because they will absorb it like sponges.) Cut off the tough part of the stems. Combine the olive oil, garlic, thyme, and pepper in a small bowl and mix well. Brush the mixture on the mushrooms, being careful to paint the entire surface of each. Put the mushrooms on a rack, stem side down, over a broiler pan or a baking sheet and roast them in the preheated oven for 15 to 20 minutes, or until they are well browned and can be pierced easily with a fork.

4. To serve, spoon 1/4 cup of the vinaigrette in the center of each plate. Place a roasted mushroom, stem side down, on top. Garnish with grilled vegetables and a sprig of fresh thyme, if desired.

MAKES 4 SERVINGS

48

• EACH SERVING CONTAINS APPROXIMATELY:

CALORIES: 113 | FAT: 6 g | CHOLESTEROL: 0 | SODIUM: 304 mg | CARBOHYDRATES: 15 g | PROTEIN: 2 g

roasted red peppers

Roasted bell peppers make a wonderful appetizer with just a little extra-virgin olive oil drizzled over them. They are also almost a magical ingredient in other recipes because they add taste, texture, and brilliant color.

4 large red bell peppers

1 tablespoon extra-virgin olive oil

handling hot chiles
When roasting spicy hot chile peppers, such as jalapeños, wear rubber gloves to avoid burning your skin and never rub your eyes after handling chile peppers or they will burn for hours. If you do make the mistake of touching your eyes, immediately splash them repeatedly with cool water.

1. Roast or char the peppers until the skins are completely black and blistered. This can be done with tongs over an open flame, on an outdoor grill, under a broiler, in a hot oven, or on a grate over an electric burner. Make sure the skins are totally blistered or they won't peel off easily.
2. While the peppers are still very hot, place them in a Ziploc plastic freezer bag or in a bowl tightly covered with plastic wrap and leave them for at least 20 minutes to "sweat." This loosens the skin so that it comes off more easily.
3. When the peppers are cool enough to handle safely, remove the skins, scraping off any tough pieces with a knife. (Do not rinse them in water to remove the skin — it will also wash away much of the flavor.) Cut the peppers in half and remove the seeds and membranes. Rub them with the olive oil and either leave them in large pieces or slice or chop to desired size. They will keep for several days if stored, tightly covered, in the refrigerator.

MAKES 4 SERVINGS

49

• EACH WHOLE-PEPPER SERVING CONTAINS APPROXIMATELY:

CALORIES: 50 | FAT: 3 g | CHOLESTEROL: 0 | SODIUM: 1 mg | CARBOHYDRATES: 5 g | PROTEIN: negligible

ecuadorian shrimp ceviche

Ceviche is extremely popular all over Ecuador, and it differs from Mexican ceviche in that the fish or seafood is cooked rather than raw. My favorite Ecuadorian ceviche is made with shrimp, and the best version of it that I had while I was in Ecuador last year was at Pinsaqui, a gorgeous old hacienda in Otavalo, the famous Indian market town in the northern part of the country. When I asked the owner, Pedro Freile Larrea, if I could have the recipe, he graciously introduced me to his chef, who told me how to make it. I was fascinated by the fact that his delicious Ecuadorian sauce was seasoned with American ketchup and English Worcestershire sauce. He started out with raw shrimp and reserved some of the cooking water to add to the sauce. In order to save the time it takes to peel, devein, and cook shrimp, I have used cooked shrimp in this recipe and substituted clam juice for the cooking liquid. If you prefer to start with raw shrimp, cook them just until they turn pink and opaque, which takes only a few seconds. Overcooking them will make them tough. Also, instead of leaving the shrimp whole and pouring the liquid over them, you may prefer to chop them up and stir them into the sauce.

1 teaspoon salt

1/2 cup lime juice

2 cups fresh orange juice

3/4 cup clam juice

1/2 teaspoon freshly ground black pepper

3/4 cup ketchup

2 teaspoons worcestershire sauce

1 small white onion, thinly sliced (1 cup)

2 medium tomatoes, peeled and diced (1 cup)

1 pound cooked medium shrimp

shrimp sizes
Shrimp are priced and sold according to size. In general, the larger the shrimp, the greater the price. The size categories are determined by the number of shrimp to the pound. Colossal is for 10 or less shrimp per pound; jumbo for 11 to 15 per pound; extra-large for 16 to 20 per pound; large for 21 to 30 per pound; medium for 31 to 35 per pound; small for 36 to 45 per pound; and miniature for about 100 per pound. However, terms may vary greatly from one region to another and, in some cases, from one market to another.

50

1. Combine the salt and lime juice in a bowl and stir until the salt is completely dissolved. Add the orange juice, clam juice, pepper, ketchup, and Worcestershire sauce and mix well. Add the onion and tomatoes and again mix well.

2. To serve, divide the shrimp equally among 8 small bowls, about 4 or 5 shrimp per serving, and spoon 3/4 cup of the sauce over each serving.

MAKES 8 SERVINGS

• **EACH SERVING CONTAINS APPROXIMATELY:**

CALORIES: **112** | FAT: **negligible** | CHOLESTEROL: **111 mg** | SODIUM: **751 mg** | CARBOHYDRATES: **13 g** | PROTEIN: **13 g**

soups

Soups are very popular at Canyon Ranch, and they run the gamut from practically calorie-free first courses to hearty main dishes. They are also uniquely different, ranging from one culture to another, and you will find a variety of national and ethnic recipes in this chapter.

When possible it is always better to make your own stocks. Even though there are very acceptable frozen and canned fat-free stocks available in most markets now, making your own not only ensures a better quality, but it is also much less expensive. When making your own stock, simmer it over very low heat, never allowing it to actually come to a full boil, especially when clarifying. In days gone by someone was always designated to make sure this didn't happen, thus the old cliché: "A watched pot never boils."

At Canyon Ranch we don't add salt or much seasoning to stocks so that we can adjust the salt and seasonings for every individual recipe.

In your own home where you won't be using as much stock as we do at Canyon Ranch it is a good idea to freeze it. After defatting your stock, freeze it in containers of a volume you most often use or store it in ice cube trays. When the stock is solidly frozen, remove the cubes from the trays and place them in plastic bags. Two cubes equal $\frac{1}{4}$ cup, so measuring is very simple.

All the soups in this chapter are uniquely flavorful and light. Even the chowders and bisques contain very little fat. In other words they are all soups you can enjoy, either as a first course or as an entree.

chicken stock

You can now buy canned, fat-free chicken stock in any grocery store. However, making your own is much less expensive and provides an infinitely more flavorful ingredient. The method below can also be used for making turkey stock.

If you don't have the fresh herbs called for in this recipe make a dried herb bouquet garni (see Consommé, page 70).

4 pounds chicken parts
(except the liver)

10 cups cold water, or to cover
ingredients by a depth of 2 inches

2 stalks celery without leaves,
cut in half

1 carrot, scraped and halved

1 leek, white part only, halved

1 small onion, quartered

3 or 4 sprigs parsley or chervil

2 sprigs fresh thyme

1 bay leaf

1. Preheat the oven to 350°F.

2. Place the chicken parts in a shallow baking dish and roast in the 350°F. oven until golden brown, approximately 35 to 45 minutes. Drain off the excess fat and discard.

3. Transfer the browned chicken to a large pot, add cold water, and bring slowly to a boil, skimming off any foam that rises to the top.

4. Add all the remaining ingredients, reduce the heat to low, and simmer, with the lid ajar, for at least 3 hours. Do not stir the stock at any point.

5. Strain the stock into a non-aluminum container. Discard the bones and vegetables. Place the container in an ice bath until cooled completely or refrigerate, uncovered, overnight or until the fat has congealed on the top. Remove and discard the fat. Stock should not be kept in the refrigerator more than 2 or 3 days. It can be kept, tightly sealed, in the freezer for several months.

MAKES APPROXIMATELY 8 CUPS

54

• EACH 1-CUP SERVING CONTAINS APPROXIMATELY:

CALORIES: **12** | FAT: **negligible** | CHOLESTEROL: **0** | SODIUM: **11 mg** | CARBOHYDRATES: **3 g** | PROTEIN: **negligible**

fish stock

Call ahead to your favorite fish market to have bones saved for you. For best results, use bones from fish low in fat such as sole or turbot. If you don't have the fresh herbs called for in the recipe, then make a Dried Herb Bouquet Garni (see page 70). When you don't have the time or the ingredients to make fish stock, use bottled clam juice.

2¹/₂ pounds fish bones

3 or 4 sprigs parsley or chervil

1 bay leaf

2 sprigs fresh thyme

1 leek, white part only

2 stalks celery without leaves, halved

1 carrot, scraped and chopped

1 small onion, chopped

6 cups water

1 cup dry white wine

1. Combine all the ingredients in a large stockpot and simmer, uncovered, for 45 minutes to 1 hour, skimming off the scum that rises to the surface as the stock cooks.

2. Line a strainer or colander with a double thickness of cheesecloth. Strain the stock through the cheesecloth into a bowl. Discard the solids. Use the stock immediately or cool and store in the refrigerator or freezer. Stock should not be kept in the refrigerator more than 2 or 3 days. It can be kept, tightly sealed, in the freezer for several months.

MAKES 5 CUPS

55

• EACH 1-CUP SERVING CONTAINS APPROXIMATELY:

CALORIES: **54** | FAT: **negligible** | CHOLESTEROL: **0** | SODIUM: **24 mg** | CARBOHYDRATES: **4 g** | PROTEIN: **negligible**

vegetable stock

Vegetable stock is an essential ingredient for vegetarian cooking. It also adds enormously to the flavor of many soups, sauces, and salad dressings and is far better than water for cooking rice and beans. It is easy and inexpensive to make and can be stored in the freezer in ice cube trays so that you always have it on hand. As soon as it's frozen, remove it from the trays and store the cubes in tightly sealed Ziploc bags. To add parsley flavor to the stock but not the bitterness that comes from boiling the leaves for a long time, use only the stems. Cut off the leafy ends of a bunch of parsley and reserve them for other uses. Either Italian flat-leaf or curly parsley may be used. Any difference in the flavor provided is negligible.

1 leek, well rinsed, trimmed, and chopped

2 medium onions, chopped

3 carrots, scraped and chopped

5 stalks celery, without leaves, chopped

1 cup chopped parsley stems

2 bay leaves, broken into halves

1 teaspoon dried marjoram, crushed

$1/4$ teaspoon dried thyme, crushed

12 cups cold water

1. Combine all the ingredients in a large pot and bring to a boil over high heat. Reduce the heat and simmer, uncovered, for 1 hour.

2. Line a strainer or colander with a double thickness of cheesecloth and set it over a very large bowl or pot. Strain the stock through the cheesecloth, discard the solids, and let the stock cool. Store, tightly covered, in the refrigerator for 1 week or in the freezer for several months.

MAKES ABOUT 9 CUPS

56

• EACH 1-CUP SERVING CONTAINS APPROXIMATELY:

CALORIES: 10 | FAT: negligible | CHOLESTEROL: 0 | SODIUM: 21 mg | CARBOHYDRATES: 3 g | PROTEIN: negligible

fruit gazpacho

This colorful fruit soup is a delightful first course for a summer meal. It is also an unusual and refreshing dessert. The freshly ground black pepper adds just the right amount of hot spiciness to contrast with the sweetness of the fruit. For a prettier presentation, garnish each serving with a sprig of fresh mint.

1/2 cup diced pineapple

1/2 cup diced strawberries

1 cup sliced grapes

3/4 cup blueberries

1 cup apple juice

1/2 cup fresh orange juice

1/4 teaspoon freshly ground
  black pepper

1/2 orange, peeled and separated
  into segments, for garnish

sprigs fresh mint for garnish, optional

1. Combine the pineapple, strawberries, grapes, and blueberries in a bowl.

2. Add the apple juice, orange juice, and pepper to the fruit and mix well. Cover the bowl tightly and refrigerate until ready to serve.

3. Spoon 3/4 cup of the mixture into each of 6 bowls and garnish with orange segments and fresh mint sprigs, if desired.

MAKES 6 SERVINGS

57

• EACH 3/4-CUP SERVING CONTAINS APPROXIMATELY:

CALORIES: 60 | FAT: negligible | CHOLESTEROL: 0 | SODIUM: 3 mg | CARBOHYDRATES: 15 g | PROTEIN: negligible

gazpacho

This cold soup is so popular at Canyon Ranch that we keep it on our menus all year round. It is better if made the day before you plan to serve it so that the flavors can marry.

½ cup peeled and diced cucumbers

¾ cup peeled and diced red and green bell peppers

¾ cup diced onion

2 plum tomatoes, peeled and diced (1 cup)

2½ cups tomato juice

2 garlic cloves, pressed or minced

¼ teaspoon freshly ground black pepper

¼ teaspoon worcestershire sauce

2 tablespoons fresh lemon juice

chopped chives or scallion tops for garnish

2 lemons, cut into 4 wedges each, for garnish

1. Combine all the ingredients, except the chives or scallion tops and lemon wedges, and mix thoroughly. Pour the soup into a container, cover tightly, and refrigerate until cold.

2. Serve in chilled bowls and garnish with the chopped chives or scallion tops and lemon wedges.

MAKES 8 SERVINGS

peeling tomatoes
Bring a pan of water to a boil. Using a sharp paring knife, cut a shallow X in the tops of the tomatoes. Drop the tomatoes into the boiling water for about 30 seconds. Remove the tomatoes and place in cold water. They will literally slip right out of their skins!

58

• EACH ½-CUP SERVING CONTAINS APPROXIMATELY:

CALORIES: **29** | FAT: **negligible** | CHOLESTEROL: **0** | SODIUM: **336 mg** | CARBOHYDRATES: **7 g** | PROTEIN: **1 g**

mixed melon soup

This delightfully refreshing cold soup also makes an unusual and very light summer dessert. For an even more colorful presentation, use 2 cups each of cantaloupe, honeydew, and watermelon, and pour the three colors together into the bowls.

3 cups diced cantaloupe

3/4 teaspoon fresh lemon juice

3 cups diced honeydew melon

3/4 teaspoon fresh lime juice

6 sprigs fresh mint for garnish, optional

1. Combine the cantaloupe and lemon juice in a blender, puree, and pour into a bowl. Combine the honeydew and lime juice in a blender, puree, and pour into another bowl. Cover both bowls tightly and refrigerate until cold before serving.

2. To serve, pour $1/4$ cup of each melon puree into each of 6 bowls, pouring from opposite sides of the bowl to create divided colors. Garnish with fresh mint sprigs, if desired.

MAKES 3 CUPS, OR 6 ($1/2$-CUP) SERVINGS

• EACH SERVING CONTAINS APPROXIMATELY:

CALORIES: **58** | FAT: **negligible** | CHOLESTEROL: **0** | SODIUM: **15 mg** | CARBOHYDRATES: **14 g** | PROTEIN: **2 g**

purple vichyssoise

Classic French vichyssoise is actually a recipe for leftover leek and potato soup, in which the cold leftover soup is pureed and mixed with heavy cream. The creaminess in this soup comes from non-fat milk and light sour cream rather than from heavy cream, making it a much lighter, lower-calorie soup. I prefer this jewel-toned variation made with purple potatoes over the traditional white version because it is so much more attractive. For an even more interesting-looking presentation, make both colors and combine them in a soup plate, creating the look of a lavender-and-white painting.

12 ounces purple potatoes, peeled and sliced

1/2 cup chopped leeks, white part only

3/4 cup fat-free chicken stock (see page 54)

1/4 cup non-fat milk

1/4 cup light sour cream

1/4 teaspoon salt (omit if using salted stock)

1/4 teaspoon freshly ground black pepper

1 teaspoon fresh lemon juice

chopped chives for garnish

1. Put the potatoes in a saucepan and cover with water. Cook over high heat until the water comes to a boil. Reduce heat to low and simmer until the potatoes can be pierced easily with a fork, about 14 minutes. Drain the potatoes and set aside.

2. In the same pan combine the leeks and chicken stock and bring to a boil. Cover and cook for 5 minutes.

3. Add the potatoes and cook for 5 more minutes. Spoon the mixture into a food processor, add all the remaining ingredients except the chives, and blend until smooth. Transfer to a bowl, cover, and refrigerate until cold.

4. To serve, pour 1/2 cup of soup into each of 4 chilled bowls and garnish with a sprinkling of chopped chives.

MAKES 4 SERVINGS

• EACH 1/2-CUP SERVING CONTAINS APPROXIMATELY:

CALORIES: **90** | FAT: **negligible** | CHOLESTEROL: **1 mg** | SODIUM: **213 mg** | CARBOHYDRATES: **19 g** | PROTEIN: **3 g**

62

creamy white bean and mushroom soup

This incredibly rich-tasting soup is both unusual and delicious. The addition of the marinated beans at the end adds an exciting flavor contrast.

8 ounces dried white beans (1 cup), soaked overnight in water and drained

1/2 cup chopped onion

1 cup diced celery

6 garlic cloves, finely chopped

1 teaspoon salt

1 1/4 teaspoons freshly ground black pepper, divided use

1 tablespoon white wine vinegar

2 tablespoons extra-virgin olive oil

1 tablespoon chopped fresh rosemary

1 teaspoon butter

1 pound fresh mushrooms, wiped clean, stemmed, and sliced (4 cups)

1/4 cup madeira

1 1/2 cups canned evaporated skim milk (12 ounces)

2 phyllo sheets for garnish

1. Rinse and drain the beans and set aside.

2. Put the onion, celery, and garlic in a large, heavy pot or soup kettle and cook, covered, until the onion is soft and translucent, about 3 minutes. Add a little water if necessary.

3. Add the drained beans, salt, and 3/4 teaspoon of pepper, cover with 1 inch of water, and bring to a boil. Reduce the heat to low and cook, covered, for 50 minutes, or until the beans are soft. Remove 1/2 cup of beans from the soup and combine with the vinegar, olive oil, rosemary, and the remaining 1/2 teaspoon of pepper. Mix well and set aside to marinate.

4. Melt the butter in a large skillet. Add the mushrooms and cook over medium heat, stirring frequently, until tender. Add the Madeira and cook over high heat until the liquid has been reduced by half. Set aside.

5. Spoon the cooled soup into a blender and puree. Pour back into the pot through a strainer for a smoother texture. Add the milk and mushrooms; simmer for 10 minutes.

6. Preheat the oven to 400 F. Spray a baking sheet with non-stick cooking spray.

7. Cut each sheet of phyllo into four 3-inch-wide strips and place them on the sprayed baking sheet. Bake until crisp and lightly browned, about 2 minutes.

8. To serve, spoon 3/4 cup of soup into each of 8 bowls. Spoon 1 tablespoon of marinated beans into each bowl, drizzling the marinade over the top. Place a baked phyllo strip across the top of each serving.

63

MAKES 8 SERVINGS

• EACH 3/4-CUP SERVING CONTAINS APPROXIMATELY:

CALORIES: **199** | FAT: **4 g** | CHOLESTEROL: **3 mg** | SODIUM: **381 mg** | CARBOHYDRATES: **28 g** | PROTEIN: **12 g**

white bean soup with pesto

Both the bean soup and the pesto in this recipe can be served separately. The soup is good served cold with chopped leftover vegetables added to it and the pesto is a wonderful sauce for pasta. This simple faux pesto sauce has fewer ingredients than the Pesto Sauce in the Sauces and Spreads chapter, which also contains miso and pine nuts. However, like the other sauce, it can be served for vegan-vegetarian menus at Canyon Ranch because it does not contain cheese. It is also a good garnish on the Minestrone in this chapter.

3/4 cup dried white beans, soaked overnight in water and drained

2¹/2 teaspoons canola oil

3 tablespoons chopped onion

1 garlic clove, chopped

1 small leek, white part only, chopped

7 cups vegetable stock (see page 56)

2 medium potatoes, peeled and diced (about 2 cups)

¹/2 teaspoon chopped fresh thyme

1 teaspoon sodium-reduced soy sauce

pinch freshly ground black pepper

PESTO:

2 cups packed fresh basil leaves

2 garlic cloves

2¹/2 teaspoons extra-virgin olive oil

1 teaspoon chopped shallot

1¹/2 tablespoons water

1. Rinse and drain the beans and set aside.
2. Heat the oil in a large saucepan. Add the onion, garlic, and leek and cook over medium heat until the onion is translucent, about 3 minutes, being careful not to burn it. Add the drained beans and vegetable stock to the pan and cook until the beans are tender, about 1¹/2 hours.
3. Add the potatoes, thyme, soy sauce, and pepper and continue to cook for 30 more minutes.
4. Meanwhile, combine the pesto ingredients in a food processor and blend until smooth. Transfer the pesto to a bowl and set aside.
5. Spoon 3/4 cup of the soup into a blender and puree. Pour the puree back into the pan with the remaining soup.
6. Ladle ¹/2 cup of soup into each of 8 bowls and garnish each serving with 2 teaspoons pesto.

MAKES 8 SERVINGS

• EACH ¹/2-CUP SERVING CONTAINS APPROXIMATELY:

CALORIES: 125 | FAT: 3 g | CHOLESTEROL: 0 | SODIUM: 70 mg | CARBOHYDRATES: 21 g | PROTEIN: 5 g

cream of broccoli and salsify soup

This non-dairy cream soup made with soy milk is perfect for vegan menus and for anyone who is allergic to milk. Of course, if neither of these categories apply, you may use cow's milk in this recipe.

$^1/_2$ tablespoon canola oil

$^1/_4$ cup chopped onion

$^1/_4$ cup chopped leeks

2 cups vegetable stock
(see page 56)

2 tablespoons fresh thyme leaves

1 garlic clove, pressed or minced

$^1/_4$ teaspoon curry powder

$^3/_4$ cup chopped peeled salsify

$^1/_2$ cup peeled and diced potatoes

$1^1/_4$ cups chopped broccoli

$^3/_4$ cup soy milk

$^1/_2$ teaspoon salt

$^1/_2$ teaspoon freshly ground
black pepper

1. Heat the canola oil in a medium saucepan. Add the onion and leeks and cook over medium heat, stirring frequently, until the onion is translucent. Add the vegetable stock, thyme, garlic, curry powder, salsify, and potatoes and simmer until the potatoes are tender, about 10 to 12 minutes.

2. Add the broccoli and cook for an additional 3 to 5 minutes. Do not overcook or the broccoli will lose its bright green color.

3. Transfer the mixture to a blender and puree. Pour the pureed soup back into the saucepan, stir in the soy milk, salt, and pepper, bring to a simmer, and serve.

MAKES 4 SERVINGS

66

salsify

Salsify, a root vegetable, is also known as the oyster plant because its taste resembles that of a delicately flavored oyster. Shaped like a parsnip, salsify is a white-fleshed root with a grayish skin. When purchasing, select well-formed roots that are heavy for their size. You can purchase it fresh or canned. If using the canned vegetable, rinse it well.

• EACH 1-CUP SERVING CONTAINS APPROXIMATELY:

CALORIES: 100 | FAT: 2 g | CHOLESTEROL: 0 | SODIUM: 338 mg | CARBOHYDRATES: 17 g | PROTEIN: 3 g

butternut squash and cider soup

This delightful autumn soup is perfect for fall picnics and tailgate parties. It can be transported in a thermos and served in mugs. At Canyon Ranch we serve it in a soup plate garnished with diced red apple and cracked black pepper.

1 tablespoon minced shallot

1 garlic clove, pressed or minced

3 cups cubed, seeded, and peeled butternut squash (about 1 pound)

1/2 cup fat-free chicken stock
(see page 54)

3/4 cup apple cider

1/4 cup light sour cream

1/2 unpeeled red delicious apple, finely diced, for garnish

cracked black pepper for garnish

1. Combine the shallot and garlic in a saucepan and cook over low heat until translucent, adding a little water if necessary to prevent scorching.

2. Add the squash and chicken stock and cook until soft, about 20 minutes. Pour into a blender and puree.

3. Add the cider and sour cream and continue to blend until well mixed.

4. Divide the soup among 4 bowls and garnish each with 1 teaspoon of diced apple and a pinch of cracked black pepper.

67

MAKES 4 SERVINGS

butternut squash
Butternut squash is a large winter vegetable weighing about 2 to 3 pounds and shaped like a pear. The smooth shell ranges from yellow to a dark gold in color, and the flesh is orange and very sweet. In fact, it is so sweet that it is often used in place of sweet potatoes in casseroles and pies. When buying butternut squash, select those that are firm and heavy with no cracks or soft spots. Those with the stub of the stem still attached will keep for a longer time. Do not refrigerate uncut squash. Store it in a cool, dry, well-ventilated area where it will keep for about 1 month.

• EACH 3/4-CUP SERVING CONTAINS APPROXIMATELY:

CALORIES: 80 | FAT: 1 g | CHOLESTEROL: 5 mg | SODIUM: 31 mg | CARBOHYDRATES: 16 g | PROTEIN: 2 g

borscht

This easy-to-make soup combines great taste with brilliantly beautiful color. It is wonderful for entertaining because it can be made the day before a party and served hot or cold. In this Canyon Ranch borscht we use buttermilk, rather than sour cream, for the tartness. This also makes it lower in both calories and fat than most other borscht recipes.

4 beets (1¹/₂ pounds)

2 garlic cloves, roasted and peeled
(see page 332)

1 teaspoon salt

1¹/₂ tablespoons sugar

2 cups buttermilk

1 lemon, sliced (8 slices), for garnish

1. Scrub the beets thoroughly, being careful not to break the skins. Cut off the roots and tops and reserve the tops for another use if desired.

2. Place the beets and roasted garlic in a pot. Cover with water and simmer until tender, about 35 to 40 minutes.

3. Remove the beets from the pot, reserving ¹/₂ cup of the water. Peel the beets and discard the skins.

4. Chop the beets and place them in a blender. Add the reserved cooking liquid and all the remaining ingredients, except the lemon slices, and blend until smooth.

5. Serve hot or cold, each serving garnished with a lemon slice.

MAKES 8 SERVINGS

68

• EACH 3/4-CUP SERVING CONTAINS APPROXIMATELY:

CALORIES: 85 | FAT: 1 g | CHOLESTEROL: 0 | SODIUM: 303 mg | CARBOHYDRATES: 19 g | PROTEIN: 4 g

consommé

Follow these instructions to turn your homemade chicken stock into a clear, rich-tasting consommé. You can use these same steps for making veal or beef consommé. If using an electric stove top that doesn't have an extremely low heat setting, offset the pan on the burner to avoid excessive evaporation.

8 cups fat-free chicken stock
(see page 54)

**3 ounces raw ground chicken
(3/4 cup)**

1 small onion, diced (1 cup)

1 small carrot, scraped and diced

1 stalk celery without leaves, diced

2 teaspoons fresh lemon juice

2 egg whites

1/8 teaspoon kosher salt

dried herb bouquet garni (see below)

1. Bring the chicken stock to a boil in a large stockpot.
2. Meanwhile, combine all the remaining ingredients, except the dried herb bouquet garni, and shape into a loaf. Add the loaf and the bouquet garni to the chicken stock and simmer over very low heat for 2 to 3 hours.
3. Skim when necessary during cooking time, but do not stir.
4. Remove the pan from the heat and strain the consommé into a clean bowl.

MAKES ABOUT 2 QUARTS (64 OUNCES)

dried herb bouquet garni
To make a dried herb bouquet garni wrap dried herbs, coarsely crumbled, not powdered, in 4- or 5-inch squares of cheesecloth and tie tightly with string. Include 3 or 4 sprigs of fresh parsley, 1 tablespoon each of dried thyme and marjoram, and 2 bay leaves.

70

• EACH 6-OUNCE (3/4-CUP) SERVING CONTAINS APPROXIMATELY:

CALORIES: **15** | FAT: **negligible** | CHOLESTEROL: **negligible** | SODIUM: **66 mg** | CARBOHYDRATES: **1 g** | PROTEIN: **4 g**

corn bisque

The complexity of flavor in this rich-tasting soup makes it an ideal first course for a dinner party or for a light luncheon menu. It has all the texture of a rich and creamy traditional bisque, but almost none of the cream—pureed vegetables create the thickness and contribute to the illusion.

1½ teaspoons olive oil

2 tablespoons finely diced leeks

½ cup finely diced onion

2 tablespoons finely diced celery

2 teaspoons whole-wheat flour

1 cup peeled and diced potatoes

1 cup frozen corn kernels

1½ cups fat-free chicken stock
(see page 54)

1 bay leaf

pinch chopped fresh thyme

½ teaspoon worcestershire sauce

1 drop tabasco sauce

1 teaspoon mrs. dash seasoning

1 teaspoon white pepper

2 tablespoons whipping cream

1. Heat the olive oil in a medium saucepan over medium-high heat. Add the leeks, onions, and celery and cook, stirring constantly, until the onion is soft and translucent.

2. Sprinkle the flour over the vegetables and cook for 2 more minutes.

3. Add the remaining ingredients, reserving the cream, and cook until the potatoes are tender. Remove from the heat and allow to cool slightly. Remove the bay leaf and discard.

4. Transfer two-thirds of the vegetable mixture to a blender and puree until smooth.

5. Add the puree to the remaining mixture and stir in the cream.

MAKES 8 SERVINGS

• EACH ½-CUP SERVING CONTAINS APPROXIMATELY:

CALORIES: **65** | FAT: **2 g** | CHOLESTEROL: **5 mg** | SODIUM: **18 mg** | CARBOHYDRATES: **10 g** | PROTEIN: **1 g**

corn chowder with chipotle pepper

Dried chipotle pepper adds a subtle smoky flavor to this Southwestern-inspired soup. It is an ideal first course for a vegan-vegetarian menu, or you can add beans of any kind to it and serve it as an entree. For a lacto-vegetarian dish you may use cow's milk in place of the soy milk.

1 dried chipotle pepper

1 teaspoon olive oil

1/2 small onion, diced (1/2 cup)

3 garlic cloves, pressed or minced

2 cups fresh or frozen corn kernels

1/2 teaspoon chili powder

1/2 teaspoon cumin

2 cups vegetable stock (see page 56)

1/2 cup soy milk

1/2 teaspoon salt

1 tablespoon chopped cilantro

1 red bell pepper, diced

1 green bell pepper, diced

chipotle chiles
The chipotle is a large, dried, smoked jalapeño. About 20 percent of Mexico's jalapeño crop is processed as chipotles because their smoky flavor is very popular in soups, salsas, and sauces.

1. Bring a small pot of water to a boil. Add the chipotle pepper, remove from the heat, and allow to soak until soft, about 5 to 10 minutes. Drain, cut the pepper in half, remove the seeds, and chop the pepper.

2. Heat the olive oil in a saucepan. Add the onion, garlic, and chipotle pepper and cook, stirring frequently, until soft.

3. Add the corn kernels, chili powder, and cumin and continue to cook for 5 more minutes, mixing well.

4. Add the vegetable stock. Simmer for about 10 minutes, or until the corn is tender. Add the soy milk and heat through.

5. Transfer the mixture to a blender and puree. Add the salt and cilantro.

6. Ladle 3/4 cup into each of 6 bowls and garnish with diced bell peppers.

MAKES 6 SERVINGS

73

quick clam and cheese chowder

For variety you can add a sprinkle of fresh herbs to this easy-to-make soup. This is a wonderful recipe for spur-of-the-moment entertaining because it can literally be made in minutes.

12 ounces canned chopped clams, undrained

2 garlic cloves, pressed or minced

1/2 teaspoon freshly ground black pepper

4 cups low-fat (1 percent) milk

1/4 cup freshly grated parmesan cheese

1. Drain the clams and pour the juice into a saucepan. Add the garlic and pepper to the juice and bring to a boil. Boil for 2 minutes.

2. Add the drained clams and milk and heat to desired temperature. Do not boil.

3. To serve, ladle 1 cup of soup into each of 4 soup bowls and sprinkle each serving with 1 tablespoon of Parmesan cheese.

MAKES 4 SERVINGS

74

• EACH 1-CUP SERVING CONTAINS APPROXIMATELY:

CALORIES: **254** | FAT: **6 g** | CHOLESTEROL: **71 mg** | SODIUM: **312 mg** | CARBOHYDRATES: **17 g** | PROTEIN: **33 g**

five onion bisque

The combination of so many kinds of onions gives this soup a depth of flavor which is truly satisfying. It is so low in both fat and calories that it is an excellent first course for many meals and ideal for dinner parties.

8 whole garlic cloves, peeled

1 teaspoon butter

1 medium sweet vidalia or imperial onion, thinly sliced

1/2 maui onion, thinly sliced

1/2 cup chopped well-rinsed leeks, white part only

4 scallions, chopped

1/4 cup non-alcoholic champagne

4 cups fat-free chicken stock
(see page 54)

1 teaspoon kosher salt

1/4 teaspoon freshly ground black pepper

1/2 cup chopped chives

1/2 cup fat-free sour cream

fresh basil leaves for garnish

18 sourdough croutons for garnish

1. Preheat the oven to 350°F.

2. Lightly spray a baking sheet with non-stick cooking spray. Spread the garlic cloves on the sheet and bake until very soft, about 10 minutes. Set aside.

3. Melt the butter in a 4-quart stockpot. Add the Vidalia and Maui onions and slowly cook them until caramelized, or a golden brown in color, about 30 to 40 minutes. Add the leeks and scallions and cook for an additional 10 to 15 minutes. Add the roasted garlic and champagne and cook until almost dry. Add the stock, salt, and pepper and simmer for 30 minutes.

4. Remove from the heat. Add the chives and allow to cool slightly. Spoon the mixture into a blender and puree while adding the sour cream.

5. Pour the puree back into the saucepan and reheat it to serving temperature. Garnish each serving with basil leaves and 3 sourdough croutons.

MAKES 6 SERVINGS

75

• EACH 2/3-CUP SERVING CONTAINS APPROXIMATELY:

CALORIES: 76 | FAT: negligible | CHOLESTEROL: 2 mg | SODIUM: 374 mg | CARBOHYDRATES: 14 g | PROTEIN: 4 g

hot and sour soup

This popular Asian soup has a mildly sharp, tart taste which is a refreshing way to start a meal. If you prefer a soup not quite as hot and spicy, just reduce the amount of red pepper flakes, or add them to taste at the end.

1 teaspoon minced garlic

2 tablespoons chopped red onion

1/2 teaspoon red pepper flakes

4 1/2 cups vegetable stock
(see page 56)

8 ounces canned bamboo shoots, drained

10 ounces firm tofu, drained and cubed

1 large shiitake mushroom, sliced

1 scallion, chopped

1 1/2 tablespoons rice vinegar

2 tablespoons cornstarch

1 cup loosely packed thinly sliced fresh spinach leaves

1. Combine the garlic, onion, and red pepper flakes in a heavy saucepan and cook, covered, over low heat until the onion is translucent, adding a little water if necessary to prevent scorching.

2. Stir in the stock. Add the bamboo shoots, tofu, mushroom, scallion, and rice vinegar and heat to boiling.

3. Combine enough water with the cornstarch to form a thin paste. Slowly pour the cornstarch mixture into the boiling soup, reduce the heat to medium, add the spinach, and continue to cook for 5 minutes.

MAKES 6 SERVINGS

• EACH 1-CUP SERVING CONTAINS APPROXIMATELY:

CALORIES: 60 | FAT: 2 g | CHOLESTEROL: 0 | SODIUM: 53 mg | CARBOHYDRATES: 9 g | PROTEIN: 4 g

kale soup

Even though kale grows best in cold climates, it is available all year round in most parts of the country, making this hearty recipe a soup for all seasons.

¼ cup dried chickpeas, soaked overnight in water

¼ cup dried kidney beans, soaked overnight in water

4½ cups fat-free chicken stock (see page 54)

1 cup chopped green kale

1 medium carrot, peeled and diced

½ onion, diced (½ cup if small; 1½ cups if large)

1 cup thinly sliced green cabbage

½ large potato, peeled and diced

1 garlic clove, minced

2 teaspoons red wine vinegar

1. Drain and rinse the chickpeas and beans. In a large pot combine them with the chicken stock and bring to a boil over high heat. Reduce the heat to medium and cook for 40 minutes.

2. Add the remaining ingredients and simmer until the beans are cooked through and tender, about 20 minutes.

MAKES 6 SERVINGS

77

kale

Kale is a member of the cabbage family and grows best in cold climates. It has a mild cabbage-like flavor and comes in a variety of colors. It is very high in vitamins A, C, folic acid, calcium, and iron. It also contains vitamin K, essential to the clotting of blood. Kale contains other protective substances called phytochemicals that are thought to play a role in cancer prevention. In other words, this is a very healthy vegetable!

• EACH 1-CUP SERVING CONTAINS APPROXIMATELY:

CALORIES: 85 | FAT: 2 g | CHOLESTEROL: 10 mg | SODIUM: 96 mg | CARBOHYDRATES: 14 g | PROTEIN: 5 g

minestrone

Minestra, the Italian word for soup, usually refers to a meat soup. A thin broth-type soup is called *minestrina,* and minestrone refers to a thick vegetable soup containing not only vegetables but also peas, beans, and some type of pasta. It is usually served topped with freshly grated Parmesan cheese and is hearty enough to be a whole meal.

¹/₄ cup black-eyed peas

¹/₂ cup orzo pasta or small shells

1 teaspoon olive oil

1 teaspoon minced garlic

3 tablespoons diced onion

¹/₄ cup diced carrots

¹/₄ cup diced celery

¹/₄ cup sliced leeks, white part only

¹/₄ teaspoon finely chopped
  fresh thyme

¹/₂ teaspoon finely chopped fresh
  parsley

pinch freshly ground black pepper

pinch salt

¹/₄ cup peeled and diced tomatoes

¹/₄ cup finely shredded savoy cabbage

3 cups vegetable stock (see page 56)

¹/₄ cup low-sodium V–8 juice

¹/₄ cup drained rinsed canned red
  kidney beans

¹/₂ cup freshly grated parmesan
  cheese

2 teaspoons chopped chives

1. Prepare the black-eyed peas and pasta according to the directions on the packages. Rinse and set aside.

2. In a medium soup pot, heat the oil and sauté the garlic and onion until the onion is translucent, being careful not to burn or brown it.

3. Add the carrots, celery, leeks, herbs, and spices and continue to sauté for 5 minutes.

4. Add the tomatoes, cabbage, stock, and V–8 juice and bring the soup to a boil. Stir in the cooked peas, pasta, and kidney beans and continue to cook over low heat until warmed through.

5. Ladle 3/4 cup of soup into each of 8 serving bowls and top each serving with 1 tablespoon Parmesan cheese and ¹/₄ teaspoon chopped chives.

MAKES 8 SERVINGS

• EACH SCANT 1-CUP SERVING CONTAINS APPROXIMATELY:

CALORIES: **94** | FAT: **3 g** | CHOLESTEROL: **4 mg** | SODIUM: **203 mg** | CARBOHYDRATES: **13 g** | PROTEIN: **5 g**

miso soup

Miso, also called bean paste, is a basic flavoring in much Japanese cooking. It comes in a variety of colors and flavor intensities. The lighter colors are usually used in soups and sauces and the darker ones in heavier dishes. At Canyon Ranch, to accommodate our vegan-vegetarian guests, we always have this soup on our menus.

1/2 teaspoon dark sesame oil

1/3 cup finely chopped shallots

3 tablespoons red miso

1 quart vegetable stock
   (see page 56)

1/4 cup diced firm tofu for garnish

3 tablespoons sliced scallions
   for garnish

miso

Miso is a fermented soybean paste that has three basic categories, rice miso, barley miso, and soybean miso. The category is determined by whether the koji, or mold used for fermentation, is cultivated in a rice, barley, or soybean base before being added to cooked soybeans. The color, flavor, and texture are affected by the amounts of soybeans, koji, and salt which are combined, and by the length of time the miso is aged, which can range from three months to three years. Red miso is derived from white rice and brown miso comes from brown rice.

1. Heat the sesame oil in a saucepan over medium heat, add the shallots, and cook until translucent.

2. Add the miso paste and mix well. Add the vegetable stock and bring to a simmer. Reduce the heat to low and simmer for 15 minutes.

3. To serve, ladle into 4 bowls and garnish each serving with tofu and scallions.

79

MAKES 4 SERVINGS

• EACH 1-CUP SERVING CONTAINS APPROXIMATELY:

CALORIES: **45** | FAT: **1 g** | CHOLESTEROL: **0** | SODIUM: **322 mg** | CARBOHYDRATES: **0** | PROTEIN: **negligible**

seafood chowder

This soup is very easy to make and no one will even notice the absence of the classic eddies of melted butter on top. Leftover soup can be pureed and used as a sauce over pasta or rice.

1 cup peeled and diced potatoes, divided use

1 small onion, diced (1/2 cup)

1 stalk celery, diced

1 garlic clove, minced

pinch white pepper

2 1/3 cups fish stock
(see page 55), divided use

1 bay leaf

pinch salt

1 teaspoon dried thyme, crushed

1/3 cup non-fat milk

1/3 pound sea scallops

1/4 pound small shrimp, peeled and deveined

1/4 pound halibut, cut into chunks

1. Steam the potatoes over boiling water for about 10 minutes, or until tender. Set aside.

2. Lightly spray a large saucepan with non-stick cooking spray. Add the onion, celery, and garlic and cook until the onion is soft and translucent, adding a few tablespoons of water if needed to prevent scorching.

3. Add half of the potatoes, white pepper, half of the fish stock, bay leaf, salt, and thyme, and simmer for 10 minutes.

4. Place the milk, remaining potatoes, and fish stock in a blender. Process until smooth. Pour the puree into the soup.

5. Add the seafood to the soup and simmer until it turns from translucent to opaque. Remove bay leaf before serving.

MAKES 8 SERVINGS

chowder

Chowder is a thick, chunky soup usually associated with seafood, clam being the most popular. The name comes from the French *chaudière*, a caldron in which fishermen made their stews with the catch of the day. A seafood chowder can contain any of several varieties of seafood and vegetables. New England–style chowder is made with milk or cream, Manhattan-style with tomatoes. The term chowder is also used to describe any thick, rich soup containing chunks of food, such as corn chowder.

80

• EACH 3/4-CUP SERVING CONTAINS APPROXIMATELY:

CALORIES: **100** | FAT: **2 g** | CHOLESTEROL: **44 mg** | SODIUM: **83 mg** | CARBOHYDRATES: **3 g** | PROTEIN: **17 g**

mulligatawny

This flavorful classic originated in southern India and the name actually means "pepper water." Based on the use of a rich stock highly seasoned with curry and other spices, mulligatawny usually includes pieces of cooked chicken and often chopped fruits, vegetables, and rice. It can be served hot or cold and is delicious garnished with a dollop of chutney.

3/4 cup peeled and diced potatoes

1¼ cups peeled and diced carrots, divided use

½ cup diced celery

½ cup diced onion

3½ cups fat-free chicken stock
(see page 54)

1½ teaspoons curry powder

pinch salt

1 teaspoon freshly ground black pepper

pinch thyme

½ cup finely diced cooked chicken breast

½ cup finely diced apple

½ teaspoon minced lemon zest, yellow part only

⅓ cup cooked white rice
(see boiled rice, page 171)

ground cinnamon for garnish

1. Combine the potatoes, 3/4 cup of carrots, celery, onion, and chicken stock in a medium saucepan. Bring to a boil, then lower the heat and simmer until the vegetables are tender, about 15 minutes.

2. Transfer the mixture to a blender. Add the curry powder, salt, pepper, and thyme and puree. Pour the mixture back into the saucepan.

3. Add the chicken, apple, remaining carrots, and lemon zest and simmer for 10 minutes. Add the cooked rice and cook until heated through.

4. To serve, ladle 3/4 cup into each of 6 soup bowls and garnish each serving with a dusting of ground cinnamon.

MAKES 6 SERVINGS

• EACH 3/4-CUP SERVING CONTAINS APPROXIMATELY:

CALORIES: **95** | FAT: **negligible** | CHOLESTEROL: **8 mg** | SODIUM: **236 mg** | CARBOHYDRATES: **18 g** | PROTEIN: **5 g**

sweet potato soup

This colorful soup makes an excellent sauce for fish and poultry. You can also whisk a little extra-virgin olive oil into leftover soup for an unusual salad dressing.

1 pound sweet potatoes, peeled and diced

1 medium sweet onion, chopped

4 garlic cloves, pressed or minced

1/4 teaspoon cinnamon

1/4 teaspoon salt

1/4 teaspoon freshly ground black pepper

1 1/2 cups fat-free chicken stock (see page 54)

2 cups fresh orange juice

1. Combine the sweet potatoes and onion in a large saucepan and cook, covered, over low heat until the onion is soft and translucent, about 12 minutes. Add the garlic, cinnamon, salt, and pepper and cook for 3 more minutes. Add the chicken stock and orange juice and cook until the sweet potatoes are soft.

2. Spoon the mixture into a blender and blend until smooth.

3. Serve hot or cold.

MAKES 6 SERVINGS

83

sweet potatoes

The sweet potato is a wonderful vegetable from a nutritional standpoint. A medium-sized sweet potato has about 140 calories and contains four times the daily allowance of beta carotene, twice the daily allowance of vitamin A, and one-third of the daily recommended vitamin C. Sweet potatoes also contribute vitamin B_6, iron, and potassium, as well as other valuable vitamins and minerals, are low in sodium, and contain no fat or cholesterol.

• EACH 1-CUP SERVING CONTAINS APPROXIMATELY:

CALORIES: **129** | FAT: **negligible** | CHOLESTEROL: **0** | SODIUM: **271 mg** | CARBOHYDRATES: **29 g** | PROTEIN: **3 g**

cream of tomato soup

Like the other non-dairy soups in this chapter, this creamy, fresh tomato soup is perfect for vegan menus and for anyone who is allergic to milk. Also, the use of Mrs. Dash seasoning adds a distinctive flavor without adding any calories, fat, or sodium and it is available in the spice section of all supermarkets.

1 teaspoon olive oil

3 tablespoons minced onion

2 teaspoons pressed or minced garlic

2 tablespoons tomato paste

3 tablespoons non-alcoholic
   white wine

3/4 cup tomato juice

5 plum tomatoes, chopped

2 1/2 cups vegetable stock
   (see page 56)

3/4 cup soy milk

1 teaspoon mrs. dash seasoning

1 teaspoon dried basil

pinch salt

dash tabasco sauce

1 1/2 teaspoons cornstarch

pinch freshly ground black pepper

6 teaspoons chopped chives
   for garnish

6 tablespoons croutons
   (see page 122) for garnish

1. Heat the olive oil in a medium saucepan. Add the onion and garlic and cook over medium heat until golden brown.

2. Add the tomato paste and continue to cook, stirring frequently, until it has a rusty color and a sweet aroma. Add the wine and cook until slightly reduced, about 10 to 15 minutes. Add all the remaining ingredients, except the chives and croutons, and cook for 30 more minutes.

3. Remove the saucepan from the heat, spoon the mixture into a blender, and puree.

4. Pour 1 cup of the soup into each of 6 bowls and garnish each serving with 1 teaspoon of chopped chives and 1 tablespoon of croutons.

MAKES 6 SERVINGS

84

soy milk
Soy milk is available in most supermarkets and all health food stores. Soy milk is made by pressing ground, cooked soybeans. It is very high in iron, and higher in protein than cow's milk. It is cholesterol-free and low in sodium and calcium. Most soy milk sold as a substitute for cow's milk is fortified with calcium.

• EACH 1-CUP SERVING CONTAINS APPROXIMATELY:

CALORIES: 75 | FAT: 1 g | CHOLESTEROL: 1 mg | SODIUM: 291 mg | CARBOHYDRATES: 12 g | PROTEIN: 3 g

fresh tomato and basil soup

This tasty, and practically fat-free, soup is the creation of Jean-François Meteigner, the chef and owner of La Cachette restaurant in Los Angeles. His highly-acclaimed French cuisine has a light touch. He suggests serving this soup hot, but I also like it cold, especially in the summertime when both tomatoes and fresh basil are at their best. For the easiest way to peel a tomato, see page 58.

5 organic tomatoes, peeled and seeded

1 medium onion, diced (1½ cups)

1 leek, white part only, chopped

6 garlic cloves, peeled

½ teaspoon salt

1 teaspoon fresh rosemary

1 cup water

½ cup tomato puree

½ cup tightly packed fresh basil leaves

1. Combine the tomatoes with the onion, leek, and garlic in a large skillet or saucepan and cook over medium heat, stirring frequently, for 5 minutes. Add all the remaining ingredients, except the basil, and cook for 15 more minutes. Add the basil and cook for only 2 minutes.

2. Puree the mixture in a blender, 2 cups at a time. (Remember to vent the blender to allow the steam to escape; otherwise, it might blow the top off the blender.)

3. If serving hot, pour the pureed soup back into the saucepan and heat to desired temperature.

MAKES 4 SERVINGS

• EACH 1-CUP SERVING CONTAINS APPROXIMATELY:

CALORIES: **65** | FAT: **negligible** | CHOLESTEROL: **0** | SODIUM: **495 mg** | CARBOHYDRATES: **15 g** | PROTEIN: **3 g**

zucchini bisque

The key to making this soup flavorful is a good, rich-tasting chicken stock. Should you prefer a vegetarian version of this tasty bisque, just substitute vegetable stock for the chicken stock, but reduce the volume of the vegetable stock by one-half for a better-tasting soup.

1 cup chopped onion

4 cups fat-free chicken stock
(see page 54), **divided use**

3/4 cup soy milk

3 medium zucchini, chopped
(3^1/$_2$ cups)

pinch salt

^{1}/$_2$ teaspoon curry powder

1. Combine the onion and ^{1}/$_4$ cup of stock in a medium saucepan and cook over medium heat until the onion is soft and translucent.

2. Add the remaining stock and bring to a boil over medium heat. Stir in the soy milk and zucchini and continue to boil for 5 minutes. Remove from the heat and stir in the salt and curry powder.

3. Puree the mixture in a blender, 2 cups at a time. (Remember to vent the blender to allow the steam to escape; otherwise, it might blow the top off the blender.) Pour the pureed soup back into the saucepan and heat to desired temperature.

MAKES 6 SERVINGS

87

• EACH 1-CUP SERVING CONTAINS APPROXIMATELY:

CALORIES: 40 | FAT: **negligible** | CHOLESTEROL: 0 | SODIUM: 236 mg | CARBOHYDRATES: 70 g | PROTEIN: 2 g

salads and salad dressings

A salad can be a small, almost calorie-free side dish or an entire meal. Quite literally, anything you can eat can be an ingredient in a salad.

To make salads more interesting there should always be an element of surprise. Combine a variety of colors and textures, the sweetness of fresh fruit, and the subtlety of well-seasoned dressings. Add colorful, crisp vegetables like carrots, jicama, radishes, and water chestnuts along with fruit—diced apples, oranges, or pineapple. Nuts and seeds also add texture as well as flavor and nutrition. Because they are quite high in fat, use them sparingly. Try toasting them, which greatly enhances their flavor. Never add nuts or seeds to a salad until you are ready to serve it because the moisture will soften them and destroy their delightful crunchiness. Consider pasta of all kinds, rice, beans, lentils, and grains such as corn, bulgar, or couscous.

When choosing lettuce, try something other than iceberg. The darker greens, such as romaine, endive, spinach, escarole, and kale, are much more nutritious than their pale cousins because they are richer in calcium, iron, and vitamins A and C. Also available in many markets is a mixture of baby greens called mesclun. For other ideas refer to the Glossary of Salad Greens in this chapter. When preparing salad greens, it is important to wash them thoroughly. Nothing is worse than a gritty salad. It is also important to dry them well before storing them in bags or wrapping them in towels in the refrigerator because wet greens dilute the dressing so that more of it is required.

For most salads it's the dressing that's the calorie culprit, but there are several solutions to this dilemma. The best way to solve the high-fat dressing dilemma is to make your own low-fat dressings using the recipes in this chapter. Homemade dressings are always better-tasting and much less expensive than their commercial counterparts. However, a regular creamy bottled dressing can be diluted with non-fat milk or buttermilk to reduce the fat, and a standard vinegar-based dressing can be diluted with water, juice, wine, or a little more vinegar.

For a fat-free dressing, try our Jet Fuel recipe on page 144 or one of its variations. You can create your own renditions just by substituting a different vinegar, such as raspberry, balsamic, or an herbed variety. If you want to add the taste of an oil, choose the most flavorful, aromatic one you can find, such as a good-quality extra-virgin olive oil or a dark, roasted sesame oil. Add just a teaspoon or two of it to a cup of fat-free dressing and you will be amazed at the enormous amount of flavor it provides. All of our salad dressing recipes can be made quickly and most will keep, tightly covered, in the refrigerator for a week or two. If you love blue cheese, try our Canyon Ranch version, which is also delicious on baked potatoes.

Salsas, even the bottled varieties, make for a tasty salad dressing. To give a little zing to your next fruit salad, try topping it with our Mango or Papaya Salsa on page 321.

Unless a salad dressing is salt-free, never dress the salad until you are ready to serve it because it's the salt that wilts the greens. If you want to dress a salad ahead of time, leave the salt out of the dressing and it will remain crisp and attractive for hours.

When you're eating salads in restaurants, order the dressing on the side and use the famous Canyon Ranch "dip and spear" technique. Your fork goes first into the dressing and then into the salad. You'll have dressing with every bite, but only a fraction of the amount you'd ordinarily use. Using this technique, you needn't shy away from your favorite creamy dressings.

Salads can be served at any temperature or combination of temperatures. In fact, two of my favorite salads in this chapter are Salad Niçoise with Grilled Tuna and Warm Chicken and Smoked Vegetable Salad.

Salads are so important at Canyon Ranch that we have a large salad bar available for both lunch and dinner. The salad bar offers such an enormous variety of ingredients that guests can use it for a quick buffet meal when they're in a hurry.

GLOSSARY OF SALAD GREENS

I am using the term greens to include not only lettuces, but also herbs and leafy vegetables, which we routinely have on our salad bars at Canyon Ranch for more varied, interesting, and refreshing salads.

ARUGULA:

Sprigs of dark green leaves with a strong nutlike flavor. It combines well with mild-flavored lettuces or with equally intensely flavored greens, such as watercress. It does not come in heads but is sold in small bunches, often with the roots attached. It is very perishable and should be kept, tightly wrapped, in the refrigerator. If properly stored it will last up to three days.

BELGIAN ENDIVE:

Six- to eight-inch heads of crisp, tender, yellow-white leaves with a green tinge. The small heads are so compact that they resemble bullets in shape and have a delicately bitter flavor. Use whole or in bite-size pieces of julienne cut. Mixes well with other greens. Expensive but little waste.

BIBB LETTUCE:

Small, cup-shaped leaves held together loosely. Dark green, crisp, tender leaves are succulent; considered by some to be the aristocrat of lettuces. The whole leaves are ideal "bowls" for salad mixtures. Mixes well with other greens.

BOSTON LETTUCE:

Soft, small head with delicate leaves. Outer leaves are green and inner are light yellow and buttery. Mixes well with other greens.

CHICORY:

Yellow-white stem with curly, fringed tendrils. Somewhat bitter taste. The outer leaves are darker and stronger-flavored than the inner. A prickly texture to add to tossed salad. An attractive garnish.

CHINESE CELERY CABBAGE:

Celery-colored, white-ribbed leaves in a tightly packed head. Serve alone, as a base for salad mixtures, or mix with other greens. The flavor is between celery and cabbage, as the name implies.

DANDELION GREENS:

A noteworthy weed with a slightly bitter, tangy flavor. It grows wild and is cultivated especially for salads. The youngest leaves are the most tender. Look for bright green, not yellowed or wilted, tips.

ESCAROLE:

The leaves are less curly and broader than endive and are a paler green; they should snap easily.

FENNEL:

The stalks are similar to celery and grow from a bulbous root with lacy, fernlike leaves. The licorice-like flavor is more intense in the leaves, which are usually used as an herb. Substitute for celery in stuffings and casseroles. Slices of the bulb provide a uniquely different taste in salads.

FIDDLEHEAD:

A fern frequently described as tasting like a cross between an asparagus and a green. Fiddleheads often grow along stream banks and are best in early spring when very young. Served raw in salads they add a wonderful taste and texture.

ICEBERG LETTUCE:

Large, compact heads with crisp leaves tightly packed. The outer leaves are a medium green and the inner leaves are a paler green. Slice, shred, or tear to add crunch to any salad. Longer shelf life than most lettuces.

ITALIAN PARSLEY:

The sprigs have a flat, broad leaf rather than the tight, curly leaf of regular parsley, with a slightly milder flavor. A frequently used herb and good garnish for Italian dishes.

LEAF LETTUCE:

Loose, tender leaves with green or red tips growing from a central stalk.

MÂCHE OR LAMB'S LETTUCE:

Small, oval-shaped, smooth green leaves in a loosely formed head. Tangy flavor. Good for tossed salads or as cooked greens.

MESCLUN:

A mixture of young greens, washed, bagged, and ready to use. These time-saving salad greens are a wonderful addition to the produce section when you're in a hurry.

MINT:

An herb, but important as a salad green in the Middle East, where it is an essential ingredient for the classic salad, tabbouleh.

NAPA CABBAGE:

Similar to Chinese celery cabbage, but the head is shorter and the base broader. Use for the same purposes, alone or with other greens.

PARSLEY:

Dark green sprigs of tightly crimped leaves with a strong, refreshing flavor. Usually thought of as a garnish, parsley is good in soup and for flavoring stocks. It is also good in salads of all types.

RADICCHIO:

There are several varieties of this red-leafed Italian chicory. However, the two most frequently available in this country are Verona and Treviso. Verona has burgundy-colored leaves with white ribs and grows in small, loose heads. The leaves of the Treviso are narrow and pointed and the heads are more tightly formed and tapered. They also have white ribs, but can range in color from pink to dark red. All varieties have firm leaves with a slightly bitter taste. Use as a garnish or mix with other greens to provide color and a different taste to a salad.

ROMAINE LETTUCE:

An elongated head of loose dark green leaves that are firm and crisp. The pungent flavor adds tang to salads. Classically used for Caesar salad.

SORREL:

Many edible varieties, both cultivated and wild. The arrow-shaped green leaves have a sour, almost bitter taste; the very young leaves are best. Best mixed with milder greens. Most frequently used in soups and sauces.

WATERCRESS:

Dark green, glossy leaves, dime-size, on crisp sprigs. The leaves and the tender part of the stems are spicy and peppery. Good addition to tossed salads. Also often used as a garnish.

YOUNG OR BABY GREENS:

All lettuce-type greens grow from the inside out. Therefore the centers of the heads are where you will find the young or baby greens.

antipasto salad

The reason the broccoli is added just before serving in this recipe is that if it is allowed to marinate in the dressing it loses its beautiful, bright color. Pressing or mincing the garlic releases more of its essential oils and provides a sharper, stronger flavor than slicing it or leaving it whole.

2 cups quartered white mushrooms

1 small red bell pepper, seeded and cut into matchstick pieces

1¼ cups drained and quartered water-packed canned artichoke hearts

2 small plum tomatoes, quartered

2 garlic cloves, pressed or minced

1 tablespoon chopped fresh basil

2 teaspoons extra-virgin olive oil

1 cup jet fuel dressing
(see page 144)

1½ cups broccoli florets, lightly steamed

1 cup mixed young greens

1. Combine all the ingredients, except the broccoli and greens, in a bowl and mix well. Cover and refrigerate for at least 1 hour. Just before serving stir in the broccoli.

2. Arrange ¼ cup of greens on each serving plate and top with 1½ cups of the antipasto mixture.

MAKES 4 SERVINGS

95

• EACH SERVING CONTAINS APPROXIMATELY:

CALORIES: 90 | FAT: 3 g | CHOLESTEROL: 0 | SODIUM: 102 mg | CARBOHYDRATES: 15 g | PROTEIN: 4 g

artichoke bowls with shrimp in dill sauce

Artichoke bowls can be used in an almost infinite variety of ways. You can serve them hot or cold, plain as a vegetable side dish, or filled as an entree. Filled with dilled shrimp, as they are in this recipe, they present an unusual entree for a luncheon or a dramatic first course for a more formal meal. If you want to serve extra dill sauce for dipping the artichoke leaves, just double the recipe for Dill Sauce. The easiest way to remove the furry, thistle-like covering on the heart of an artichoke — the choke — is with a serrated grapefruit spoon.

ARTICHOKE BOWLS:

4 large artichokes, thoroughly washed

2 garlic cloves, halved

lemon slices

DILL SAUCE:

1 cup plain non-fat yogurt

1/4 cup rice vinegar

1/4 teaspoon salt

1/8 teaspoon freshly ground black pepper

2 teaspoons sugar

2 tablespoons finely chopped fresh dill

1/2 teaspoon dried dill, crushed

2 cups (3/4 pound) cooked and cleaned small shrimp

1 cup diced celery

1. To make artichoke bowls, first pull off and discard the toughest outer leaves on each artichoke. Using scissors or kitchen shears, cut off the thorny tips of the remaining outer leaves. Using a large, sharp knife, cut off the pointed top on each artichoke so that the top is flat. Cut off each stem so that the bottom is flat. Then invert the trimmed artichoke on a flat surface and press down firmly on it to open up the leaves as much as possible, making it look like a flower.

2. Fill a pan large enough to hold all four of the artichokes with water to a depth of 2 inches. Add the garlic and lemon slices and bring to a boil. Place the artichokes in the pan, bottom side down, and cook, covered, over low heat for about 40 minutes, or until the bottom can be pierced easily with a fork. Remove the artichokes from the water and let them drain, upside down, until cool enough to handle.

3. Remove and discard the small center leaves and spread the artichoke open to expose the heart. Remove the remaining tiny leaves and then, using a grapefruit spoon, carefully scrape out the furry choke. Wrap tightly and refrigerate until cold.

artichoke

The word artichoke is sometimes confusing because it is the name given to three unrelated plants: the globe artichoke, Jerusalem artichoke, and Chinese (or Japanese) artichoke. When not otherwise specified in a recipe, artichoke almost always refers to the globe, grown mainly in the mid-coastal region of California. It is actually the bud of a large plant in the thistle family and has tough, petal-shaped leaves, part of which can be eaten when cooked by drawing the base of the leaf through your teeth to remove the soft portion at the end. It has an inedible prickly choke that must be cut or scraped out and discarded before the tender heart and meaty bottom can be eaten. Globe artichokes are grown year round, but their peak season is from March through May. When buying artichokes, look for ones that are heavy for their size and dark green with a tight leaf formation. Hearts and bottoms are available both frozen and canned.

4. To make the dill sauce, combine the yogurt, vinegar, salt, pepper, sugar, and dill in a bowl and mix well.

5. Add the shrimp and celery to the sauce and again mix well. Divide the mixture evenly among the chilled, hollowed-out artichoke bowls.

6. Serve with additional Dill Sauce on the side as a dip for the artichoke leaves, if desired.

MAKES 4 SERVINGS

97

asparagus vinaigrette

Because vinegar-based marinades and dressings dull the bright green color of asparagus, the bold red of pimiento adds important color here, making an attractive dish. This combination also works well with steamed celery hearts, canned artichoke hearts, and hearts of palm. Don't leave off the pimiento in any of these variations; its color and flavor count.

2 ounces whole pimientos, undrained

1/2 cup jet fuel tarragon dressing
(see page 144)

24 asparagus spears, steamed and chilled

1 1/2 tablespoons capers, drained

1. Pour the juice from the jar of pimientos into the dressing and mix well.

2. Cut the drained pimientos into 1/4-inch strips, cover, and refrigerate until needed.

3. Arrange the asparagus spears in a shallow glass serving dish and pour the dressing over the top.

4. Sprinkle the capers evenly over the top. Cover and refrigerate for several hours before serving.

5. To serve, place 6 asparagus spears on each plate. Sprinkle the top with the capers used to marinate them. Garnish each serving with strips of chilled pimiento.

MAKES 4 SERVINGS

98

• EACH SERVING CONTAINS APPROXIMATELY:

CALORIES: **96** | FAT: **negligible** | CHOLESTEROL: **0** | SODIUM: **45 mg** | CARBOHYDRATES: **19 g** | PROTEIN: **9 g**

coleslaw

This colorful, crunchy slaw will keep well for several days if tightly covered in the refrigerator. For faster preparation, substitute 5 cups of pre-shredded coleslaw mix for the cabbage and carrots.

3 cups shredded green cabbage

1 cup shredded red cabbage

1 cup shredded carrots

1 cup shredded jicama

1/2 small red onion, finely chopped

2 medium red delicious apples, finely diced (1 1/2 cups)

DRESSING:

1/2 cup fat-free mayonnaise

1/3 cup white vinegar

2 tablespoons plus 2 teaspoons fructose

2 tablespoons plus 2 teaspoons dijon mustard

1 1/2 teaspoons caraway seed

1/4 teaspoon salt

pinch white pepper

1. Combine the vegetables and apples in a large bowl and mix well.

2. Combine all the dressing ingredients in a small bowl and mix well.

3. Pour the dressing over the salad and toss until evenly coated. Cover tightly and refrigerate until cold before serving.

MAKES 12 SERVINGS

• EACH 1/2-CUP SERVING CONTAINS APPROXIMATELY:

CALORIES: 5 | FAT: negligible | CHOLESTEROL: 0 | SODIUM: 236 mg | CARBOHYDRATES: 13 g | PROTEIN: 1 g

cold pea salad

This unique salad is wonderful for entertaining because it can be made ahead of time. In fact, I like it even better the day after it is made. Because it is so easy to serve it is perfect for buffet-style service, a delightful addition to holiday menus, and great for picnics and tailgate parties.

2 cups fresh or frozen green peas

⅓ cup light sour cream

⅓ cup non-fat plain yogurt

¾ cup chopped scallions

¼ teaspoon seasoned salt

1. If using fresh peas, steam them until tender, but still firm. Remove from the heat and place the steamer basket under cold water to stop the cooking and preserve the color. If using frozen peas, which have already been slightly cooked, it is only necessary to thaw them.

2. Combine the sour cream, yogurt, scallions, and salt and mix well. Add the peas and gently fold them in until completely combined.

3. Cover tightly and refrigerate until cold before serving.

MAKES 8 SERVINGS

• EACH ⅓-CUP SERVING CONTAINS APPROXIMATELY:

CALORIES: **41** | FAT: **negligible** | CHOLESTEROL: **1 mg** | SODIUM: **80 mg** | CARBOHYDRATES: **7 g** | PROTEIN: **3 g**

carrot and raisin salad

Carrot and raisin salad is practically an American classic and it is always a popular item on the salad bar at Canyon Ranch. The ingredients are available all year round and the combination of flavors goes well with a variety of other dishes.

1/2 cup canned crushed pineapple, with juice

6 tablespoons non-fat plain yogurt

6 tablespoons fat-free mayonnaise

2 1/4 pounds carrots, grated (about 6 cups)

1/2 cup raisins

1. Drain the pineapple, reserving the juice. Combine 3 tablespoons of the reserved juice, yogurt, and mayonnaise in a large bowl and mix well.

2. Add the drained crushed pineapple and the carrots and raisins and mix well. Cover tightly and refrigerate until cold before serving.

MAKES 8 SERVINGS

bromelain — the enzyme in fresh pineapple Canned pineapple is the pineapple of choice in this salad because fresh pineapple contains bromelain, a potent enzyme that makes combining fresh pineapple with other ingredients extremely difficult. It can't be used with gelatin because bromelain prevents jelling; if used in breads and cakes, it causes an overmoist, almost gooey texture; when combined with fish, poultry, or meat, it will quickly destroy the firm texture of the protein, causing it to become mushy, and in this recipe it will curdle the yogurt. Cooking inactivates the bromelain, and therefore canned pineapple, which must be cooked before being canned, does not cause any of these problems and is the one to use in this salad.

102

• EACH 1/2-CUP SERVING CONTAINS APPROXIMATELY:

CALORIES: **69** | FAT: **negligible** | CHOLESTEROL: **0** | SODIUM: **75 mg** | CARBOHYDRATES: **17 g** | PROTEIN: **2 g**

fresh fennel salad

This simple salad has a delightfully refreshing taste that is perfect for fish and poultry. When possible make it the day before you plan to serve it to give the flavors a chance to marry.

1 tablespoon extra-virgin olive oil

1/4 cup fresh lemon juice

1/4 teaspoon salt

1/2 teaspoon freshly ground
   black pepper

1 fennel bulb (8 ounces), very thinly
   sliced (2 cups)

1 plum tomato, peeled and diced

1. Combine the olive oil, lemon juice, salt, and pepper and mix well. Add the fennel and mix well. Cover and marinate at room temperature for at least 30 minutes.

2. Just before serving, stir in the diced tomato.

MAKES 4 SERVINGS

fennel
There are two types of fennel, Florence fennel and common fennel. Both have celerylike stems and bright green feathery foliage. But it is Florence fennel, also called finocchio, that has a broad bulbous base that is treated like a vegetable, and its fernlike top can be used as a garnish or snipped and added to recipes as a flavor enhancer. Both the base and the top can be eaten raw or cooked. It has a mild anise flavor, which is even more subtle when cooked. Common fennel produces the long, oval-shaped brown seeds used as a spice in many Mediterranean and Middle Eastern dishes.

103

• EACH 1/2-CUP SERVING CONTAINS APPROXIMATELY:

CALORIES: 58 | FAT: 3 g | CHOLESTEROL: 0 | SODIUM: 166 mg | CARBOHYDRATES: 7 g | PROTEIN: 1 g

curried shrimp salad in pineapple boats

Most salads are better if assembled just before serving, but with this salad it is essential to literally wait until the last minute before combining all the component parts. The enzymes in fresh pineapple break down the protein in the shrimp, making them mushy in texture if combined ahead of time.

½ cup chopped raw walnuts

1 fresh pineapple

1 pound papaya, peeled and cut into bite-size pieces (2 cups)

1 cup curried chutney dressing
(see page 142)

8 bibb lettuce leaves for lining plates

3/4 pound small cooked cleaned shrimp (about 2 cups)

1. Place the walnuts in a preheated 350°F. oven for 8 to 10 minutes, or until golden brown. Or toast them in a small skillet over medium heat. Whichever method you use, watch them carefully because they burn easily. Set aside.

2. Cut the pineapple into quarters, leaving the leaves attached at the top. Remove the pineapple from its shell. Slice off the center core and cut the pineapple into bite-size pieces to use in the salad. You should have 2 cups. Trim the pineapple leaves, cutting off any dead leaves, and set aside.

3. Combine the papaya, pineapple, and dressing and toss thoroughly. Line 4 chilled plates with 2 Bibb lettuce leaves each and place the pineapple boats on top.

4. Just before serving, stir the shrimp into the salad mixture. Spoon 1 3/4 cups into each pineapple boat. Top each serving with 2 tablespoons of toasted walnuts. Serve immediately.

MAKES 4 SERVINGS

• EACH 13/4-CUP SERVING CONTAINS APPROXIMATELY:

CALORIES: **414** | FAT: **12 g** | CHOLESTEROL: **129 mg** | SODIUM: **167 mg** | CARBOHYDRATES: **60 g** | PROTEIN: **23 g**

gado-gado

This classic Indonesian salad is traditionally garnished with emping, homemade potato chips. Because of the high percentage of calories from fat in this salad, it is necessary to balance the menu by adding low-fat foods.

MARINADE:

1/4 cup fresh lime juice

3 tablespoons seasoned rice vinegar

2 tablespoons reduced-sodium soy sauce

1 garlic clove, pressed or minced

2 teaspoons finely chopped fresh gingerroot

2 teaspoons dark sesame oil

1/2 teaspoon crushed red pepper flakes

2 cups cubed and well-drained extra-firm silken tofu, divided use

1/4 cup whole-wheat flour

1 pound cabbage, coarsely chopped (4 cups), lightly steamed

10 ounces carrots, diagonally sliced (2 cups), lightly steamed

2 cups pea pods, lightly steamed

2 cups bean sprouts, lightly steamed

1 cup cooked pink lentils

1 cup seeded and thinly sliced cucumber

1/4 cup unhomogenized peanut butter (see page 329)

1. To marinate the tofu, combine the lime juice, rice vinegar, soy sauce, garlic, ginger, oil, and red pepper flakes in a shallow bowl and mix well. Add 1 1/2 cups of the tofu cubes to the marinade and allow to marinate for 1 hour. Set the remaining 1/2 cup of tofu aside.

2. Drain and reserve the marinade. Set aside.

3. Place the whole-wheat flour on a large plate and dip the marinated tofu cubes in the flour to coat. Spray a large skillet or wok with non-stick cooking spray and place over medium-high heat. Carefully stir-fry the tofu until golden brown. Remove from the heat and set aside.

4. Arrange the browned tofu cubes, cabbage, carrots, pea pods, bean sprouts, cooked lentils, and cucumbers evenly and attractively in separate piles on 4 plates or bowls.

5. To make the dressing, combine the reserved marinade, peanut butter, and remaining 1/2 cup of tofu in a blender and blend until smooth. Spoon 1/4 cup of the dressing over the top of each salad.

MAKES 4 SERVINGS

• EACH SERVING CONTAINS APPROXIMATELY:

CALORIES: **439** | FAT: **17 g** | CHOLESTEROL: **0** | SODIUM: **316 mg** | CARBOHYDRATES: **50 g** | PROTEIN: **29 g**

greek salad

This simple salad, served with crusty bread, is my favorite lunch whenever I'm in Greece. The secret to its success is the freshness of all the ingredients. Even though the calories from fat in this recipe are high, it is served as a side dish with crusty bread and other dishes so that the total percentage of fat for the whole meal can easily be balanced.

4 cups lettuce torn into bite-size pieces

4 plum tomatoes, quartered

1 small green bell pepper, seeded, membrane removed, and cut into strips

12 kalamata olives

1 small red onion, cut into rings

2 ounces feta cheese, crumbled

1 tablespoon extra-virgin olive oil

4 tablespoons fresh lemon juice

1/4 teaspoon freshly ground black pepper

1. For each salad place 1 cup of the lettuce on a dinner plate. On top of the lettuce arrange 4 tomato quarters, 1/4 of the bell pepper strips, 3 olives, 1/4 of the onion rings, and 1/2 ounce of feta cheese.

2. Combine the olive oil, lemon juice, and pepper in a small bowl, mix well, and drizzle over the salads.

MAKES 4 SERVINGS

107

feta cheese

Feta is a white, crumbly Greek cheese traditionally made with goat's milk. It is cured and stored in brine and therefore often called pickled cheese. Feta has a rich, tangy flavor and is a classic ingredient in Greek salads. Though not considered a low-fat cheese, it is also not a high-fat cheese, and just a very small amount of it can add enormously to anything it's on.

• EACH SERVING CONTAINS APPROXIMATELY:

CALORIES: **143** | FAT: **8 g** | CHOLESTEROL: **13 mg** | SODIUM: **291 mg** | CARBOHYDRATES: **15 g** | PROTEIN: **5 g**

jicama slaw

This is a salad created by Mark Militello, the Floridian chef famous for the ambitious menus in all of his Miami restaurants and named Chef of the Year in 1995 by *Seafood Magazine*. It is both unusual and delicious and was easily modified to meet Canyon Ranch nutritional guidelines. It is not only easy to make but can be made ahead of time, making it ideal for party menus. Do not peel the jicama until you are ready to use it or the pristine white color may darken.

DRESSING:

1/2 teaspoon salt

1/2 teaspoon sugar

2 tablespoons champagne vinegar

1/2 cup fresh orange juice

2 tablespoons extra-virgin olive oil

1/2 poblano chile

1 large jicama (1 1/2 pounds), peeled and cut into matchstick-size pieces

1/2 red bell pepper, seeded, membrane removed, and cut into matchstick-size pieces

1/2 yellow bell pepper, seeded, membrane removed, and cut into matchstick-size pieces

1 large orange, peeled and diced

1/4 cup finely chopped cilantro leaves

2 tablespoons finely chopped fresh mint leaves

1. To make the dressing, in a small bowl dissolve the salt and sugar in the vinegar. Add the orange juice and mix well. Slowly stir in the oil.

2. Combine all the remaining ingredients in a large bowl, add the dressing, and toss well.

MAKES 6 CUPS

jicama

Jicama is often called the Mexican potato because of its appearance. It is a large, bulbous root vegetable with a thin, light brown skin. The flesh is very white, crunchy, and quite sweet and can be served raw or cooked. When cooked, it resembles a water chestnut in both taste and texture. It used to be found only in Mexican markets, but jicama is now available in most supermarkets from November through May.

• EACH 1-CUP SERVING CONTAINS APPROXIMATELY:

CALORIES: 119 | FAT: 4 g | CHOLESTEROL: 0 | SODIUM: 187 mg | CARBOHYDRATES: 18 g | PROTEIN: 2 g

kamut and butternut squash salad with orange-almond dressing

This recipe was developed at Canyon Ranch to familiarize the guests with this ancient grain. The salad is such a popular item on the menu that I decided to include it in this book for anyone looking for a totally different vegetarian combination that can be made ahead of time. If butternut squash is not available, diced carrots or sweet potatoes can be substituted for it. When peeling and separating the oranges for this salad, hold them over the salad bowl so that you capture any of the juice that would otherwise be lost. This salad is wonderful for picnics served with whole-wheat pita bread.

½ cup **kamut wheat** (see box)

½ cup **unsweetened apple juice**

1 cup **water**

1 cup **peeled and diced butternut squash**

ORANGE-ALMOND DRESSING:

4 **oranges, peeled and separated into segments** (2 cups)

1 tablespoon **fresh lemon juice**

2 tablespoons **chopped parsley**

2 tablespoons **chopped fresh rosemary, or 2 teaspoons dried, crushed**

¼ cup **slivered almonds, toasted**

1 cup **raisins**

kamut

Kamut is a variety of high-protein wheat. In fact, the name kamut is the ancient Egyptian word for wheat. The kernels, which have never been hybridized, are two to three times the size of regular wheat and when cooked have a slightly chewy texture and a delicious nutty flavor. It is usually necessary to go to a health food store to buy kamut.

1. Put the kamut in a medium saucepan and cover with cold water. Cook over medium-high heat until it comes to a boil. Drain the kamut thoroughly and return it to the pan.

2. Add the apple juice and water. Cook, covered, over low heat until all the liquid is absorbed, about 35 minutes.

3. While the kamut is cooking, steam the squash until just crisp-tender and set aside.

4. Combine all the remaining ingredients in a large bowl and mix well. Stir in the cooked kamut and squash, and allow the salad to stand at room temperature for at least 1 hour before serving to marry the flavors.

MAKES 4 SERVINGS

109

• EACH 1¼-CUP SERVING CONTAINS APPROXIMATELY:

CALORIES: 115 | FAT: 3 g | CHOLESTEROL: 0 | SODIUM: 7 mg | CARBOHYDRATES: 22 g | PROTEIN: 3 g

bulgar lentil salad

This tasty salad combines lentils, a legume, with bulgar, a grain, thus providing a complete protein. Serve either in small, appetizer-size portions, or in larger amounts, as an entree.

⅓ cup medium-grind bulgar

¼ cup minced shallots

1 tablespoon white wine vinegar

2 tablespoons uncooked green lentils

½ cup water

¼ teaspoon salt

⅓ cup diced celery

⅓ cup diced carrots

1 tablespoon finely chopped fresh
   tarragon

1 teaspoon extra-virgin olive oil

1 tablespoon chopped walnuts

pinch white pepper

1. Put the bulgar in a small bowl, cover with warm water, and let soak for at least 30 minutes. Drain and set aside.

2. Combine the shallots and vinegar in a bowl and set aside.

3. Place the lentils in a medium saucepan and cover with 2 inches of water. Bring to a boil, reduce the heat to low, and simmer until tender, about 15 to 20 minutes. Drain the lentils and add them to the shallots and vinegar.

4. Add the drained bulgar and all the remaining ingredients and mix well. Serve at room temperature.

MAKES 4 SERVINGS

110

bulgar

When buying the ingredients for this salad be sure to purchase bulgar, also spelled bulgur and bulghur, rather than cracked wheat. Bulgar is often confused with cracked wheat, which is the wholewheat berry, ground and broken into either coarse, medium, or fine grinds, and is best cooked. Bulgar consists of wheat kernels that have been steamed, dried, and crushed. It has a tender, chewy texture and also comes in coarse, medium, and fine grinds. It can be served cooked as well as soaked, as it is in this salad and in the popular Middle Eastern salad tabbouleh, also in this chapter. It is available in most supermarkets and all health food stores and Middle Eastern markets.

• EACH SERVING CONTAINS APPROXIMATELY:

CALORIES: 104 | FAT: 3 g | CHOLESTEROL: 0 | SODIUM: 154 mg | CARBOHYDRATES: 19 g | PROTEIN: 5 g

melon bowls with curried crab

If you are having a party and want a fancier presentation of this salad, cut the melons into halves in a sawtooth pattern.

2 small ripe cantaloupes

2 cups chopped cooked crabmeat

3/4 teaspoon curry powder

1/2 teaspoon ground ginger

chopped scallion tops for garnish

1. Cut the melons into halves and remove the seeds. Use a melon baller to remove the melon from the rinds.

2. Combine the melon balls in a bowl with all the remaining ingredients, except the chopped scallion tops, and mix thoroughly.

3. Divide the salad equally among the 4 melon bowls and sprinkle the top of each serving generously with chopped scallion tops.

MAKES 4 SERVINGS

111

• EACH 1 1/2-CUP SERVING CONTAINS APPROXIMATELY:

CALORIES: 162 | FAT: 2 g | CHOLESTEROL: 60 mg | SODIUM: 249 mg | CARBOHYDRATES: 23 g | PROTEIN: 16 g

minted cucumber salad

This refreshing salad is excellent served with fish and seafood of all types. It is particularly good as a light side dish with poached salmon.

3 large cucumbers, peeled and very thinly sliced

salt

1/2 cup fresh lemon juice

1 tablespoon fructose

1/4 cup finely chopped fresh mint

sprigs fresh mint for garnish

cucumber preparation
Salting cucumber is an important step. The salt draws out the liquid and most of the bitterness. It also softens the cucumber flesh, which is desirable in this recipe. Many people who get indigestion from eating raw cucumbers can eat them without any problem after they have been salted and well drained. Always thoroughly rinse the drained cucumber to remove the salt.

1. Spread the cucumber slices in a large glass baking dish and sprinkle evenly with salt. Cover and allow to stand for at least 2 hours.

2. Drain the cucumbers and rinse thoroughly.

3. Combine the lemon juice and fructose in a medium bowl and mix thoroughly. Add the cucumber slices and chopped mint and mix well. Chill before serving. To serve, garnish with mint sprigs.

MAKES 8 SERVINGS

112

• EACH 3/4-CUP SERVING CONTAINS APPROXIMATELY:

CALORIES: 26 | FAT: negligible | CHOLESTEROL: 0 | SODIUM: 20 mg | CARBOHYDRATES: 6 g | PROTEIN: 1 g

marinated mushroom salad

These tangy marinated mushrooms are always a big hit as a salad or as an appetizer. For a more colorful presentation, top each serving with a sprinkle of diced tomato or red bell pepper. These are also good in sandwiches and other salads.

1/2 cup red wine vinegar

1/3 cup water

1/2 teaspoon fructose

2 tablespoons canola oil

1 tablespoon finely diced onion

1 tablespoon finely chopped parsley

1/2 teaspoon dried oregano, crushed

2 garlic cloves, pressed or minced

1/4 teaspoon salt

1/4 teaspoon freshly ground black pepper

3/4 pound mushrooms, such as oyster, chanterelle, or shiitake

lettuce leaves for serving

1. Combine all the ingredients, except the mushrooms and lettuce leaves, in a saucepan. Bring to a boil, remove from the heat, and cool for 30 minutes.

2. Clean and slice the large mushrooms, leaving the small ones whole. Place in a non-aluminum bowl.

3. Pour the marinade over the mushrooms and allow to cool to room temperature.

4. Line 8 plates with lettuce leaves. Drain the mushrooms. Arrange 1/4 cup of the mushrooms on each plate.

MAKES 8 SERVINGS

113

• EACH 1/4-CUP SERVING CONTAINS APPROXIMATELY:

CALORIES: 47 | FAT: 3.6 g | CHOLESTEROL: 0 | SODIUM: 76 mg | CARBOHYDRATES: 4 g | PROTEIN: 1 g

salad niçoise with grilled tuna

This salad is a variation of the classic French salade niçoise made with canned tuna. You may want to get creative and use another type of fish, or turn it into a chicken niçoise with a grilled chicken breast.

8 small red boiling potatoes, quartered

1/2 pound green beans

1/2 medium onion, thinly sliced

1 small red bell pepper, seeded and sliced

8 cherry tomatoes, quartered

4 canned artichoke hearts, drained and quartered

2 tablespoons capers, drained and rinsed

1/2 cup canyon ranch dressing (see page 138)

4 tuna fillets (4 ounces each)

4 cups baby greens, washed and well drained

4 whole scallions for garnish, optional

1. Arrange a steamer basket in a saucepan over boiling water. Add the quartered potatoes and green beans and cover. Remove the beans with tongs when tender but still crisp. Continue cooking the potatoes until they can be pierced easily with a fork.

2. Lightly spray a small skillet with non-stick vegetable cooking spray and place over medium heat. Add the onion and bell pepper and cook until tender but still slightly crunchy.

3. Combine the cooked onion, pepper, beans, and potatoes in a bowl with the tomatoes, artichoke hearts, and capers. Add the dressing and mix well. Refrigerate, tightly covered, for about 15 minutes.

4. Prepare hot coals for grilling or preheat the broiler. Grill or broil the fish fillets for about 3 minutes per side.

5. Add the greens to the vegetables and mix well.

6. Divide the salad among 4 serving plates and arrange a tuna fillet on each bed of salad. Garnish each serving with a whole scallion, if desired.

MAKES 4 SERVINGS

114

• EACH SERVING CONTAINS APPROXIMATELY:

CALORIES: **280** | FAT: **5 g** | CHOLESTEROL: **51 mg** | SODIUM: **80 mg** | CARBOHYDRATES: **29 g** | PROTEIN: **31 g**

new potato salad

This recipe calls for red potatoes because they provide a prettier presentation. However, if they are not available, use the round white boiling potatoes.

1 pound small red potatoes, cut into 1-inch cubes (3 cups)

1/2 cup non-fat plain yogurt

1/4 cup reduced-calorie mayonnaise

1/2 tablespoon cider vinegar

1 teaspoon dijon mustard

1 tablespoon minced parsley

3/4 cup minced celery

1/2 cup finely chopped scallions

1/4 cup diced red pepper

pinch celery seed

pinch freshly ground black pepper

pinch salt

2 tablespoons sweet pickle relish

1. Place the potatoes in a small pan with enough water to cover. Cover and cook until tender but not mushy, about 10 minutes. Drain and cool.

2. Combine the yogurt, mayonnaise, vinegar, and mustard in a large bowl and mix well. Add the parsley, celery, scallions, red pepper, seasonings, and relish and mix well. Fold in the cooled potatoes.

3. Store, tightly covered, in the refrigerator until well chilled, about 2 hours. Serve cold.

MAKES 8 SERVINGS

boiling potatoes
Round red and white boiling potatoes are almost identical except for their color. The red potatoes have a reddish brown skin and the white ones have a freckled beige-colored skin. Both have a waxy flesh that contains less starch and more moisture than russets or the long white potatoes.

116

• EACH 1/2-CUP SERVING CONTAINS APPROXIMATELY:

CALORIES: **85** | FAT: **negligible** | CHOLESTEROL: **negligible** | SODIUM: **226 mg** | CARBOHYDRATES: **18 g** | PROTEIN: **3 g**

hearts of palm and endive salad with papaya vinaigrette

Papaya Vinaigrette is also an excellent topping for fruit salads of all types and an excellent sauce on fish and poultry.

PAPAYA VINAIGRETTE:

1½ pounds papaya, peeled, seeded, and diced (3 cups)

2 teaspoons fresh lime juice

2 teaspoons frozen pineapple juice concentrate, undiluted

2 teaspoons raspberry vinegar

1 teaspoon peanut oil

pinch freshly ground black pepper

SALAD:

2 heads belgian endive

4 heads bibb lettuce

13½ ounces canned water-packed hearts of palm, drained

1. To make the vinaigrette, combine the papaya with the remaining dressing ingredients in a blender and blend until smooth. Pour into a bowl, cover, and refrigerate. This can be made a day ahead of time.

2. Rinse the endive and Bibb lettuce under cold water. Set on a cloth towel to dry. Tear the Bibb lettuce into bite-size pieces.

3. Cut hearts of palm into matchstick-size pieces.

4. Assemble 8 salad plates with 3 endive leaves, 1 cup of Bibb lettuce, and one-eighth of the hearts of palm on each plate. Top with 2 tablespoons of the vinaigrette.

MAKES 8 SERVINGS

117

heart of palm

Heart of palm is the center portion of the stem of the cabbage palm, which grows only in tropical climates. In this country it is grown only in Florida, where it is the official state tree. The heart is shaped like a large asparagus without the head, ivory in color, and tastes similar to an artichoke heart. Generally heart of palm is available fresh only where it is grown due to the fact that it is extremely perishable. However, canned hearts of palm packed in water are readily available and can be found in most supermarkets.

• EACH SERVING CONTAINS APPROXIMATELY:

CALORIES: 70 | FAT: negligible | CHOLESTEROL: 16 mg | SODIUM: 3 mg | CARBOHYDRATES: 16 g | PROTEIN: 1 g

pasta primavera salad

Be careful not to overcook whole-wheat pasta. If not cooked al dente, it becomes mushy much faster than regular semolina pasta. I like this salad best served at room temperature. If you prefer to serve it cold, cover the salad before refrigerating it and add the broccoli just before serving.

1 cup diced carrots

1 cup diced yellow squash

1 cup diced onion

1 cup cauliflower in small florets

1 cup broccoli in small florets

1/2 cup canyon ranch dressing
(see page 138)

2 cups cooked whole-wheat noodles
(1/2 pound dry)

1/4 cup freshly grated parmesan
cheese

1 1/2 cups diced tomatoes
for garnish

1. Steam all the vegetables until crisp-tender. Transfer all the vegetables, except the broccoli, to a large bowl and marinate for several hours in the dressing.

2. Combine the cooked pasta and Parmesan cheese in a bowl and mix well.

3. To serve, combine the marinated vegetables, broccoli, and pasta and mix thoroughly. Garnish each serving with diced tomatoes.

MAKES 4 SERVINGS

• EACH 2-CUP SERVING CONTAINS APPROXIMATELY:

CALORIES: 236 | FAT: 3 g | CHOLESTEROL: 4 mg | SODIUM: 276 mg | CARBOHYDRATES: 44 g | PROTEIN: 10 g

positive power salad

This is a salad I designed especially for Mel Zuckerman shortly after we opened in Tucson in 1979, and I included his favorite foods as ingredients. I named it after our most advanced fitness class because it was indeed an energy-packed dish. Everyone who saw the salad back then wanted one so we put it on our menu and for years it was one of our most popular dishes. In fact, so many returning guests ask about it that I decided to put it in this book. It is higher in fat than most of our salads, but it is also very high in protein and complex carbohydrates and can easily be included in a healthy menu plan for a whole day.

½ cup raw almonds, chopped and toasted

2 cups chopped broccoli

2 cups sliced mushrooms

1½ cups chopped cauliflower

1½ cups diced jicama

1 cup diced carrots

½ cup diced yellow squash

½ cup diced zucchini

½ cup alfalfa sprouts

¼ cup chopped scallions

2 red delicious apples, unpeeled and diced

½ cup raisins

4 ounces part-skim mozzarella cheese, diced (1 cup)

¼ cup freshly grated parmesan cheese

½ cup italian jet fuel dressing (see page 144)

⅓ cup toasted sunflower seeds

If preparing this salad ahead of time, don't add the dressing, almonds, or sunflower seeds until you're ready to serve it. The salt in the dressing will soften the other ingredients, and the nuts and seeds won't be as crunchy.

1. Combine all the ingredients, except the sunflower seeds, in a large bowl and mix thoroughly.

2. Sprinkle 2 teaspoons of toasted sunflower seeds over the top of each serving.

MAKES 8 SERVINGS

• EACH 1½-CUP SERVING CONTAINS APPROXIMATELY:

CALORIES: **226** | FAT: **11 g** | CHOLESTEROL: **10 mg** | SODIUM: **151 mg** | CARBOHYDRATES: **25 g** | PROTEIN: **12 g**

romaine with parmesan and dijon mustard

This light and delicious salad is the Canyon Ranch version of a classic Caesar salad.

1 large head romaine lettuce

¼ cup pasteurized egg whites
(see box)

1 teaspoon dijon mustard

1 tablespoon red wine vinegar

½ tablespoon extra-virgin olive oil

2 tablespoons chopped fresh basil

½ garlic clove, pressed or minced

1 tablespoon chopped scallions

1 tablespoon freshly grated
parmesan cheese

1 cup whole-grain croutons
(see page 122)

1. Prepare the lettuce by removing the base of the head and thoroughly washing the lettuce in cool water. Shake out as much of the water as possible and tear the lettuce into big, bite-size pieces. Roll the torn lettuce in towels to absorb any remaining moisture and refrigerate until cold.

2. Prepare the dressing by whipping the egg whites with the Dijon mustard and vinegar. Add the olive oil and mix well. Stir in the basil, garlic, scallions, and Parmesan cheese.

3. In a large bowl lightly toss the lettuce with the dressing.

4. Divide the salad equally among 4 plates and top each serving with ¼ cup of the croutons.

MAKES 4 SERVINGS

pasteurized egg whites

If you can't buy pasteurized egg whites in your market, use liquid egg substitute, which is also pasteurized. Do not use raw egg whites. Cooking eggs destroys salmonella, a strain of bacteria that is difficult to detect because it gives no obvious warnings such as an off color or bad taste or smell. It can enter the system through contaminated water or food. Any food can be contaminated just by touching salmonella-carrying foods or being placed on unwashed surfaces such as cutting boards that have had contact with them. It can attack in as little as 6 hours or as long as 3 days.

• EACH 2-CUP SERVING CONTAINS APPROXIMATELY:

CALORIES: 75 | FAT: 3 g | CHOLESTEROL: 2 mg | SODIUM: 147 mg | CARBOHYDRATES: 9 g | PROTEIN: 4 g

croutons

Making your own croutons is far better than buying them. They are fresher, better-tasting, and usually much lower in fat. Croutons add a delightful look, taste, and texture to many types of salads and soups.

4 slices whole-grain bread, or any firm bread of your choice

1. Allow the bread to dry out for several hours, turning it occasionally to speed up the process.

2. Preheat the oven to 300°F.

3. Cut the bread into ¼-inch squares and spread out on a baking sheet. Bake in the preheated oven for 20 minutes, or until well browned, stirring occasionally for even browning.

MAKES 2 CUPS

122

• EACH ¼-CUP SERVING CONTAINS APPROXIMATELY:

CALORIES: **30** | FAT: **negligible** | CHOLESTEROL: **0** | SODIUM: **67 mg** | CARBOHYDRATES: **6 g** | PROTEIN: **1 g**

shrimp louis

A seafood Louis is a perennial favorite on lunch menus throughout the country. Shrimp is called for in this recipe, but you can substitute crab or lobster, or use a combination of all three. Using this quick and easy recipe it's possible to make it at home in minutes.

8 large lettuce leaves

1 large head lettuce, shredded (8 cups)

3/4 cup thousand island dressing (see page 151)

12 ounces medium cooked shrimp (about 2 cups)

2 tomatoes, quartered, for garnish

sprigs fresh parsley and lemon wedges for garnish

1. Wash and dry the lettuce leaves and place them, wrapped in towels, in the refrigerator to chill.

2. Combine the shredded lettuce and dressing in a large bowl and mix thoroughly.

3. Arrange the lettuce leaves on 4 large plates or in bowls. Top the lettuce leaves with 2 cups of dressed lettuce. Arrange 1/2 cup of the shrimp on top of each serving.

4. Garnish each serving with tomato, lemon wedges, and parsley sprigs.

123

MAKES 4 SERVINGS

• EACH SERVING CONTAINS APPROXIMATELY:

CALORIES: 95 | FAT: 2 g | CHOLESTEROL: 76 mg | SODIUM: 109 mg | CARBOHYDRATES: 9 g | PROTEIN: 13 g

sweet potato salad

This colorful combination is a delightful variation of the more usual versions of potato salad. It's easy to serve buffet style, and a great addition to holiday menus.

1¹/₂ pounds sweet potatoes, peeled and cut into 3/4-inch cubes (4 cups)

1 tablespoon chopped fresh thyme

¹/₄ cup vegetable stock
(see page 56)

¹/₂ teaspoon capers

1¹/₂ tablespoons chopped parsley

1 tablespoon whole-grain mustard

1¹/₂ teaspoons honey

1¹/₄ teaspoons balsamic vinegar

¹/₄ teaspoon salt

¹/₂ teaspoon extra-virgin olive oil

1. Preheat the oven to 350°F.

2. Spray a baking sheet with non-stick cooking spray. Spread the sweet potatoes on the baking sheet in a single layer and spray again. Bake for about 20 minutes, or until tender.

3. Combine all the remaining ingredients in a bowl and mix well. Add the baked sweet potatoes and toss gently to coat. Tightly cover and refrigerate for about 1 hour, or until well chilled.

MAKES 6 SERVINGS

124

• EACH 3/4-CUP SERVING CONTAINS APPROXIMATELY:

CALORIES: **95** | FAT: **negligible** | CHOLESTEROL: **0** | SODIUM: **164 mg** | CARBOHYDRATES: **21 g** | PROTEIN: **21 g**

szechuan noodles with spicy peanut sauce

This cold noodle dish is as popular at Canyon Ranch as it is in most Chinese restaurants.

10 ounces dry asian-style noodles
(4 cups cooked)

1½ teaspoons dark sesame oil

1 cup spicy peanut sauce
(see page 329)

½ cup chopped scallion tops
for garnish

red bell pepper, diced, for garnish,
optional

4 scallion flowers (see box) for
garnish, optional

1. Cook the noodles until al dente according to package directions. Drain and rinse with cold water. Drain again thoroughly.

2. Combine the noodles and sesame oil and toss to coat all the noodles with the oil. Cover tightly and refrigerate to chill slightly.

3. To serve, place 1 cup of noodles on each plate. Pour ¼ cup of the peanut sauce over the top. Sprinkle with 2 tablespoons of the chopped scallion tops. Sprinkle diced red pepper over the top of each serving and garnish with a scallion flower, if desired.

125

MAKES 4 SERVINGS

scallion flowers

To make a scallion flower, first cut the root end off, and then cut the green top off about 2 inches above the white part of the scallion. Using a sharp paring knife, shred the green end, then drop the scallion into ice water to "bloom." The cold water causes the scallion greens to curl and resemble a flower.

• EACH SERVING CONTAINS APPROXIMATELY:

CALORIES: **329** | FAT: **7 g** | CHOLESTEROL: **68 mg** | SODIUM: **33 mg** | CARBOHYDRATES: **54 g** | PROTEIN: **12 g**

tabbouleh

This Middle Eastern salad is so popular that it is available in most delicatessens and take-out food counters across the country. However, most recipes for it include olive oil; our low-fat version does not.

1 cup uncooked bulgar

2 cups water

1/3 cup fresh lemon juice

1/2 teaspoon salt

1/4 teaspoon freshly ground
  black pepper

2 garlic cloves, pressed or minced

3 medium tomatoes, finely chopped

1 cup finely chopped parsley

1 cup finely chopped scallions

1/2 cup finely chopped mint leaves

1. Combine the bulgar and water in a bowl and allow to soak for at least 45 minutes.

2. In another bowl combine the lemon juice, salt, pepper, and garlic and mix well.

3. Drain the bulgar well, add it to the lemon juice mixture, and combine thoroughly.

4. Add all the remaining ingredients and mix well. Cover tightly and refrigerate for several hours before serving.

MAKES 6 CUPS

bulgar
For information on bulgar see the box following Bulgar Lentil Salad on page 110.

126

• EACH 1/2-CUP SERVING CONTAINS APPROXIMATELY:

CALORIES: 70 | FAT: **negligible** | CHOLESTEROL: 0 | SODIUM: **120 mg** | CARBOHYDRATES: **15 g** | PROTEIN: 4 g

taco salad

This simple salad is a wonderful entree for a Southwestern luncheon. It is even easier and faster to make if you buy already baked corn tortilla chips and prepared fresh salsa at the supermarket. Serve the salad with Canyon Ranch Guacamole (page 36) on the side and fresh tropical fruit for dessert.

8 corn tortillas, cut into wedges

2 heads iceberg lettuce, finely chopped

3 large tomatoes, diced

1 cup jet fuel mexican dressing (see page 144)

4 ounces canned whole green chiles, cut into strips

3 cups diced cooked chicken or turkey

1/2 cup grated reduced-fat cheddar or monterey jack cheese

1/2 cup light sour cream

2 cups tomato salsa (see page 324)

1. Toast the tortillas in a low preheated oven until crisp. Set aside. Combine the lettuce, tomatoes, and dressing in a medium bowl and toss thoroughly.

2. Divide the salad among 8 dinner plates. Garnish with the tortilla pieces and green chile strips.

3. Sprinkle equal amounts of chicken and cheese evenly over the top of each salad. Top each with 1 tablespoon of the sour cream.

4. Serve with a side dish of 1/4 cup salsa.

MAKES 8 SERVINGS

127

• EACH 2-CUP SERVING CONTAINS APPROXIMATELY:

CALORIES: 314 | FAT: 10 g | CHOLESTEROL: 86 mg | SODIUM: 204 mg | CARBOHYDRATES: 21 g | PROTEIN: 33 g

tuna and black bean salad

This tangy tuna and bean salad is a perfect spa meal for boating and camping trips because all the ingredients can be stored safely without refrigeration and the dish is best served at room temperature. For picnics combine all the ingredients except the tuna. Pack a can opener in your basket and add the tuna, drained and flaked, just before serving.

30 ounces canned black beans, rinsed and drained

1 teaspoon freshly ground black pepper

2 teaspoons grated or finely chopped lemon zest

1/4 cup fresh lemon juice

4 tablespoons capers

1/2 cup (4 ounces) sliced pimientos

12 ounces canned solid-pack white tuna in water, drained and flaked

1. Combine the beans and all the other ingredients, except the tuna, and mix well.

2. Just before serving, carefully fold the tuna into the mixture.

MAKES 4 SERVINGS

128

• EACH 1 1/4-CUP SERVING CONTAINS APPROXIMATELY:

CALORIES: **418** | FAT: **2 g** | CHOLESTEROL: **13 mg** | SODIUM: **171 mg** | CARBOHYDRATES: **68 g** | PROTEIN: **34 g**

wild rice salad

We serve this salad as a vegetarian entree at Canyon Ranch. However, it is also good with water-packed tuna or diced cooked poultry or meat added to it. It is a wonderful portable meal for picnics and al fresco parties of all types.

1/2 cup chopped walnuts

1 medium onion, finely chopped (1 1/2 cups)

2 cups broccoli florets

3/4 cup wild rice

1 1/2 cups water

2 teaspoons reduced-sodium soy sauce

1 tablespoon dried thyme, crushed in a mortar and pestle

2 medium carrots, scraped and finely chopped (1 cup)

2 stalks celery, without leaves, finely chopped (1 cup)

1/2 cup caper dressing (see page 137)

lettuce leaves for lining plates

4 cups greens torn into bite-size pieces

4 sprigs fresh thyme for garnish

1. Preheat the oven to 350°F.

2. Toast the walnuts in the preheated oven for 8 to 10 minutes. Watch them carefully because they burn easily. Set aside.

3. Steam the onion and broccoli separately and set aside.

4. Combine the wild rice, water, soy sauce, and thyme and bring to a boil. Reduce the heat and cook, covered, for about 30 to 35 minutes, or until all the liquid has been absorbed and the rice is fluffy.

5. Allow to cool to room temperature.

6. Combine the wild rice with the steamed onions, chopped carrots, chopped celery, and the dressing and mix well. Refrigerate until cold before serving. Refrigerate the broccoli in a separate bowl.

7. To serve, add the steamed chilled broccoli and toss again thoroughly.

8. Line 4 chilled plates with lettuce leaves and top each serving with 1 cup of greens. Place 2 cups of the wild rice mixture over the greens. Garnish with a sprig of fresh thyme. Top each serving with 2 tablespoons of toasted walnuts.

MAKES 4 SERVINGS

• EACH 2-CUP SERVING CONTAINS APPROXIMATELY:

CALORIES: 307 | FAT: 12 g | CHOLESTEROL: 0 | SODIUM: 380 mg | CARBOHYDRATES: 41 g | PROTEIN: 12 g

winter pear and stilton salad with port dressing and toasted walnuts

The variety of tastes and textures in this recipe combine to create a distinctively different and truly delicious salad. It only takes about 15 minutes to make and you can prepare it hours before your guests arrive. Always toast nuts before using them because it enhances their flavor. In this recipe I toast the walnuts in a pan on the top of the stove because I'm not using the oven for anything else. However, if the oven is already preheated you can also toast the walnuts at 350°F. for 8 to 10 minutes, or until a golden brown. Watch them carefully.

¼ cup chopped walnuts

1½ cups port wine

6 cups assorted young greens torn into bite-size pieces

2 pears, peeled, cored, sliced, and broiled until lightly browned

¼ cup crumbled stilton cheese

2 shallots, sliced (¼ cup)

1 garlic clove, pressed or minced

1 tablespoon dijon-style mustard

2 tablespoons balsamic vinegar

walnut storage
Shelled walnuts will remain fresh for at least 6 months stored in the refrigerator in airtight containers or Ziploc bags. A freezer is the best place for long-term storage where they will keep their flavor for a year.

130

1. Put the walnuts in a heavy saucepan and place over medium heat. Cook, stirring frequently, until nicely toasted. Put the toasted walnuts in a bowl and set aside.

2. Pour the port into the same pan used to toast the walnuts. Bring to a boil over medium-high heat. Continue to boil until reduced in volume by half. Remove from the heat and cool.

3. Place 1½ cups of the greens on each of 4 plates. Arrange the broiled pear slices evenly over the top of the greens. Sprinkle 1 tablespoon of the Stilton over each salad.

4. Pour the reduced port into a blender. Add the shallots, garlic, mustard, and vinegar and puree. Pour an equal amount of the dressing over each salad. Top each serving with 1 tablespoon of the toasted walnuts.

MAKES 4 SERVINGS

• EACH 1½-CUP SERVING CONTAINS APPROXIMATELY:

CALORIES: **291** | FAT: **7 g** | CHOLESTEROL: **6 mg** | SODIUM: **187 mg** | CARBOHYDRATES: **30 g** | PROTEIN: **6 g**

warm chicken and smoked vegetable salad

This layered chicken dish is as attractive as it is tasty. The vegetable assortment adds brilliant colors to the plate, and smoking them lends an interesting and unusual flavor.

VINAIGRETTE:

1 medium shallot, finely chopped

1 tablespoon honey

¼ cup red wine vinegar

1 teaspoon finely chopped fresh thyme

¼ cup fat-free chicken stock
(see page 54)

pinch freshly ground black pepper

SMOKED VEGETABLES:

1 cup mesquite chips

2 medium yellow squash (8 ounces), sliced

2 medium zucchini squash (8 ounces), sliced

2 large tomatoes, quartered

4 boned skinless chicken breasts (1 pound)

4 cups assorted young greens

1. To make the vinaigrette, combine the shallot, honey, and vinegar in a saucepan and bring to a boil. Reduce by half. Add the thyme and stock to the honey mixture and reduce by one-third. Stir in the pepper and set aside.

2. To smoke the vegetables, first soak the mesquite chips in lukewarm water until saturated, about 1 hour. Drain well.

3. Prepare the coals for grilling. When the coals are glowing, lightly coat the grill rack with oil or spray with non-stick cooking spray. Place the soaked wood chips on top of the coals. Arrange the vegetables to be smoked on the grill rack. Cover the grill and smoke the vegetables for 3 to 5 minutes. Uncover, turn the vegetables over, and smoke them for an additional 3 to 5 minutes.

4. To prepare the chicken, place each breast on a flat surface and cover with wax paper or plastic wrap. Pound the chicken with the flat side of a meat mallet to slightly flatten. Spray a hot skillet with non-stick cooking spray. Add the chicken and cook until golden brown on both sides, about 3 minutes per side.

5. To serve, place 1 cup of greens on each plate. Top the greens with a chicken breast. Arrange the smoked vegetables over the chicken. Spoon 3 tablespoons of the vinaigrette over each serving.

MAKES 4 SERVINGS

• EACH SERVING CONTAINS APPROXIMATELY:

CALORIES: **185** | FAT: **2 g** | CHOLESTEROL: **66 mg** | SODIUM: **104 mg** | CARBOHYDRATES: **14 g** | PROTEIN: **29 g**

132

warm scallop salad

This salad is as pretty as it is delicious. Cooking the scallops in the dressing gives them a uniquely different and appealing flavor. You can also cut the portions in half for a superb appetizer.

green leaf lettuce to line plates

endive lettuce to frame plates

6 cups assorted young greens torn in bite-size pieces

1 red delicious apple, cored and sliced into thin wedges

1 cup raspberry walnut dressing and marinade (see page 149)

1 pound sea scallops

1/2 cup chopped and toasted walnuts

1/2 cup enoki mushrooms

3 ounces (about 1 cup) fresh pea pods, lightly steamed

1. Line 4 large plates with the lettuce leaves and frame with the endive.

2. On each plate place 1 1/2 cups assorted greens and arrange 1/4 of the apple wedges decoratively in a spiral pattern.

3. Heat the dressing in a large skillet. Add the scallops and cook just until they turn opaque, about 1 to 2 minutes. Remove the scallops, reserving the dressing.

4. Arrange 1/4 of the cooked scallops over each salad, then drizzle a little of the warm dressing over the greens. Top each salad with 1 tablespoon of the toasted walnuts and enoki mushrooms and 2 tablespoons of the pea pods.

MAKES 4 SERVINGS

134

enoki mushrooms
The cultivated variety of enoki (en-oh-kee) mushrooms comes in clumps with spaghetti-like stems about 5 inches long topped with tiny white caps. They have a slightly crunchy texture and a mild, almost fruity flavor, unlike the earthier taste of most other mushrooms. They are best eaten raw because cooking tends to make them tough.

• EACH SERVING CONTAINS APPROXIMATELY:

CALORIES: 249 | FAT: 10 g | CHOLESTEROL: 37 mg | SODIUM: 202 mg | CARBOHYDRATES: 16 g | PROTEIN: 25 g

balsamic dijon dressing

The tangy sweetness of this dressing comes from the use of a high-quality, well-aged balsamic vinegar. It makes a good sauce for meat and poultry and is also good served on baked potatoes.

5 teaspoons canola oil

6 tablespoons balsamic vinegar

1 1/2 cups vegetable stock
(see page 56)

2 tablespoons chopped shallots

2 tablespoons dijon mustard

1 1/2 tablespoons white grape juice

1 teaspoon whole-grain mustard

1 small garlic clove, pressed or minced

1 1/2 tablespoons reduced-sodium
soy sauce

pinch white pepper

1 tablespoon rice vinegar

1 tablespoon cornstarch dissolved in
1 tablespoon water

1. Combine all the ingredients, except the cornstarch mixture, in a medium saucepan and mix well.

2. Bring the dressing to a boil over medium heat. Add the cornstarch mixture and cook until slightly thickened, about 2 to 3 minutes. Remove from the heat and let cool. While the dressing is still hot it should not be too thick; it will thicken as it cools. It will keep for at least a week if stored, tightly covered, in the refrigerator.

MAKES 1 1/4 CUPS

135

balsamic vinegar
The highly prized Italian balsamic vinegar is made from white Trebbiano grape juice. It obtains its characteristic dark color and pungent sweetness from being aged in various woods in graduating sizes over a period of many years.

• EACH 2-TABLESPOON SERVING CONTAINS APPROXIMATELY:

CALORIES: **35** | FAT: **2 g** | CHOLESTEROL: **0** | SODIUM: **209 mg** | CARBOHYDRATES: **3 g** | PROTEIN: **negligible**

blue cheese dressing

You can use any blue cheese in this recipe; see the box below for some easily available choices. Or you can substitute goat cheese or aged Cheddar for a totally different flavor range. Blending the blue cheese into the other ingredients in this dressing infuses its flavor throughout the mixture. Stirring the cottage cheese, rather than blending it, provides texture. Also, the lumps of the cottage cheese absorb the flavor and make it seem as if there is more of the higher-fat blue cheese included than there actually is.

3/4 cup buttermilk

1/3 cup fat-free mayonnaise

1/2 teaspoon minced garlic

1/4 cup crumbled blue cheese

2 tablespoons fat-free cottage cheese

blue cheese

The unusual, sharp flavor of blue cheese and the blue or green veins running through it come from molds injected into it during the curing process. There are many varieties of blues, each with slightly different characteristics. Some of the best known are Stilton from England and Gorgonzola from Italy, both made from cow's milk, and Roquefort from France, which is made from sheep's milk cured in damp caves.

1. Combine the buttermilk, mayonnaise, garlic, and blue cheese in a blender and blend until smooth.
2. Transfer to a medium bowl and stir in the cottage cheese. Chill, covered, until ready to serve.

MAKES 1 1/2 CUPS

136

• EACH 2-TABLESPOON SERVING CONTAINS APPROXIMATELY:

CALORIES: 30 | FAT: 1 g | CHOLESTEROL: 4 mg | SODIUM: 175 mg | CARBOHYDRATES: 2 g | PROTEIN: 2 g

caper dressing

This is a tasty dressing for green, grain, and vegetable salads. It is also a nice light-textured sauce for fish and poultry. It can literally turn a simple piece of grilled fish or a skinless chicken breast into gourmet fare.

¼ cup rice vinegar

¼ teaspoon salt

¼ teaspoon freshly ground black pepper

1 shallot, finely chopped

1 tablespoon capers, drained and chopped

1 teaspoon dijon mustard

½ cup water

2 tablespoons canola oil

1. Combine the vinegar and salt in a bowl and stir until the salt has completely dissolved.

2. Add the remaining ingredients, except the oil, and mix well. Slowly whisk in the oil. Mix well again just before using.

MAKES 1 CUP

137

• EACH 2-TABLESPOON SERVING CONTAINS APPROXIMATELY:

CALORIES: 34 | FAT: 3.4 g | CHOLESTEROL: 0 | SODIUM: 85 mg | CARBOHYDRATES: 1.1 g | PROTEIN: negligible

canyon ranch dressing

This dressing is much better if made a day before you plan to use it. In addition to its enhancing almost any salad, it can also be used as a marinade for cooked vegetables or uncooked fish, poultry, and meat.

1/2 **cup vegetable stock**
(see page 56)

2 **tablespoons balsamic vinegar**

4 **tablespoons red wine vinegar**

pinch freshly ground black pepper

1/4 **cup chopped shallots**

1 **tablespoon minced parsley**

2 **tablespoons extra-virgin olive oil**

1. Combine all the ingredients in a blender and blend until smooth.
2. Transfer the dressing to a jar or storage container. Cover tightly and store in the refrigerator.

MAKES 1 1/4 CUPS

138

• EACH 2-TABLESPOON SERVING CONTAINS APPROXIMATELY:

CALORIES: **30** | FAT: **3 g** | CHOLESTEROL: **negligible** | SODIUM: **5 mg** | CARBOHYDRATES: **2 g** | PROTEIN: **negligible**

creamy curry dressing

The satin texture of the silken tofu gives this non-dairy, practically fat-free dressing a creaminess that makes it seem much richer than it is. It is particularly good on fruit salads.

2 cups soft silken tofu

¹/₂ cup water

1 teaspoon salt

2 teaspoons sugar

1¹/₂ teaspoons curry powder

¹/₄ teaspoon ground ginger

4 teaspoons fresh lemon juice

1. Combine all the ingredients in a blender and blend until smooth.

2. Cover tightly and refrigerate for several hours before using.

MAKES 2 ¹/₂ CUPS

139

• EACH 2-TABLESPOON SERVING CONTAINS APPROXIMATELY:

CALORIES: **20** | FAT: **1 g** | CHOLESTEROL: **0** | SODIUM: **120 mg** | CARBOHYDRATES: **1 g** | PROTEIN: **2 g**

creamy kiwi dressing

This dressing can be used on salads of all types, or as a sauce on cold fish, poultry, or meat. Also, by substituting white wine or pineapple juice for the rice vinegar called for, it can be served as a dessert or a chilled fruit soup. The exotic sweet-tart flavor of the kiwi works equally well in both sweet and savory dishes, making it an exceedingly versatile ingredient.

**3 kiwi, peeled and finely diced
(9 ounces or 1 cup diced)**

1 banana, mashed

3/4 cup non-fat vanilla yogurt

2 tablespoons rice vinegar

1/2 teaspoon coconut extract

Combine all the ingredients and mix well. Refrigerate, tightly covered, until cold. Serve well chilled.

MAKES 2 CUPS

kiwi

The kiwi is grown in many countries in the Southern Hemisphere and also abundantly in California. Since the seasons in the Southern Hemisphere are exact opposites to ours, the fruit is available year round. Also known as the Chinese gooseberry, the kiwi looks like a large brown egg covered with fine downy hair. However, this rather unattractive exterior hides beautiful, brilliantly green flesh dotted with tiny, edible black seeds. It is ripe when slightly soft to the touch. Ripe kiwis can be stored in the refrigerator for up to 3 weeks. The easiest way to peel a kiwi is to first cut off both ends, then insert the bowl of a teaspoon up under the peel, carefully running it all the way around the fruit just under the peel and then slipping it off.

• **EACH SERVING CONTAINS APPROXIMATELY:**

CALORIES: **46** | FAT: **negligible** | CHOLESTEROL: **0** | SODIUM: **18 mg** | CARBOHYDRATES: **10 g** | PROTEIN: **2 g**

curried chutney dressing

For plain curry dressing, just omit the chutney in this recipe. For a dairy-free rendition, simply omit the yogurt and double the amount of fat-free mayonnaise.

¹/₃ cup fat-free mayonnaise

¹/₃ cup plain non-fat yogurt

1¹/₂ teaspoons curry powder

4 teaspoons sugar

¹/₈ teaspoon crushed red pepper
    flakes

Pinch freshly ground black pepper

1 small garlic clove, pressed or minced

1 shallot, finely chopped

¹/₈ teaspoon worcestershire sauce

¹/₂ teaspoon freshly squeezed
    lemon juice

1¹/₂ teaspoons reduced-sodium
    soy sauce

1 tablespoon red wine vinegar

¹/₄ cup chutney

1. Combine all the ingredients, except the chutney, in a blender and blend until smooth. Pour into a bowl and stir in the chutney.

2. Store, tightly covered, in the refrigerator.

MAKES 1 CUP

fat-free mayonnaise
Fat-free mayonnaise is not a good substitute for real mayonnaise on sandwiches because it tends to make the bread soggy, rather than sealing it. However, it is a useful ingredient in sauces and salad dressings where it can be used as a flavor carrier, as it is in this recipe, without contributing any additional fat.

142

• **EACH 2-TABLESPOON SERVING CONTAINS APPROXIMATELY:**

CALORIES: **40** | FAT: **negligible** | CHOLESTEROL: **0** | SODIUM: **132 mg** | CARBOHYDRATES: **9 g** | PROTEIN: **negligible**

curried date dressing

This recipe is a good example of how dried fruit can be used to thicken a dressing or sauce. Delicious on fruit and vegetable salads, this is wonderful as a sauce on poultry and most meats as well. It will keep, tightly covered, in the refrigerator for at least 2 weeks.

8 ounces pitted dates, chopped
    (about 1 cup chopped)

1 medium onion, quartered

2 tablespoons curry powder

1/2 teaspoon salt

1/4 cup red wine vinegar

3/4 cup water

1/4 cup canola oil

Combine all the ingredients, except the oil, in a blender or a food processor and blend for 1 minute. While the blender is still running, slowly add the oil.

MAKES 2 1/2 CUPS

143

• EACH 1/4-CUP SERVING CONTAINS APPROXIMATELY:

CALORIES: **128** | FAT: **5 g** | CHOLESTEROL: **0** | SODIUM: **163 mg** | CARBOHYDRATES: **21 g** | PROTEIN: **negligible**

jet fuel dressing

This fat-free salad dressing was in a book of mine, *Jet Fuel, The New Food Strategy for the High Performance Person*, published in 1984. The dressing has remained so popular with our guests at Canyon Ranch that we keep it on our menus and we still call it Jet Fuel Dressing. The flavor is better if the combination is made the day before you plan to use it, allowing the flavors to marry.

½ teaspoon salt

½ cup red wine vinegar

¼ teaspoon freshly ground black pepper

1 tablespoon sugar

2 garlic cloves, minced

2 teaspoons worcestershire sauce

1 tablespoon dijon mustard

1 tablespoon fresh lemon juice

1 cup water

1. Combine the salt and vinegar and stir until the salt is completely dissolved. Add all the remaining ingredients, except the water, and mix well.
2. Add the water and mix well. Refrigerate in a tightly covered container.

MAKES 2 CUPS

italian dressing
Add 1 tablespoon each of fresh oregano, basil, and tarragon, finely chopped, or 1 teaspoon of each of the same herbs, dried, crushing them first in a mortar and pestle.

asian dressing
Add 1 teaspoon curry powder and ¹/8 teaspoon ground ginger.

mexican dressing
Add ¹/2 teaspoon ground cumin.

tarragon dressing
Add 3 tablespoons fresh tarragon, finely chopped, or 1 teaspoon dried, crushed before using in a mortar and pestle.

• EACH 2-TABLESPOON SERVING CONTAINS APPROXIMATELY:

CALORIES: 5 | FAT: 0 | CHOLESTEROL: 0 | SODIUM: 93 mg | CARBOHYDRATES: 2 g | PROTEIN: negligible

poppy seed dressing

This low-fat, non-dairy salad dressing has a zesty, refreshing flavor if used soon after it is made. It is a good sauce for seafood and poultry and an excellent topping for fresh fruit.

5 ounces (3/4 cup) soft silken tofu

2½ tablespoons frozen apple juice concentrate, undiluted

1/8 teaspoon salt

1 teaspoon dry mustard

1⅓ tablespoons reduced-fat mayonnaise

1/3 cup rice vinegar

1/2 cup chopped onion

3/4 cup drained and chopped oranges or mandarin oranges

1 tablespoon poppy seeds

1. Combine all the ingredients, except the poppy seeds, in a blender and blend until creamy smooth. Pour into a bowl and stir in the poppy seeds.

2. Store, tightly covered, in the refrigerator.

MAKES ABOUT 2 CUPS

• EACH 2-TABLESPOON SERVING CONTAINS APPROXIMATELY:

CALORIES: 25 | FAT: 1 g | CHOLESTEROL: 0 | SODIUM: 36 mg | CARBOHYDRATES: 3 g | PROTEIN: 1 g

provençal vinaigrette

At Canyon Ranch we serve this dressing as a cold sauce on our Chicken Roulade with Lobster (see page 246). However, it is good on many other dishes and can also be used as a warm sauce or, more predictably, as a salad dressing.

1 garlic clove, pressed or minced

¼ cup sliced shallots

½ cup sliced fresh mushrooms

½ cup diced tomato

⅓ cup red wine vinegar

⅔ cup vegetable stock
(see page 56)

2¼ teaspoons extra-virgin
olive oil

¾ teaspoon minced fresh dill

½ teaspoon minced fresh tarragon

pinch freshly ground black pepper

pinch salt

1. Spray a small skillet with non-stick cooking spray. Add the garlic, shallots, and mushrooms and cook over medium heat until just tender.

2. Put the cooked mixture and all the remaining ingredients in a blender and blend until smooth.

3. Store, tightly covered, in the refrigerator.

MAKES 2 CUPS

146

• EACH ¼-CUP SERVING CONTAINS APPROXIMATELY:

CALORIES: **20** | FAT: **1 g** | CHOLESTEROL: **0** | SODIUM: **33 mg** | CARBOHYDRATES: **3 g** | PROTEIN: **negligible**

ranch dressing

This recipe is the Canyon Ranch version of the popular, all-purpose buttermilk dressing. Actually, the ingredients aren't too different from the original; we just eliminated most of the fat.

6 tablespoons buttermilk

2 tablespoons non-fat mayonnaise

1/2 cup non-fat sour cream

1/4 cup non-fat plain yogurt

1/2 teaspoon freshly ground
  black pepper

1/2 teaspoon salt

1/2 teaspoon dried basil, crushed

1 tablespoon rice vinegar

fresh lemon juice to taste

1/2 tablespoon minced
  parsley leaves

1/2 tablespoon minced chives

2 garlic cloves, pressed or minced,
  or 1 teaspoon garlic powder

pinch onion powder

1. Combine all the ingredients in a small bowl and mix well.

2. Refrigerate, tightly covered, until ready to serve.

MAKES 1 1/4 CUPS

147

• EACH 2-TABLESPOON SERVING CONTAINS APPROXIMATELY:

CALORIES: 15 | FAT: 0 | CHOLESTEROL: 0 | SODIUM: 173 mg | CARBOHYDRATES: 3 g | PROTEIN: 1 g

raspberry vinaigrette

This is a uniquely different raspberry vinaigrette in that it uses fresh raspberries as well as raspberry vinegar. This combination gives the dressing a thick, rather pleasing texture. It can also be used as a sauce on fish, poultry, and meat.

1½ cups thawed frozen or fresh raspberries

¼ teaspoon ground thyme

¼ teaspoon freshly ground black pepper

¼ cup water

3 tablespoons raspberry vinegar

2 teaspoons canola oil

1½ teaspoons reduced-sodium soy sauce

1 tablespoon sugar

1. Combine all the ingredients in a blender and blend until smooth.
2. Store, covered tightly, in the refrigerator.

MAKES 1½ CUPS

• EACH 2-TABLESPOON SERVING CONTAINS APPROXIMATELY:

CALORIES: 30 | FAT: 1 g | CHOLESTEROL: 0 | SODIUM: 38 mg | CARBOHYDRATES: 5 g | PROTEIN: negligible

raspberry walnut dressing and marinade

This dressing makes a wonderful marinade. It can also be used to cook the ingredients in a warm salad as it is in the Warm Scallop Salad on page 134.

1/2 cup raspberry vinegar

1/4 teaspoon salt

1/8 teaspoon freshly ground
  black pepper

1 tablespoon sugar

1 tablespoon dried tarragon, crushed

2 garlic cloves, pressed or minced

1 1/2 teaspoons worcestershire
  sauce

1 1/2 teaspoons dijon mustard

1 tablespoon fresh lemon juice

2 tablespoons walnut oil

1. Combine the vinegar and salt in a bowl and stir until the salt has completely dissolved. Add all the remaining ingredients, except the oil, and mix well.

2. Slowly whisk in the oil.

3. Store, tightly covered, in the refrigerator. Always mix well before serving.

MAKES 2 CUPS

149

• EACH 2-TABLESPOON SERVING CONTAINS APPROXIMATELY:

CALORIES: 22 | FAT: 2 g | CHOLESTEROL: 0 | SODIUM: 45 mg | CARBOHYDRATES: 2 g | PROTEIN: negligible

sun-dried tomato vinaigrette

Dried tomatoes add intense, zesty flavor to everything from soups and stews to salads, and they are decidedly the star in this incredibly delicious vinaigrette. It is superb used as a dressing on fresh garden greens and vegetables and as a marinade for fish, poultry, or meat. It is also a wonderful sauce spooned over grilled vegetables, pasta, rice, or beans. The ingredients can all be stored in a pantry, which means that you can enjoy this recipe year round. For easier preparation, it is faster to cut dried tomatoes with a pair of scissors than with a knife.

1 cup sun-dried tomatoes (2 ounces), cut into quarters

1/4 cup red wine vinegar

1/4 teaspoon salt

1/2 teaspoon freshly ground black pepper

1/4 teaspoon fresh rosemary, finely chopped, or 1/4 teaspoon dried rosemary, crushed

3 tablespoons extra-virgin olive oil

1 tablespoon capers, drained

150

1. Put the tomatoes in a bowl and cover with hot water. Let stand for 15 minutes.

2. Meanwhile, in another bowl, combine the vinegar, salt, pepper, and rosemary and stir until the salt is completely dissolved. Slowly stir in the oil, then add the capers.

3. Drain the tomatoes, reserving 1/4 cup of the soaking water. Add both the tomatoes and the reserved water to the vinegar mixture and mix well.

4. If stored in a tightly covered container in the refrigerator, it will last for several weeks.

MAKES 2 CUPS

• EACH 1/4-CUP SERVING CONTAINS APPROXIMATELY:

CALORIES: 64 | FAT: 5 g | CHOLESTEROL: 0 | SODIUM: 157 mg | CARBOHYDRATES: 4 g | PROTEIN: 1 g

thousand island dressing

Thousand Island dressing is versatile in any number of ways: Use it as a dip for raw vegetables, as a salad dressing, or spread it on sandwiches or burgers. With our low-calorie version you can enjoy it often, but be careful with commercial varieties. Some of them pack in a whopping 120 calories for 2 tablespoons. For a dairy-free rendition, omit the yogurt and double the amount of fat-free mayonnaise.

1/2 cup non-fat plain yogurt

1/2 cup fat-free mayonnaise

1/2 cup chili sauce

1/4 cup sweet pickle relish

1/4 teaspoon salt

2 tablespoons red wine vinegar

1/2 teaspoon sugar

1/8 teaspoon freshly ground
   black pepper

fresh lemon juice to taste

1. Combine all the ingredients in a bowl and mix thoroughly.

2. It will keep, tightly covered, in the refrigerator for 1 week.

MAKES ABOUT 1 3/4 CUPS

151

• EACH 2-TABLESPOON SERVING CONTAINS APPROXIMATELY:

CALORIES: **25** | FAT: **6 g** | CHOLESTEROL: **0** | SODIUM: **165 mg** | CARBOHYDRATES: **6 g** | PROTEIN: **negligible**

tropical fruit dressing

This versatile dressing can be served over both fruit and vegetable salads and used as a sauce on fish, poultry, and meat. It is essential to use silken tofu in this recipe to achieve the desired creamy texture. For more information on tofu, see page 35. If stored tightly covered in the refrigerator, this dressing will keep for several days.

Combine all the ingredients in a blender and puree.

MAKES 1 3/4 CUPS

¼ cup silken tofu (about 2 ounces)

¾ cup vegetable stock
(see page 56)

1 tablespoon extra-virgin olive oil

1 tablespoon cornstarch

1 tablespoon pineapple juice

1 tablespoon grapefruit juice

1 tablespoon apple juice

2 tablespoons orange juice

2 tablespoons peeled and diced mango

½ teaspoon chopped fresh mint

• EACH 2-TABLESPOON SERVING CONTAINS APPROXIMATELY:

CALORIES: 25 | FAT: 1 g | CHOLESTEROL: 0 | SODIUM: 6 mg | CARBOHYDRATES: 4 g | PROTEIN: negligible

tofu mayonnaise

This recipe offers a very viable alternative to real mayonnaise and, unlike real mayonnaise, is made without eggs.

10 1/2 ounces firm light tofu

6 tablespoons balsamic vinegar

1 tablespoon dijon mustard

1. Combine all the ingredients in a blender and blend until smooth.

2. Store, tightly covered, in the refrigerator for up to 4 days.

MAKES 1 1/4 CUPS

153

• EACH 1-TABLESPOON SERVING CONTAINS APPROXIMATELY:

CALORIES: 10 | FAT: negligible | CHOLESTEROL: 0 | SODIUM: 24 mg | CARBOHYDRATES: negligible | PROTEIN: 1 g

vegetarian dishes

Vegetarian eating is not some trendy food fad. It's been around throughout recorded history, and there's been a definite rise in interest in recent years. About 4 percent of Americans called themselves vegetarians in the 1960s, while almost 7 percent make that claim today.

The Canyon Ranch menu largely focuses on plant-based eating. We emphasize whole-grain products, legumes, fruits, vegetables, nuts, and seeds in our recipes. By using spices, herbs, and cooking techniques creatively, we develop dishes that are tasty and satisfying for anyone who enjoys fine dining— vegetarian or not.

In general, research shows positive links between

vegetarian eating and good health. Vegetarians are usually less likely to have heart disease, high blood pressure, adult-onset diabetes, obesity, and some forms of cancer. They also appear to be at lower risk for kidney stones, gallstones, osteoporosis, and breast cancer.

At Canyon Ranch, our daily menus always offer delicious and satisfying vegetarian dishes to meet the dietary requirements of vegetarians and to give all our guests a chance to discover how satisfying and delightful vegetarian cuisine can be.

Canyon Ranch vegetarian recipes run the gamut from exciting, new interpretations of popular dishes like Tamale Pie to meatless versions of the classics such as Vegetarian Cassoulet and Vegetable Lasagna. For those days when you're in a hurry to get a meal on the table, try the Asian Pasta (recipe follows) and serve it with a colorful vegetable stir-fry, using vegetables from the salad bar section of your market—washed, chopped, and ready to cook.

asian pasta

This spicy pasta is a sensational side dish for any type of Asian menu, and it can be made, start to finish, in about 5 minutes. It is also wonderful served cold as a pasta salad, either by itself or combined with fish, poultry, or meat.

6 tablespoons rice vinegar

3 tablespoons reduced-sodium soy sauce

3 tablespoons honey

1 1/2 teaspoons chinese chili paste

3 tablespoons finely chopped fresh ginger

3 scallions, finely chopped

1 tablespoon finely chopped fresh gingerroot

12 ounces fresh angel hair pasta

1 tablespoon dark sesame oil

1. Put a large pot of water on to boil. Combine all the ingredients, except the pasta and sesame oil, in a small bowl and mix well. Set aside.

2. Cook the pasta in boiling water for about 1 1/2 minutes, or until tender but still firm to the bite.

3. Drain the pasta well and toss with the sesame oil. Add the sauce and toss well again.

MAKES 4 SERVINGS

157

• EACH 1 1/2-CUP SERVING CONTAINS APPROXIMATELY:

CALORIES: 281 | FAT: 3 g | CHOLESTEROL: 0 | SODIUM: 249 mg | CARBOHYDRATES: 55 g | PROTEIN: 8 g

pasta alla checca

Interestingly enough, this popular Italian dish originated in the most humble of circumstances. People who didn't have access to any real cooking facilities, but could boil a pot of water over an open fire, created this spicy, uncooked pasta sauce and served it over piping hot fettuccini. It is my favorite pasta dish and I like it topped with a sprinkle of freshly grated Parmigiano-Reggiano. The secret to success is using really flavorful, ripe tomatoes and allowing them to drain long enough to get rid of all of the excess water, thereby concentrating the tomato flavor.

8 medium ripe plum tomatoes (about 2 pounds), peeled and diced (4 cups)

1/2 teaspoon salt

2 garlic cloves, pressed or minced

1/2 cup chopped fresh basil leaves

1/2 cup chopped fresh parsley leaves

2 tablespoons extra-virgin olive oil

1/4 teaspoon freshly ground black pepper, or to taste

1/4 teaspoon crushed red pepper flakes, or to taste

12 ounces dry fettuccini

sprigs fresh basil for garnish, optional

1. Place the diced tomatoes in a colander and sprinkle with the salt. Mix well and allow to drain for at least 1 hour.
2. Combine the garlic, basil, parsley, olive oil, and black and red pepper. Add the drained tomatoes and mix well.
3. Cook the fettuccini al dente, according to package directions.
4. To serve, place 1 1/2 cups cooked pasta on each of 4 plates. Top each serving with 3/4 cup of the sauce and garnish with a sprig of fresh basil, if desired.

MAKES 4 SERVINGS

158

• EACH SERVING CONTAINS APPROXIMATELY:

CALORIES: **420** | FAT: **9 g** | CHOLESTEROL: **0** | SODIUM: **325 mg** | CARBOHYDRATES: **79 g** | PROTEIN: **15 g**

bean and vegetable quesadillas

These spicy Southwestern sandwiches are an extremely popular item on all of the Canyon Ranch lunch menus. We serve them with our Tomato Salsa (see page 324) and Canyon Ranch Guacamole (see page 36).

3/4 cup dried black beans, picked over to remove small stones, then rinsed

1/4 cup diced red onion

2 tablespoons chopped leeks, white part only

1 tablespoon minced garlic

2 1/4 cups vegetable stock
(see page 56)

1/4 cup peeled and diced carrots

1/4 cup diced red bell pepper

1/4 cup canned diced green chiles

2 tablespoons chopped cilantro leaves

1 tablespoon minced parsley

1 1/2 tablespoons fresh lemon juice

pinch each cayenne pepper, ground cumin, and chili powder

4 whole-wheat flour tortillas, 9 inches each in diameter

1 large tomato, sliced thin into 8 rounds

1/2 cup grated low-fat monterey jack cheese

1. Cover the beans with water and soak overnight.

2. Lightly spray a medium saucepan with non-stick cooking spray and place over medium heat. Add the onion, leeks, and garlic and cook, stirring frequently, until the onion is translucent.

3. Drain the beans and add them and the vegetable stock to the pan. Continue to cook over medium heat for 45 minutes, or until the beans are tender.

4. Lightly spray a small skillet with non-stick cooking spray. Sauté the carrots, bell pepper, and green chiles until tender. Remove from the heat and add the cilantro, parsley, lemon juice, and seasonings. Mix well.

5. Transfer one-third of the bean mixture to a blender and puree. Combine the bean puree and beans with the vegetable mixture.

6. Preheat the oven to 350°F. Lightly spray a baking sheet with non-stick cooking spray and set aside.

7. Lay 1 tortilla at a time out on the work area. Spoon 3/4 cup of the mixture over half of the tortilla. Place 2 slices of tomato over the filling and sprinkle 2 tablespoons of cheese over the tomato. Fold in half and place on the baking sheet. Repeat with the remaining tortillas and filling mixture. Bake in the preheated oven for 6 to 8 minutes, or until hot.

MAKES 4 SERVINGS

159

• EACH QUESADILLA SERVING CONTAINS APPROXIMATELY:

CALORIES: **270** | FAT: **5 g** | CHOLESTEROL: **0** | SODIUM: **190 mg** | CARBOHYDRATES: **48 g** | PROTEIN: **10 g**

indonesian tempeh stir-fry

Tempeh, a traditional Indonesian food, is a tender, chunky soybean cake. It is made from whole soybeans, sometimes mixed with a grain, such as rice or millet, and fermented into a rich, high-protein cake with a nutty, smoky flavor. Tempeh is available in health food stores and in the Asian section of many supermarkets. Serve this as is or over noodles. Leftovers are good cold as a salad or vegetable side dish.

1 teaspoon dark sesame oil

1 serrano chile, finely chopped (about 1 teaspoon)

3 tablespoons reduced-sodium soy sauce

2 tablespoons light brown sugar

2 tablespoons dry sherry

1/4 cup ketchup

1/2 teaspoon ground ginger

3/4 cup vegetable stock (see page 56)

8 ounces tempeh, cut into 1-inch pieces (1 cup)

1/2 medium onion, coarsely chopped (3/4 cup)

3 garlic cloves, pressed or minced

4 cups broccoli florets

3 bell peppers, seeded and coarsely chopped (about 2 1/4 cups)

3 scallions, cut into 2-inch pieces

2 tablespoons finely chopped roasted peanuts

1 1/3 cups cooked rice (see page 171)

1. Heat the sesame oil in a large saucepan over medium heat. Add the chile and cook for about 1 minute. Add the soy sauce, brown sugar, sherry, ketchup, ginger, and vegetable stock and reduce by one-third. Set aside.

2. Spray a wok or a large skillet with non-stick cooking spray and heat until drops of water dance on the surface. Add the tempeh and onion and stir-fry until golden. Add the garlic and cook 1 minute. Add the broccoli and bell peppers and stir-fry 1 minute. Add the scallions and peanuts and stir-fry 1 more minute.

3. Add the sauce mixture and toss to combine. Continue to stir-fry until the vegetables are tender, about 1 or 2 more minutes. Do not overcook.

4. Serve 1 1/2 cups of the stir-fry over 1/3 cup rice.

MAKES 4 SERVINGS

160

• EACH SERVING CONTAINS APPROXIMATELY:

CALORIES: **360** | FAT: **8 g** | CHOLESTEROL: **0** | SODIUM: **400 mg** | CARBOHYDRATES: **57 g** | PROTEIN: **18 g**

canyon ranch stuft spuds

A baked potato doesn't have to be dripping in butter and sour cream to be really good. In fact, this stuffed baked potato has been a popular luncheon entree at Canyon Ranch ever since the day we opened in Tucson almost 20 years ago. From time to time other ingredients are added, but this original version is still my personal favorite.

2 small baking potatoes (8 ounces), baked for 50 minutes at 400°F.
(recipe follows)

1 medium onion, finely chopped

¼ cup buttermilk

½ cup low-fat cottage cheese

3 tablespoons freshly grated parmesan cheese

2 tablespoons chopped chives or scallion tops

1. Cut a thin slice from the top of each potato. Remove the pulp from the potatoes, being careful not to tear the shells. Place the potato pulp in a mixing bowl and mash. Cover and set aside. Keep the shells warm.

2. Cook the onion in a medium skillet, covered, over very low heat until soft, stirring occasionally and adding a little water if necessary to prevent scorching. Add the mashed potatoes, buttermilk, cottage cheese, and Parmesan and mix well. Heat through.

3. Stuff the potato mixture back into the warm shells. The mixture will be heaped way over the top.

4. To serve, sprinkle the top of each stuft spud with 1 tablespoon of chopped chives or scallion tops. If you have prepared the potatoes in advance, reheat them in a 350°F. oven for about 15 minutes, or until hot, before adding the chopped chives or scallions.

MAKES 2 SERVINGS

161

• EACH SERVING CONTAINS APPROXIMATELY:

CALORIES: 201 | FAT: 4 g | CHOLESTEROL: 12 mg | SODIUM: 682 mg | CARBOHYDRATES: 27 g | PROTEIN: 15 g

baked potatoes

The following method of baking potatoes can be used for preparing potatoes for stuffing, as in the recipe for Canyon Ranch Stuft Spuds, as well as for serving them plain. It can also be used for large sweet potatoes. Small sweet potatoes don't need to bake for quite as long.

2 large russet potatoes, 12 ounces each, scrubbed and dried

Note that there is no rubbing of the outside of the potato with oil or butter, or wrapping the potato in aluminum foil for baking, all of which softens the skin. You want as tough-textured a potato shell as possible for stuffing so that it won't tear.

1. Preheat the oven to 400°F.

2. Pierce each potato with the tines of a fork to keep the skins from bursting.

3. Place the potatoes in the preheated oven and bake for 1 hour.

162

MAKES 2 SERVINGS

• EACH SERVING CONTAINS APPROXIMATELY:

CALORIES: **164** | FAT: **negligible** | CHOLESTEROL: **0** | SODIUM: **16 mg** | CARBOHYDRATES: **38 g** | PROTEIN: **5 g**

cheese enchiladas

Mexican food is popular all over the world, and enchiladas are certainly one of the favorite entrees in this Southwestern cuisine. While this dish is higher in fat than most of our entrees, it contains only about half the amount of fat found in the average enchilada. This recipe can be made ahead and heated just before serving.

SAUCE:

2 tablespoons chopped onion

3 tablespoons fat-free vegetable stock
(see page 56)

2 tablespoons diced pimientos

1¹/2 cups undrained low-sodium canned diced tomatoes

2 tablespoons diced green chiles

1 tablespoon white vinegar

1 garlic clove, pressed or minced

1/2 teaspoon chili powder

1/4 teaspoon ground cumin

dash tabasco sauce

ENCHILADAS:

3/4 cup chopped onion

1/4 cup fat-free vegetable stock
(see page 56)

1/4 cup canned diced green chiles

1 tablespoon chili powder

1/2 teaspoon ground cumin

1 cup peeled and diced tomatoes

6 ounces part-skim mozzarella cheese, grated (1¹/2 cups)

6 corn tortillas, warmed

1 ounce sharp cheddar cheese, grated (1/4 cup)

1. Preheat the oven to 350°F.

2. To make the sauce, cook the onion in the stock over medium heat until soft, about 3 minutes. Add all the remaining sauce ingredients and bring to a boil. Cover and simmer 10 minutes. Allow to cool slightly.

3. Transfer approximately half of the sauce to a blender container and blend until smooth. Pour back into the remaining sauce and mix thoroughly. Set aside.

4. To make the enchiladas, combine the onion and chicken stock in a skillet and cook over medium heat until the onion is soft and translucent, about 3 minutes. Add the green chiles, spices, and tomatoes and cook for another 5 minutes. Remove from heat and cool to room temperature.

5. Add the mozzarella cheese and mix well. Spoon 3 tablespoons of the filling into each tortilla and roll it up.

Spread 1/2 cup of sauce evenly in the bottom of a 9-inch-square baking dish. Put the rolled enchiladas on top of the sauce, folded side down, and cover with the remaining sauce. Sprinkle the Cheddar cheese over the top and bake in the preheated oven for about 20 minutes, or until heated through. Serve immediately.

MAKES 6 SERVINGS

chicken enchiladas

Substitute 1 1/3 cups of diced cooked chicken breast for the mozzarella cheese.

• EACH ENCHILADA CONTAINS APPROXIMATELY.

CALORIES: **187** | FAT: **7 g** | CHOLESTEROL: **20 mg** | SODIUM: **354 mg** | CARBOHYDRATES: **20 g** | PROTEIN: **12 g**

corn tamales

The filling for these tamales can also be formed into patties and cooked in a skillet or pressed in a baking pan and baked in the oven. However, the husks provide a much more attractive presentation, especially if you are making them for a party.

14 large dried corn husks

2 3/4 cups vegetable stock
(see page 56)

10 ounces dry whole-wheat couscous

3 cups frozen corn kernels, thawed

1 cup diced onion

1/2 cup diced red or green bell pepper

1/4 cup diced green chiles

1/2 teaspoon tabasco sauce

1/4 teaspoon ground white pepper

dash chili powder

1 teaspoon chopped cilantro

3/4 cup grated reduced-fat monterey jack cheese

COUSCOUS
Couscous is a granular semolina usually associated with North African cuisine. It is an ideal accompaniment for many types of foods and can be prepared in minutes.

1. Place the corn husks in a bowl, cover with water, and soak for 24 hours. This process softens husks so they are easier to handle. When you are ready to assemble the tamales, remove the husks from the water and pat dry. Cut 24 thin, lengthwise strips from 2 of the husks to use as ties for the ends of the tamales. Set aside.

2. Pour the vegetable stock into a medium saucepan and bring to a boil. Stir in the couscous, cover tightly, and remove from the heat. Allow to stand for 5 minutes. Fluff with a fork and set aside to cool.

3. Place the corn kernels in a blender and puree.

4. Combine the couscous, pureed corn, onion, bell pepper, green chiles, seasoning, and cheese in a bowl and mix well.

5. Lay the corn husks out on a work area. Divide the corn mixture equally among the 12 remaining corn husks. Roll tightly and tie each end closed with a husk strip.

6. Place the tamales in a steamer basket over boiling water and steam for about 10 minutes, or until hot.

MAKES 6 SERVINGS

166

• EACH 2-TAMALE SERVING CONTAINS APPROXIMATELY:

CALORIES: 335 | FAT: 6 g | CHOLESTEROL: 0 | SODIUM: 312 mg | CARBOHYDRATES: 56 g | PROTEIN: 16 g

corn and quinoa casserole with roasted vegetables

This is both an unusual and a delicious vegan dish and the combination of the grains and soy milk provides a complete protein.

1/4 cup plus 2 tablespoons quinoa, rinsed and drained

1/2 teaspoon plus 1 teaspoon olive oil, divided use

1 tablespoon chopped shallots

1 tablespoon chopped carrots

1 tablespoon chopped leeks

1 tablespoon chopped celery

2 cups cooked corn kernels, divided use

2/3 cup soy milk

8 slices (1/2 inch thick) eggplant

4 whole scallions

1/4 cup finely chopped parsley

chili powder

For a more colorful presentation, thickened carrot juice may be spooned on the plates. For carrot juice, combine 3/4 cup of juice with 1/4 teaspoon of cornstarch in a small saucepan and mix well. Place over medium heat and bring to a boil, stirring constantly until thickened, about 2 minutes.

1. Preheat oven to 350°F.

2. Sprinkle the drained quinoa on a baking sheet. Place it in the preheated oven for about 10 minutes, stirring occasionally, until golden brown. Set aside.

3. Heat the 1/2 teaspoon of olive oil in a medium skillet and stir-fry the shallots, carrots, leeks, and celery for 1 to 2 minutes. Set aside.

4. Combine 1 cup of the corn and the soy milk in a blender and puree. Add the pureed mixture to the stir-fried vegetables along with the remaining corn and all but 2 tablespoons of the toasted quinoa and mix well.

5. Spoon the mixture into a small loaf pan and sprinkle the remaining 2 tablespoons of toasted quinoa over the top. Bake, covered, in the preheated oven for 40 minutes. Uncover and bake for 20 more minutes. Remove from the oven while preparing the remaining vegetables.

6. Increase the oven temperature to 450°F.

7. Brush the eggplant slices and scallions with the remaining 1 teaspoon of olive oil and arrange them in a roasting pan. Place in a hot oven for 8 to 10 minutes, or until browned.

8. Place a slice of eggplant on each of four plates. Divide the quinoa into 4 portions and spoon on top of the eggplant. Place the remaining eggplant slices on top. Garnish each serving with 1 tablespoon of chopped parsley and a pinch of chili powder. Place a scallion on top.

MAKES 4 SERVINGS

• EACH SERVING CONTAINS APPROXIMATELY:

CALORIES: 205 | FAT: 4 g | CHOLESTEROL: 0 | SODIUM: 27 mg | CARBOHYDRATES: 48 g | PROTEIN: 7 g

cuban black beans and rice

This Cuban dish has become so popular all over this country that we see it combined with everything imaginable from seafood to steak. This vegetarian recipe is still my favorite version of the Caribbean classic, and it is an ideal entree for a vegetarian menu because the combination of beans and rice forms a complete protein. When you want to make it in a hurry, substitute 2 cans of drained black beans for the dried beans; start with step 3 and add the jalapeños to the onion mixture.

1 cup dried black beans, picked over and rinsed

3 cups vegetable stock (see page 56) or water, divided use

1$\frac{1}{2}$ teaspoons minced jalapeño peppers

1 medium onion, chopped (3/4 cup)

1$\frac{1}{2}$ tablespoons minced garlic

$\frac{1}{2}$ cup seeded and chopped green bell pepper

1$\frac{1}{2}$ teaspoons freshly ground black pepper

$\frac{1}{4}$ teaspoon salt

2 tablespoons red wine vinegar

$\frac{1}{4}$ cup dry sherry

1$\frac{1}{2}$ cups cooked brown rice (recipe follows)

6 tablespoons light sour cream for garnish

chopped scallions for garnish

1. Cover the beans with enough water to cover by at least 4 inches and allow to soak overnight.

2. To cook, drain the beans and combine with the vegetable stock or water and jalapeño peppers in a heavy saucepan. Bring to a boil, reduce heat to a simmer, and cook, covered, for 1$\frac{1}{2}$ hours. The beans should be tender, not mushy.

3. Cook the onion, garlic, and bell pepper in a large saucepan, covered, over low heat until onion is translucent, adding a little water if necessary to prevent scorching.

4. When the beans are done, puree one-quarter of them in a blender or food processor, then return to the pot. Add the onion mixture and remaining ingredients except the brown rice and bring to a boil. Reduce the heat and simmer, uncovered, until slightly thickened.

5. To serve, place $\frac{1}{4}$ cup of rice and $\frac{1}{2}$ cup of black beans in a large soup plate. Top each serving with 1 tablespoon of sour cream and a sprinkle of chopped scallions.

MAKES 6 SERVINGS

• EACH SERVING OF 1/4 CUP OF RICE AND 1/2 CUP OF BEANS WITH GARNISHES CONTAINS APPROXIMATELY:

CALORIES: 240 | FAT: negligible | CHOLESTEROL: 0 | SODIUM: 215 mg | CARBOHYDRATES: 40 g | PROTEIN: 12 g

170

boiled rice

2 cups liquid

1 cup white rice

white rice

Combine the liquid and the rice in a saucepan with a tight-fitting lid and bring to a boil. Reduce the heat to low and simmer, covered, for about 15 minutes, or until all the liquid has been absorbed and the rice is tender. Fluff with a fork before serving.

MAKES 3 CUPS, OR 6 SERVINGS

• EACH 1/2-CUP SERVING CONTAINS APPROXIMATELY:

CALORIES: 133 | FAT: negligible | CHOLESTEROL: 0 | SODIUM: negligible | CARBOHYDRATES: 29 g | PROTEIN: 2 g

171

2 1/4 cups liquid

1 cup brown rice

brown rice

Bring the liquid to a boil in a saucepan with a tight-fitting lid. Stir in the rice and reduce the heat to low. Simmer, covered, for about 45 to 50 minutes, or until all the liquid has been absorbed and the rice is tender. Fluff with a fork before serving.

MAKES 3 CUPS, OR 6 SERVINGS

• EACH 1/2-CUP SERVING CONTAINS APPROXIMATELY:

CALORIES: 108 | FAT: negligible | CHOLESTEROL: 0 | SODIUM: 5 mg | CARBOHYDRATES: 22 g | PROTEIN: 3 g

egg white omelet with vegetables

The egg white omelet bar at Canyon Ranch is extremely popular with our guests. We offer a large selection of filling ingredients from which to choose so that they can literally design their own omelets. This basic vegetarian recipe gives you the preparation techniques for designing your own omelets at home with the filling ingredients of your choice.

3 egg whites

1/4 cup diced bell pepper

1/4 cup diced tomato

1/2 cup sliced mushrooms

1 tablespoon diced scallions

172

1. Put the egg whites in a small bowl and whisk just until they become frothy.

2. Heat a small skillet or omelet pan over medium-high heat. Spray the hot skillet with non-stick cooking spray and cook the vegetables, stirring constantly until tender.

3. Pour the beaten eggs over the vegetables. As the eggs start to set, use a spatula to lift the edge of the eggs and turn them over. As soon as the mixture has set, remove the pan from the heat and fold the omelet in half as you place it on the plate. Serve immediately.

MAKES 1 SERVING

• EACH SERVING CONTAINS APPROXIMATELY:

CALORIES: **70** | FAT: **negligible** | CHOLESTEROL: **0** | SODIUM: **156 mg** | CARBOHYDRATES: **6 g** | PROTEIN: **1 g**

grilled portobello sandwich with roasted pepper and wasabi mayonnaise

These spicy mushroom and pepper sandwiches are a big hit with everyone at Canyon Ranch. They are also a great alternative for hamburgers at backyard barbecue parties when you're planning a vegetarian menu.

MARINADE:

2 tablespoons extra-virgin olive oil

1/2 cup balsamic vinegar

1/2 tablespoon minced shallots

1/2 tablespoon minced garlic

4 medium-size portobello mushrooms (10 ounces)

WASABI MAYONNAISE:

1/3 cup silken tofu

1 tablespoon balsamic vinegar

1 tablespoon wasabi paste, or to taste

1/2 tablespoon fresh lime juice

1 teaspoon dijon mustard

4 multi-grain rolls, split and lightly grilled or toasted

8 large arugula leaves, washed and drained

1 cup roasted red peppers (see page 49)

1. Combine all the marinade ingredients in a large bowl or a flat dish, mix well, and set aside.

2. Cut the stems off the mushrooms so that the bottoms are flat. Using a mushroom brush or a soft damp cloth, clean the mushrooms thoroughly. Add the mushrooms to the marinade and marinate for at least 1 hour.

3. Combine all wasabi mayonnaise ingredients in a blender and blend until smooth. Set aside.

4. Prepare a grill or preheat a broiler and grill or broil the marinated mushroom caps just long enough to lightly brown on both sides.

5. To assemble each sandwich, first spread 1 1/2 tablespoons of the wasabi mayonnaise on the bottom half of a roll. Top it with 2 arugula leaves and 1/4 cup of the roasted peppers. Place a grilled mushroom on top of the peppers and place the top of the bun over it.

MAKES 4 SERVINGS

portobello mushrooms
Portobello mushrooms are large, flat, firm, and extremely flavorful. In fact, their texture is so firm that they can be grilled and served like a steak. They are becoming increasingly popular in this country and consequently more readily available.

174

• EACH SANDWICH CONTAINS APPROXIMATELY:

CALORIES: **305** | FAT: **10 g** | CHOLESTEROL: **0** | SODIUM: **457 mg** | CARBOHYDRATES: **47 g** | PROTEIN: **10 g**

grilled vegetable strudel with tomato olive sauce

This savory vegetable strudel can be served with other sauces. It is also good served cold as a light lunch or dinner entree. Grilled portobello mushrooms would be a nice accompaniment to this dish for a vegetarian dinner party menu.

MARINADE:

2 tablespoons chopped chives

2 tablespoons balsamic vinegar

1 tablespoon extra-virgin olive oil

pinch salt

pinch freshly ground black pepper

2 tablespoons finely chopped fresh basil

VEGETABLES:

1 red bell pepper, seeded and quartered

1 yellow bell pepper, seeded and quartered

2 tomatoes, seeded and quartered

1 yellow squash, diagonally cut 1/4 inch thick

1 zucchini, diagonally cut 1/4 inch thick

1 eggplant, peeled and cut into 1/2-inch-thick strips

2 artichoke hearts

6 sheets phyllo pastry

1 1/2 cups tomato olive sauce
(see page 331)

1. Combine all the marinade ingredients in a bowl and mix well.

2. Prepare the grill or preheat the broiler. Grill or broil the vegetables until tender. Remove them from the grill and allow to cool slightly. Dice the grilled vegetables, place them in a shallow dish, and spoon the marinade over them. Cover tightly and allow to marinate for several hours or overnight.

3. Preheat the oven to 350°F.

4. Layer the 6 sheets of phyllo on a flat surface, spraying between each layer with non-stick cooking spray. Arrange the vegetables lengthwise along one long edge of phyllo sheets, leaving about 1 1/2 inches on each end. Fold the ends in, overlapping the vegetables to enclose the ends of the filling. Roll the phyllo and filling over itself to form a strudel roll. Transfer to a baking sheet, seam down, and spray the strudel roll lightly with non-stick spray. Score with a knife to form 6 slices.

5. Bake in the preheated oven for 25 minutes, or until golden brown. Remove the strudel from the oven and allow it to stand for 5 minutes before slicing into 6 equal portions.

strudel

Strudel is a type of German pastry made up of many layers of very thin dough which is filled with either a savory or sweet mixture and then rolled and baked until it is golden brown. Phyllo can be substituted successfully for strudel dough to save time, and it is also much lower in fat.

Spread ¹/₄ cup of the sauce on the bottom of each serving plate and place a strudel slice on top of the sauce.

MAKES 6 SERVINGS

• **EACH SERVING CONTAINS APPROXIMATELY:**

CALORIES: 145 | FAT: 1 g | CHOLESTEROL: 0 | SODIUM: 330 mg | CARBOHYDRATES: 33 g | PROTEIN: 6 g

177

grilled vegetable sandwich on lavash

Lavash is wafer-thin bread that has been made by the Armenians for thousands of years. It is often referred to as cracker bread because it is more frequently seen after it has been toasted or baked until crisp and served as a cracker. The thinness of lavash makes it ideal for rolled sandwiches, and the fact that it contains no fat makes it a healthy choice for spa cuisine. This lavash roll-up is the Armenian version of a wrap sandwich. You can either eat it immediately while it's still warm, or you can wrap it tightly in plastic wrap and refrigerate it to have cold for a future meal. However, if you are not planning to eat it immediately, substitute low-fat cream cheese for the fat-free or the sandwich will become soggy. Roll-up sandwiches are ideal to carry in backpacks when you're hiking or biking because they are so much more durable than filling between 2 slices of bread. The soft lavash called for in this recipe is available in many supermarkets and all Middle Eastern markets.

2 small zucchini, thinly sliced

2 small yellow squash, thinly sliced

16 asparagus spears, tough ends broken off

1 teaspoon balsamic vinegar

¼ teaspoon salt

1 tablespoon extra-virgin olive oil

1 garlic clove, pressed or minced

½ cup goat cheese

½ cup fat-free cream cheese

4 half sheets of whole-wheat lavash

1 cup roasted red peppers (see page 49), cut into ½-inch strips

1 cup watercress leaves

2 plum tomatoes, diced, optional

1. Put the zucchini, yellow squash, and asparagus in a baking dish or a shallow bowl. In still another small bowl combine the vinegar and salt and stir until the salt is completely dissolved. Add the olive oil and garlic, mix well, and drizzle over the vegetables. Stir to coat them completely and allow to marinate while you get everything else ready to make the sandwiches.

2. In another bowl, combine the goat cheese and cream cheese and mash until completely blended. Set aside.

3. Prepare the grill or preheat the broiler.

4. Arrange the vegetables on a rack and place on the grill or under the broiler. Cook until the vegetables can be pierced easily with a fork. Remove from the heat and set aside.

5. Spread 1/4 cup of the cheese mixture evenly over the entire surface of each lavash half. Layer the grilled vegetables, roasted red peppers, and watercress across one end of the bread. Begin at the end with the filling and roll tightly, while tucking the filling under as you roll. The final roll with the cheese acts as a seal and holds the sandwich closed.

6. For an attractive plate presentation, slice each sandwich in half on the diagonal. Place half of the roll-up flat on a plate. Lean the other half up against it, diagonal cut against diagonal cut. Sprinkle the plate with diced tomato, if desired.

179

MAKES 4 SERVINGS

• EACH SERVING CONTAINS APPROXIMATELY:

CALORIES: **166** | FAT: **9 g** | CHOLESTEROL: **16 mg** | SODIUM: **111 mg** | CARBOHYDRATES: **15 g** | PROTEIN: **9 g**

linguini with broiled eggplant and artichoke sauce

This recipe calls for linguini, but any cut of pasta can be used. The unusual combination of ingredients in this recipe gives the sauce a uniquely different and satisfying flavor. It is also good served over rice or other vegetables.

SAUCE:

8 sun-dried tomatoes

4 teaspoons extra-virgin olive oil

1 teaspoon chopped garlic

1 teaspoon chopped shallots

1 cup vegetable stock (see page 56)

2 tablespoons balsamic vinegar

1 tablespoon cornstarch dissolved in 1 tablespoon water

3 tablespoons chopped chives

1/4 teaspoon dried tarragon, crushed

1/4 teaspoon dried thyme, crushed

1 red bell pepper, seeded and sliced

1 yellow bell pepper, seeded and sliced

1 green bell pepper, seeded and sliced

1/2 cup chopped plum tomatoes

1/4 cup tomato sauce

1 small asian eggplant, sliced 1/4 inch thick

1/2 cup drained and chopped canned artichoke hearts

3/4 pound linguini, cooked al dente

4 tablespoons freshly grated parmesan

1. To make the sauce put the sun-dried tomatoes in a small bowl and cover with boiling water. Allow to soak for 5 minutes, or until soft. Drain and cut into thin strips. Set aside.

2. Heat the olive oil in a large skillet over medium heat. Add the garlic and shallots and cook, stirring frequently, until golden brown.

3. Add the vegetable stock and balsamic vinegar and bring to a boil. Add the cornstarch dissolved in water and cook until thickened, about 7 minutes.

4. Add the chives, tarragon, thyme, bell peppers, tomatoes, and tomato sauce and continue cooking for 5 more minutes.

5. Preheat the broiler.

6. Dip the eggplant slices in the vegetable mixture and place on a baking sheet that has been sprayed with non-stick cooking spray. Place under the preheated broiler for 2 to 3 minutes, or until tender. Add the broiled eggplant, sun-dried tomatoes, and artichoke hearts to the vegetable mixture.

7. To serve, place 1 1/2 cups of cooked pasta in each of 4 bowls. Top each with the vegetable mixture. Top each serving with 1 tablespoon of Parmesan cheese.

MAKES 4 SERVINGS

• EACH SERVING CONTAINS APPROXIMATELY:

CALORIES: 430 | FAT: 7 g | CHOLESTEROL: 4 g | SODIUM: 131 mg | CARBOHYDRATES: 76 g | PROTEIN: 15 g

potato fajita with tempeh

For an unusual Southwestern vegan entree, try this spicy potato fajita. For a lacto-vegetarian dish add a dollop of light sour cream as garnish on the plate.

1 large russet potato (12 ounces), thinly sliced

FAJITA SEASONINGS:

1½ teaspoons chili powder

1½ teaspoons ground cumin

¼ teaspoon cayenne pepper

¼ teaspoon salt

½ teaspoon granulated garlic

1 cup seeded and sliced bell pepper (cut into ½-inch pieces)

8 ounces tempeh, cut into lengthwise pieces

4 whole-wheat tortillas, 9 inches each, warmed

½ cup tomato salsa (see page 324)

½ cup canyon ranch guacamole (see page 36)

¼ cup light sour cream, optional

1. Preheat the oven to 400°F.

2. Spray a baking sheet with non-stick cooking spray. Arrange the potato slices on the baking sheet and spray again. Combine all the fajita seasoning ingredients in a bowl, mix well, and sprinkle over the potatoes. Place the potatoes in the preheated oven and bake for about 15 minutes, or until browned.

3. Spray a skillet with non-stick cooking spray, add the bell pepper and tempeh, and cook until tender.

4. Remove the potatoes from the oven and divide onto 4 plates. Serve with a warm whole-wheat tortilla, 2 tablespoons of salsa, 2 tablespoons of guacamole, and one-fourth of the tempeh and bell pepper mixture. Top with a tablespoon of sour cream, if desired.

MAKES 4 SERVINGS

181

• EACH FAJITA WITH SOUR CREAM SERVING CONTAINS APPROXIMATELY:

CALORIES: 375 | FAT: 7 g | CHOLESTEROL: 0 | SODIUM: 386 mg | CARBOHYDRATES: 55 g | PROTEIN: 16 g

mushroom beignets

A classic beignet (ben-YAY), French for fritter, is a deep-fried yeast pastry. It is a traditional New Orleans dish, where it is served hot with a generous dusting of powdered sugar. However, savory beignets, such as crab or herb, are also popular. These savory mushroom beignets are the creation of John Luzader, the executive chef at the Canyon Ranch in Tucson. They have all the taste and texture associated with the classic, deep-fried version with only a fraction of the calories and fat. John serves these beignets on sautéed kohlrabi topped with oven-fried potatoes, toasted sesame seeds, and cashews, and surrounds them with reconstituted dried apricots. He then drizzles a little fresh carrot juice and mushroom essence around the rim of the plate for both taste enhancement and added color.

8 ounces chanterelle mushrooms (4 cups), cut in matchstick-size pieces

8 ounces shiitake mushrooms (4 cups), cut in matchstick-size pieces

8 ounces oyster mushrooms (4 cups), cut in matchstick-size pieces

1 medium white onion, thinly sliced

1 medium red onion, thinly sliced

1 cup cooked rice (see page 171)

1/4 teaspoon salt

1/4 teaspoon freshly ground black pepper

1/3 cup cornstarch

1 tablespoon chopped fresh sage, or 1 teaspoon dried sage, crushed

1 tablespoon chopped fresh oregano, or 1 teaspoon dried oregano, crushed

2 tablespoons chopped fresh chervil, or 2 teaspoons dried chervil, crushed

1/2 cup whole-wheat bread crumbs

These delightfully different fritters make a superb light summer supper, and leftovers are great for stuffing pita pocket sandwiches. For a less expensive dish, you can substitute both canned and fresh white mushrooms for the chanterelle, shiitake, and oyster mushrooms, and for a still faster dish you can buy them already sliced.

1. Spray a large skillet with non-stick vegetable spray and heat it until drops of water dance on the surface. Add the mushrooms and onions and cook over medium-low heat, stirring frequently, until the mushrooms are tender and the onion is translucent. Remove from the heat and allow to cool.

2. While the mushrooms are cooling, preheat the oven to

350°F. Line a standard-size 9 x 5 x 3-inch loaf pan, or a similar sized terrine, with plastic wrap.

3. Combine the rice, salt, and pepper in a food processor and puree. Set aside.

4. Sprinkle the cornstarch evenly over the mushroom mixture. Add the chopped herbs and mix well. Add the rice mixture and again mix well. Spoon the mushroom mixture into the lined pan and pack it down tightly.

5. Place the pan in a larger pan filled with water to a depth of 3/4 inch. Put it in the preheated oven and bake for about 1 hour, or until firm. Remove from the oven and cool on a rack. When it is room temperature, cover the pan and refrigerate it for several hours or overnight.

6. Cut the loaf into eight 1-inch slices. Put the bread crumbs on a plate. Gently roll each slice in the crumbs, pressing them into the surface on all sides. Shake off the excess coating.

7. Spray a large skillet with non-stick vegetable spray and heat it until drops of water dance on the surface. Cook the slices in a single layer in the hot pan over medium heat until crisp on the outside and lightly browned on all sides.

183

MAKES 4 SERVINGS

• EACH 2-SLICE SERVING CONTAINS APPROXIMATELY:

CALORIES: **504** | FAT: **2 g** | CHOLESTEROL: **0** | SODIUM: **483 mg** | CARBOHYDRATES: **121 g** | PROTEIN: **15 g**

shakshuka

This zesty recipe is practically the national dish of Israel. You will find it served in street cafés like Dr. Shakshuka's, a popular hangout in the old town of Jaffa just outside of Tel Aviv, and in very upscale dining rooms as well. This is my favorite version of this Israeli dish and it is based on a recipe given to me by Deiter Lengauer, the executive chef at the Hyatt Regency Dead Sea Resort. When serving shakshuka at home, I prefer to put three-quarters of a cup in each of 4 individual au gratin dishes. For a lower-cholesterol vegan dish just omit the eggs.

1 teaspoon olive oil

¼ cup sliced garlic

1 cup chopped onion

1 tablespoon sweet paprika

3 cups cubed tomatoes plus 2 tomatoes sliced

1 cup chopped red bell pepper

¼ teaspoon red pepper flakes

½ teaspoon ground cumin

¼ teaspoon salt

½ teaspoon freshly ground black pepper

¼ teaspoon fresh thyme leaves, or pinch of dried thyme

1 tablespoon chopped fresh basil leaves, optional

4 eggs

4 slices crusty bread

184

1. Heat the oil and garlic in a skillet just until the garlic starts to sizzle.

2. Add the chopped onion and paprika and stir for 3 minutes, or until the paprika is completely incorporated into the mixture.

3. Add the cubed tomatoes, bell pepper, red pepper flakes, cumin, salt, pepper, thyme, and basil and simmer over low heat for 30 minutes, or until all the ingredients are soft and tender.

4. Preheat the oven to 350°F.

5. Arrange the tomato slices on the bottom of a 7 x 11-inch baking dish. Spoon the cooked vegetable mixture over the tomatoes. Break the eggs over the vegetables.

6. Bake in the preheated oven for about 15 minutes, or until the eggs are set. Serve immediately with crusty bread.

MAKES 4 SERVINGS

• EACH 3/4-CUP SERVING AND 1 SLICE OF BREAD CONTAINS APPROXIMATELY:

CALORIES: **295** | FAT: **7 g** | CHOLESTEROL: **213 mg** | SODIUM: **629 mg** | CARBOHYDRATES: **47 g** | PROTEIN: **14 g**

spicy black-eyed peas

Eating black-eyed peas on New Year's Day for good luck in the coming year is an old Southern tradition. This easy-to-make fat-free vegetarian dish is so delicious and nutritious that it is a perfect entree for all of us on New Year's Day, or any other day of the year. You can eliminate step 1 below if you soak the black-eyed peas overnight. Also, you can substitute any dried beans for the black-eyed peas in this recipe. This dish is even better if made the day before and reheated.

1 pound dried black-eyed peas

6 cups water

2 garlic cloves, pressed or minced

2 medium onions, chopped

1 bell pepper, seeded and diced

1 teaspoon salt

1/2 teaspoon freshly ground black pepper

1/2 teaspoon sugar

1 teaspoon dried oregano, crushed

1 teaspoon dried thyme, crushed

26 ounces canned chopped tomatoes, undrained

4 ounces canned diced green chiles, undrained

1/4 cup red wine vinegar

1. Combine the black-eyed peas and water in a large pot and bring to a rapid boil. Allow to boil for 2 minutes and then remove from the heat. Cover and allow to stand for 1 hour.
2. While the peas are soaking, combine the garlic, onions, and bell pepper in a skillet and cook over low heat, covered, for about 10 minutes, until the onions are translucent, adding a little water if necessary to prevent scorching.
3. Add the cooked onion mixture and all the remaining ingredients to the peas and bring to a boil. Reduce the heat to low and cook, covered, for 1 1/2 to 2 hours, or until the peas are soft.

MAKES 8 CUPS

185

• EACH 1-CUP SERVING CONTAINS APPROXIMATELY:

CALORIES: 230 | FAT: 1 g | CHOLESTEROL: 0 | SODIUM: 428 mg | CARBOHYDRATES: 43 g | PROTEIN: 15 g

tamale pie

This is a wonderful dish for a buffet party. It is easy for guests to serve themselves, and all you need to go with it is a tossed green salad.

1/4 cup vegetable stock (see page 56)

1 1/4 cups finely chopped onion

1 garlic clove, pressed or minced

1/4 cup canned diced green chiles

2 cups canned chopped tomatoes

1 2/3 cups corn kernels

2 tablespoons chili powder

1/2 teaspoon salt

pinch ground cumin

1/2 teaspoon dried oregano, crushed

1/2 teaspoon dried thyme, crushed

2 cups non-fat milk

5 tablespoons yellow cornmeal

2 eggs, beaten

1/2 cup grated reduced-fat sharp cheddar cheese

1/2 cup grated part-skim mozzarella cheese

1. Preheat the oven to 350°F.

2. Spray a 9 x 1-inch pan with non-stick cooking spray.

3. Heat the vegetable stock in a saucepan over low heat. Add the onions and garlic and cook until soft and translucent, about 10 minutes. Add the green chiles, tomatoes, corn, and seasonings and simmer slowly for 10 minutes.

4. Meanwhile, bring the milk to a simmer in a double boiler over simmering water. Add the cornmeal and stir constantly until thickened. Add the beaten eggs and mix thoroughly.

5. Combine the cornmeal mixture with the vegetable mixture and blend well.

6. Spoon the mixture into the prepared pan and bake in the preheated oven for approximately 1 hour, or until set. Sprinkle the cheeses over the top and bake for 5 more minutes. Serve hot.

MAKES 8 SERVINGS

• EACH SERVING CONTAINS APPROXIMATELY:

CALORIES: 175 | FAT: 6 g | CHOLESTEROL: 68 mg | SODIUM: 427 mg | CARBOHYDRATES: 19 g | PROTEIN: 10 g

individual vegetable frittatas

A frittata is an Italian omelet. Unlike a French omelet where the ingredients are folded inside, the ingredients are mixed with the eggs and it is cooked in a round shape. It can either be cooked on top of the stove and flipped over like a pancake to cook the other side, or it can be started on top of the stove and finished in the oven. Use your imagination and what you have on hand to alter the recipe. This recipe can also be made in 1 large skillet and cut into 4 wedges.

1 egg

5 egg whites

1/2 teaspoon salt

1/2 cup water

1/2 cup low-fat (1 percent) milk

3/4 cup sliced mushrooms

1 cup diced zucchini

1/2 cup diced red bell pepper

1 garlic clove, pressed or minced

1 teaspoon chopped fresh thyme

1 teaspoon chopped scallions

3/4 teaspoon fresh lemon juice

1 tablespoon freshly grated
   parmesan cheese

1. Combine the egg, egg whites, salt, water, and milk in a bowl and whisk until well mixed. Set aside.

2. Combine the mushrooms, zucchini, red pepper, garlic, thyme, scallions, and lemon juice in a skillet and cook over medium heat, stirring constantly, until dry.

3. Remove the vegetables from the heat and stir in the Parmesan cheese.

4. Preheat the broiler.

5. Spray a small ovenproof skillet with cooking spray and place over medium heat until drops of water dance on the surface. Add 1/2 cup of the egg mixture and 1/2 cup of the vegetable mixture and cook for 1 minute to set. Remove from the heat and place the frittata under the preheated broiler until nicely browned.

6. Remove from the broiler and slide a spatula around the underside of the frittata, ensuring it does not stick to the pan. Remove the frittata to a plate and keep warm. Repeat with the remaining ingredients.

MAKES 4 SERVINGS

• EACH SERVING CONTAINS APPROXIMATELY:

CALORIES: 90 | FAT: 3 g | CHOLESTEROL: 75 mg | SODIUM: 204 mg | CARBOHYDRATES: 7 g | PROTEIN: 10 g

187

vegetable casserole

This casserole is a wonderful way to use up bits and pieces of fresh vegetables. If you don't have all the vegetables called for in the recipe, just substitute what you have available.

½ tablespoon extra-virgin olive oil

3 medium onions, thinly sliced
  (6 cups)

3 garlic cloves, pressed or minced

1 cup diced zucchini

1 cup diced yellow squash

1 cup diced eggplant

1 cup diced turnips

1 cup diced butternut squash

1 bell pepper, seeded and cut into thin
  strips

2 plum tomatoes, diced

1 scallion, chopped

1 bay leaf

1½ teaspoons freshly ground
  black pepper

½ tablespoon chopped fresh basil

½ tablespoon chopped fresh oregano

1 tablespoon chopped italian parsley

1½ cups whole-wheat bread crumbs

¾ cup freshly grated parmesan
  cheese

2 cups cooked brown rice
  (see page 171), **optional**

1. Preheat the oven to 375°F.
2. Heat the olive oil in a skillet over medium heat. Add the onions and garlic and cook, stirring frequently, until golden brown. Set aside.
3. Place the zucchini, yellow squash, eggplant, turnips, and butternut squash in a baking pan and bake in the preheated oven until the edges are golden brown.
4. Add the bell pepper, tomatoes, and scallion to the onions and garlic and cook over medium heat until soft. Add the bay leaf, pepper, and roasted vegetables and cook for 10 more minutes.
5. Remove from the heat and take out the bay leaf. Add all the fresh herbs and mix well. Spoon the mixture into 6 individual 8-ounce baking dishes. Top each one with ¼ cup of the bread crumbs and 2 tablespoons of the cheese. Put the dishes back in the oven for 10 minutes, or until browned. Place each baking dish on a dinner plate. Serve with ⅓ cup of brown rice, if desired.

MAKES 6 SERVINGS

188

• EACH SERVING CONTAINS APPROXIMATELY:

CALORIES: 381 | FAT: 7 g | CHOLESTEROL: 8 mg | SODIUM: 560 mg | CARBOHYDRATES: 70 g | PROTEIN: 13 g

vegetable lasagna

You can save lots of time making this recipe just by buying packaged prewashed spinach.

1 pound part-skim ricotta cheese

1/2 pound low-fat mozzarella cheese, grated (2 cups)

1 pound fresh or dried spinach lasagna noodles

3 cups marinara sauce (see page 326)

2 cups sliced zucchini

1 1/2 cups sliced yellow squash

3 medium bell peppers (red, yellow, and green), seeded and sliced

3/4 pound eggplant, peeled and thinly sliced

1 pound spinach, thoroughly washed and tough stems removed

1/4 cup freshly grated parmesan cheese

1. Preheat the oven to 300°F.

2. Spoon the ricotta cheese into a bowl and beat until smooth. Fold in the mozzarella cheese.

3. If using fresh pasta, there is no need to cook the noodles. If using dried pasta, cook al dente, according to package directions. Drain and reserve under a damp towel to keep from drying out.

4. Lightly spray a 9 x 13-inch baking dish with non-stick cooking spray.

5. In the baking dish, layer 1 cup of the sauce, a single layer of cooked or fresh noodles, half of the ricotta cheese mixture, half of the vegetables including the spinach, and a third of the Parmesan cheese. Repeat the steps and end with one more layer of noodles, sauce, and Parmesan cheese.

6. Cover the dish with foil and bake in the preheated oven for 30 minutes. Uncover and continue to cook for 15 more minutes, or until cooked through.

7. Remove from the oven and allow to stand 15 minutes before cutting.

MAKES 8 SERVINGS

189

• EACH 1-CUP SERVING CONTAINS APPROXIMATELY:

CALORIES: 437 | FAT: 9 g | CHOLESTEROL: 79 mg | SODIUM: 522 mg | CARBOHYDRATES: 65 g | PROTEIN: 29 g

vegetable pizza

This first-rate vegetarian pizza has always been one of the most popular entrees on Canyon Ranch lunch menus. For a vegan pizza just omit the cheese, or replace it with a soy cheese.

1 unbaked pizza crust (recipe follows)

1 cup marinara sauce (see page 326)

1/2 large onion, thinly sliced (2 cups)

1/2 cup thinly sliced mushrooms

1/2 small green bell pepper, seeded and thinly sliced

1/2 small red bell pepper, seeded and thinly sliced

1 medium zucchini, thinly sliced

1 cup shredded part-skim mozzarella cheese

1. Prepare the pizza crust.

2. Preheat the oven to 425°F.

3. Spread the sauce on the unbaked pizza crust. Arrange the onions, mushrooms, pepper slices, and zucchini decoratively on top of the sauce. Bake in the preheated oven on the lowest shelf for 10 minutes. Remove from the oven.

4. Spread the shredded cheese on the pizza and bake for an additional 15 minutes, or until the bottom is lightly browned. If the pizza begins to brown too much before the crust is done, place a square of aluminum foil lightly over the top and continue to bake until the bottom crust is lightly browned. Remove from the oven. Allow to stand for 3 to 5 minutes before slicing. Cut the pizza into 8 slices.

MAKES 1 PIZZA, OR 8 SERVINGS

190

EACH PIECE (ONE-EIGHTH OF THE PIZZA) CONTAINS APPROXIMATELY:

CALORIES: **240** | FAT: **6 g** | CHOLESTEROL: **12 mg** | SODIUM: **502 mg** | CARBOHYDRATES: **37 g** | PROTEIN: **13 g**

pizza crust

This is the whole-wheat pizza crust we use at Canyon Ranch for our popular Vegetable Pizza (preceding recipe).

2 packages dry yeast
(check date on package before using)

1 cup warm water, 90° to 100°F.

1 teaspoon sugar

1¹/₂ cups whole-wheat flour

2 teaspoons extra-virgin olive oil

3/4 cup all-purpose flour

1/4 teaspoon salt

2 teaspoons cornmeal

1. Combine the yeast and warm water in a bowl and allow to soften. Stir in the sugar. Add the whole-wheat flour and mix well. Add the olive oil and again mix well.

2. Mix the all-purpose flour and salt together and add to the yeast mixture. Turn out onto a floured board and knead until smooth and elastic, about 10 to 15 minutes, adding additional all-purpose flour if needed.

3. Lightly rub the inside of a large bowl with vegetable oil. Place the dough in the oiled bowl and cover with wax paper or plastic wrap and put in a warm spot until the dough has doubled in bulk, about 1 hour. Punch down and knead for about 30 seconds and then form into a ball.

4. Roll the dough out on a lightly floured board to about 14 inches in diameter. Sprinkle a 14-inch pizza pan with 2 teaspoons of cornmeal and transfer the crust to the pan. If you are not going to make the pizza immediately, wrap tightly and freeze. Thaw completely before placing the sauce, toppings, and cheese over the top.

MAKES 1 PIZZA CRUST, OR 8 SERVINGS

192

• EACH SERVING CONTAINS APPROXIMATELY:

CALORIES: **140** | FAT: **2 g** | CHOLESTEROL: **0** | SODIUM: **294 mg** | CARBOHYDRATES: **27 g** | PROTEIN: **6 g**

vegetable tofu stir-fry

Marinating the tofu in this tasty stir-fry not only adds enormously to the flavor of the dish, but it also further firms up the tofu. It is easier to cook when it's not breaking apart.

MARINADE:

2 tablespoons reduced-sodium soy sauce

1 garlic clove, pressed or minced

1/2 teaspoon finely chopped fresh gingerroot

3 tablespoons vegetable stock
(see page 56)

1 teaspoon dark sesame oil

12 ounces extra-firm tofu (about 3 cups), drained

1/4 cup whole-wheat flour

4 ounces whole snow peas

1 small zucchini, sliced

3/4 cup diced jicama

3/4 cup diced celery

2 small japanese eggplants, sliced

1 medium carrot, sliced

1/2 cup broccoli florets

1/2 cup sliced wild mushrooms

1/2 bell pepper, seeded and sliced

1 teaspoon cornstarch

2 teaspoons toasted sesame seeds

2 cups cooked brown rice
(see page 171)

1. Combine the soy sauce, garlic, ginger, vegetable stock, and oil in a bowl and mix well.

2. Slice the tofu into 1/4-inch-thick strips and place in a shallow baking dish. Pour the marinade over the tofu and allow to marinate for 2 hours.

3. Drain and reserve the marinade. Set aside.

4. Place the whole-wheat flour on a large plate and dip the tofu strips in the flour to coat. Spray a large skillet or wok with non-stick cooking spray and place over medium-high heat. Carefully stir-fry the tofu until golden brown. Remove from the pan and set aside. Keep warm.

5. In the same pan, add the snow peas, zucchini, jicama, celery, eggplants, carrot, and broccoli and stir-fry over medium-high heat, adding just enough water to keep from scorching. Cook until the vegetables are tender but crisp, about 4 to 5 minutes. Add the remaining vegetables and tofu and toss gently, continuing to stir-fry for 2 minutes.

6. In a small bowl, combine the cornstarch and enough cold water to make a thin paste. Add the mixture to the reserved marinade and pour over the vegetables and tofu. Stir gently and cook over low heat, covered, about 4 minutes, until the vegetables are glazed and the sauce is thickened.

7. Sprinkle the stir-fry with toasted sesame seeds and serve each portion over 1/2 cup of brown rice.

193

MAKES 4 SERVINGS

▪ EACH 2-CUP SERVING CONTAINS APPROXIMATELY:

CALORIES: 305 | FAT: 8 g | CHOLESTEROL: 0 | SODIUM: 305 mg | CARBOHYDRATES: 45 g | PROTEIN: 16 g

vegetarian cassoulet

A classic French cassoulet consists of white beans cooked with a variety of meats, such as lamb, duck, and sausages, usually left over from previous meals during the week. It is cooked, covered, very slowly to marry all the flavors. This vegetarian cassoulet varies enormously from the classic in that it combines other beans with the traditional white beans instead of leftover poultry and meat, and it is cooked uncovered and much more rapidly.

¹/₃ cup black beans

¹/₃ cup kidney beans

¹/₃ cup navy beans

8 cups water

¹/₄ cup minced shallots

3 garlic cloves, pressed or minced

4 cups vegetable stock (see page 56)

¹/₂ teaspoon salt
(omit if using salted stock)

¹/₂ teaspoon freshly ground black
pepper

¹/₂ teaspoon finely chopped fresh
lemon thyme

¹/₂ teaspoon finely chopped fresh basil

¹/₂ teaspoon finely chopped fresh
tarragon

2 cups diced plum tomatoes

fresh herb sprigs for garnish

1. Combine the beans and water to cover and soak for 4 to 5 hours or overnight. Drain the beans and discard the water. Add 8 cups of fresh water and bring the beans to a boil. Reduce the heat to low and cook, covered, for 45 minutes. Again, drain and discard the water. Set the drained beans aside.

2. In a heavy saucepan, cook the shallots in a little water over medium heat until translucent. Add the garlic and cook 2 more minutes. Add the cooked beans and mix well. Add the vegetable stock and salt to the bean mixture and cook over medium-high heat until the liquid is reduced by half. Add the pepper, chopped herbs, and diced tomatoes and mix well.

3. To serve, ladle 2 cups of the cassoulet into each of 4 large soup plates and garnish with fresh herb sprigs.

MAKES 4 SERVINGS

• EACH 2-CUP SERVING CONTAINS APPROXIMATELY:

CALORIES: **155** | FAT: **negligible** | CHOLESTEROL: **0** | SODIUM: **15 mg** | CARBOHYDRATES: **27 g** | PROTEIN: **9 g**

vegetarian chili

This truly quick and easy chili is a great recipe for a busy day. It can literally be assembled in minutes and takes very little time to cook. When served with this spicy corn bread, it is a satisfying and healthy vegetarian entree.

1 1/2 cups finely diced onions

2 garlic cloves, pressed or minced

4 ounces undrained canned diced green chiles

1 cup diced tomatoes

1/2 teaspoon no-salt seasoning, such as Mrs. Dash or Parsley Patch

1 teaspoon dried oregano, crushed

1 teaspoon ground cumin

1 1/4 teaspoons chili powder

28 ounces canned red kidney beans, drained and rinsed

5 cups low-sodium tomato juice

6 servings jalapeño corn bread (see page 340)

1. Combine the onions and garlic in a large skillet and cook, covered, over low heat until soft, adding a little water if necessary to prevent scorching.

2. Add all the remaining ingredients, except the corn bread, and mix thoroughly. Cook over medium heat until bubbling hot.

3. Serve with a piece of jalapeño corn bread on the side of each portion.

MAKES 6 SERVINGS

195

• EACH 1 1/2-CUP SERVING CONTAINS APPROXIMATELY:

CALORIES: **260** | FAT: **2 g** | CHOLESTEROL: **5 mg** | SODIUM: **599 mg** | CARBOHYDRATES: **48 g** | PROTEIN: **13 g**

vegetarian pot stickers

Pot stickers are small dumplings made of wonton skins, filled usually with either ground fish, poultry or meat, scallions, and seasonings. They are first browned and then simmered in broth. In this vegetarian recipe tempeh is used in place of the fish or meat. Pot stickers can be served as either appetizers or as an entree. These vegetarian pot stickers are great for picnics because you don't have to worry about animal protein being unrefrigerated for several hours.

1 tablespoon cornstarch

1 pound frozen spinach, thawed

1 tablespoon reduced-sodium soy sauce

¼ teaspoon chili sauce

2 teaspoons peeled and minced fresh gingerroot

¼ cup finely chopped scallions

½ pound tempeh, crumbled

SAUCE:

½ cup water

1 teaspoon low-sodium worcestershire sauce, without anchovies

½ teaspoon chili sauce

¼ teaspoon sugar

2 teaspoons grated orange rind, orange part only

32 wonton skins

2 tablespoons canola oil

1. Lightly dust a large baking sheet with the cornstarch and set aside.

2. Squeeze any excess moisture from the thawed spinach.

3. Combine the soy sauce, chili sauce, and gingerroot in a bowl and mix well. Add the spinach, scallions, and tempeh and again mix well.

4. Combine all the sauce ingredients in a small bowl, mix well, and set aside.

5. Separate the wonton skins. Place 1 tablespoon of the pot-sticker mixture onto each of the wonton skins. To form into pot stickers, bring the 4 corners of the wonton skins into the center, overlapping to cover the filling and form a ball. Place the ball, fold side down, in the soft hollow of your hand between your thumb and index finger. Squeeze your hand gently to form and seal each pot sticker.

6. Place the finished pot stickers on the prepared baking sheet and refrigerate for at least 1 hour. (The recipe can be assembled to this point several hours in advance and refrigerated until cooking time.)

7. To cook the pot stickers, heat the oil in a large non-stick

skillet over medium-high heat. Add the pot stickers and cook until the bottoms are golden brown. Carefully turn each pot sticker over to brown the other side. Pour the sauce over the pot stickers, cover, and steam for 3 minutes. Remove the cover and continue cooking until all the sauce is completely absorbed.

MAKES 4 SERVINGS

• EACH SERVING OF 8 POT STICKERS CONTAINS APPROXIMATELY:

CALORIES: 190 | FAT: 6 g | CHOLESTEROL: 0 | SODIUM: 261 mg | CARBOHYDRATES: 26 g | PROTEIN: 11 g

wild rice–stuffed acorn squash

In this recipe the wild rice is first cooked with fresh herbs and then mixed with baked squash for a truly delightful dish. I like to stuff it back into the squash for a prettier presentation as a vegetarian entree. However, it also makes a wonderful vegetable side dish with poultry or meat for a holiday meal.

3 cups vegetable stock (see page 56)

1 cup dry wild rice (5 1/3 ounces)

1 teaspoon salt, divided use

1 tablespoon chopped fresh thyme

1 tablespoon chopped fresh tarragon

4 large acorn squash (about 5 pounds), halved and seeded

1/2 medium onion, finely chopped

3 garlic cloves, pressed or minced

1/4 teaspoon ground allspice

1 tablespoon dry vermouth

1/4 cup canned evaporated skim milk

1 tablespoon walnut oil

1 cup crumbled blue cheese (4 ounces)

1/4 cup toasted pumpkin seeds

1. Preheat the oven to 350°F. Bring the stock to a boil over medium-high heat. Stir in the wild rice, 1/2 teaspoon of salt (omit if using salted stock), thyme, and tarragon and reduce the heat to low. Simmer, covered, until the rice kernels burst and are tender, about 45 to 50 minutes. Fluff with a fork before removing from the pan.

2. Place the squash halves, cut side down, in a baking dish. Add water to a depth of 1/4 inch. Cover and bake for about 45 minutes, or until pierced easily with a fork.

3. While the squash is cooking, combine the onion and garlic in a heavy pan and cook, covered, over low heat for about 10 minutes, or until the onion is soft and translucent, adding a little water if necessary to prevent scorching. Uncover and add the allspice, the remaining salt, and vermouth and continue cooking for 3 more minutes.

4. Remove the squash from the oven and allow to cool until it can be safely handled. Remove the cooked flesh from each squash half, leaving about 1/4 inch of the squash as a lining and being careful not to tear the shells. Place the cooked squash in a food processor. Add the cooked onion mixture and milk and blend until smooth. Slowly add the walnut oil while the processor is running.

5. Combine the blended squash and cooked rice and mix

more about tofu

Tofu, also called bean curd, is made from curdled soy milk, an iron-rich liquid extracted from ground, cooked soybeans. The curds are drained and pressed in much the same way that cheese is made. The firmness of the tofu is determined by how much of the liquid is pressed out. It has a custardlike texture and very little taste of its own. However, it has the chameleonlike capability of taking on the flavor of anything it is marinated in, making it an extremely versatile ingredient. Silken tofu, available both soft and firm, has the smoothest texture and is best to use whenever a satin-smooth texture is the most desirable.

well. Spoon the rice mixture into each of the 8 shells. Top each one with 2 tablespoons of the blue cheese and 1/2 tablespoon of the toasted pumpkin seeds.

MAKES 8 SERVINGS

• EACH FILLED CHEESE-TOPPED ACORN SQUASH HALF CONTAINS APPROXIMATELY:

CALORIES: 260 | FAT: 6 g | CHOLESTEROL: 11 mg | SODIUM: 384 mg | CARBOHYDRATES: 448 g | PROTEIN: 8 g

wild mushroom risotto

Risotto is becoming increasingly popular in this country. Remember, the two ingredients most necessary for a perfect risotto are arborio rice and quite a bit of patience.

3 ounces dried wild mushrooms (3 cups), such as shiitake, oyster, or porcini

10 cups hot water

1 teaspoon sugar

2 tablespoons extra-virgin olive oil

1 cup arborio rice

1 cup shredded parmesan or romano cheese

arborio rice
Arborio rice is a small, white, opaque grain unique to the Po Valley region of northern Italy. Risotto is made by cooking this rice slowly, adding the liquid, a little at a time, and stirring almost constantly between additions until a creamy, cereal-like consistency is achieved.

1. Combine the mushrooms, hot water, and sugar in a large bowl and allow to stand for 30 minutes. Pour the liquid into a pan through a fine strainer or through cheesecloth to remove any sand or grit, and bring it to a simmer.

2. Carefully wash the mushrooms, remove the tough stems, and cut them into thin strips. Set aside.

3. Heat the olive oil in a heavy pan over medium heat. Add the rice and stir until each grain of rice is coated and shiny, about 2 minutes. Spoon 1/2 cup of the hot mushroom liquid into the rice and cook, stirring frequently, until it is almost absorbed. Add the mushrooms and mix well. Continue to add the liquid, 1/2 cup at a time, stirring constantly between additions, until it has all been added, about 20 minutes. Always wait until the previous 1/2 cup has been almost absorbed, but do not wait until the rice is dry before adding more liquid. There should always be a veil of liquid over the top of the rice and the final consistency should be slightly runny, like a soft-textured cooked cereal.

4. Remove from the heat and stir the cheese into the risotto. Serve immediately.

MAKES 4 SERVINGS

• **EACH 2-CUP SERVING CONTAINS APPROXIMATELY:**

CALORIES: **380** | FAT: **13 g** | CHOLESTEROL: **16 mg** | SODIUM: **401 mg** | CARBOHYDRATES: **53 g** | PROTEIN: **14 g**

marinated tofu

This marinated tofu can also be diced and added to other dishes such as salads and stir-fries. It would be good sprinkled over salads or vegetables or in soups.

6 ounces firm tofu

1 tablespoon reduced-sodium
   soy sauce

1 tablespoon chopped scallions

1 teaspoon finely chopped lemongrass

1 garlic clove, pressed or minced

1/4 teaspoon freshly ground
   black pepper

1 teaspoon sesame oil

pinch fructose

1. Cut the tofu into 1-ounce slices. Lay the slices flat in a glass baking dish.

2. Combine all the remaining ingredients and spoon over the tofu. Allow to marinate for 2 to 3 hours.

MAKES 6 SERVINGS

201

• EACH SERVING CONTAINS APPROXIMATELY:

CALORIES: 40 | FAT: 3 g | CHOLESTEROL: 0 | SODIUM: 103 mg | CARBOHYDRATES: negligible | PROTEIN: 3 g

fish and shellfish

Most fish and shellfish are lower in fat than either poultry or meat and are our best source of animal protein. Also, even in higher-fat fish, the fats they do contain are primarily unsaturated, and they are the best source of omega−3 fatty acids, considered helpful in preventing heart attacks and in controlling high blood pressure.

Because of its superb nutritional profile and to take advantage of the many varieties of seasonal fish available from all over the world, we have a fresh fish special on all Canyon Ranch menus every day.

When buying fresh fish, you should be sure it smells fresh. Never buy fish with a fishy smell. Whole fish should have clear, shiny eyes and shimmering scales. Filleted fresh fish should look moist and lay flat. When buying shellfish, the shells should be tightly closed. All fresh fish and shellfish are extremely perishable. If you must keep fish for more than a day before using it, then wash it under cold running water, pat it dry, and wrap it tightly in plastic wrap. Place it on a pan of crushed ice in the coldest part of your refrigerator. If you have to keep it longer than 2 days it should be frozen.

When using frozen fish, always put it in the refrigerator to thaw. Force-thawing fish will cause the texture to become mushy. Also, it should never be refrozen.

Fish is divided into several categories, such as freshwater and saltwater and lean and oily. Freshwater fish, such as catfish, perch, and trout, tend to have more tender flesh and more numerous small bones. Saltwater fish, such as ahi tuna, halibut, and snapper, have more solid flesh and larger bones that are more easily removed. Lean fish, such as sole and halibut, are more delicate and will dry out more easily. For this reason they are better cooked with additional fat or liquid, while oilier fish, such as salmon and swordfish, can be grilled or broiled.

When cooking fish, remember it doesn't take long to cook no matter which method you're using. When fish turns from translucent to opaque it is done. Prolonged cooking will dry it out and toughen it. Allow for shrinkage of about 25 to 30 percent in the ounce weight from raw to cooked fish; for a 3-ounce cooked serving you should start with 4 ounces of raw fish.

light rouille

Rouille is the French word for rust, which aptly describes the color of this hot garlicky sauce. It is frequently served with fish and fish stews such as Bouillabaisse (recipe follows).

3/4 cup roasted red peppers
(see page 49)

2 garlic cloves, halved

2 slices whole-wheat bread, broken into pieces

1/4 cup fish stock or clam juice

1/4 teaspoon salt

1/4 teaspoon freshly ground black pepper

1/4 teaspoon crushed red pepper flakes, or to taste

1 tablespoon extra-virgin olive oil

1. Combine all the ingredients, except the olive oil, in a blender and blend until smooth. With the blender running, slowly add the oil.

2. Store, tightly covered, in the refrigerator. It will keep for a couple of days. If you wish to keep it longer you can freeze it — but the texture will not be as smooth when thawed.

MAKES 1 1/4 CUPS

205

• EACH 2-TABLESPOON SERVING CONTAINS APPROXIMATELY:

CALORIES: **28** | FAT: **1 g** | CHOLESTEROL: **0** | SODIUM: **82 mg** | CARBOHYDRATES: **3 g** | PROTEIN: **negligible**

bouillabaisse

This hearty seafood stew was created by the fishermen living in and around the French seaport of Marseilles, who used whatever fish and shellfish they hadn't sold at the end of each day to make their dinner. Even though this dish has taken on a much more sophisticated aura over the years, the predominant seasonings in bouillabaisse are still the same saffron and fennel favored by these savvy fishermen. However, in Marseilles they serve this stew over crusty French bread which I prefer to serve on the side so that it remains crunchy. Serve with a dollop of the Canyon Ranch garlicky sauce called Light Rouille, a lighter version of the classic, high-fat French sauce, which precedes this recipe.

1 medium onion, finely chopped (1½ cups)

1 leek, white part only, thinly sliced (1 cup)

1 garlic clove, pressed or minced

2 medium tomatoes, peeled, seeded, and diced (1½ cups)

2 tablespoons finely chopped parsley

1 stalk celery, finely chopped (½ cup)

1 bay leaf

¼ teaspoon dried thyme, crushed

¼ teaspoon dried fennel seeds, crushed

¼ teaspoon dried saffron threads dissolved in a little defatted chicken or fish stock

⅛ teaspoon freshly ground black pepper

2 cups fat-free fish stock (see page 55) or chicken stock (see page 54)

1 cup dry white wine

½ pound firm white fish, cut into strips (2 cups)

½ pound shellfish, shelled and cleaned

sprigs fresh thyme or fennel for garnish

4 slices crusty French bread

1. Combine the onion, leek, and garlic in a large saucepan or pot and cook, covered, over very low heat until soft, about 10 minutes, adding a little stock if necessary to prevent scorching. Add all the other ingredients except the fish, shellfish, garnish, and bread. Mix well and bring to a boil. Reduce the heat and simmer, covered, for 10 minutes.

2. Add the fish and shellfish and continue to simmer until they turn from translucent to opaque, 2 to 5 minutes.

3. Serve in 4 casseroles and garnish with sprigs of thyme or fennel. Serve a slice of French bread on the side.

MAKES 4 SERVINGS

• EACH 2-CUP SERVING CONTAINS APPROXIMATELY:

CALORIES: **363** | FAT: **4 g** | CHOLESTEROL: **130 mg** | SODIUM: **577 mg** | CARBOHYDRATES: **25 g** | PROTEIN: **40 g**

fish 'n' chips

You will be amazed at how close to the original version of the famous British street food this tastes. In fact, you might even want to serve it in a folded newspaper with malt vinegar on the side for dipping! At Canyon Ranch we serve it with our Coleslaw (see page 99).

1 pound russet potatoes, cut into wedges

½ cup whole-wheat flour

6 tablespoons whole-wheat bread crumbs

pinch freshly ground black pepper

1 egg white, beaten

1 pound sole or scrod fillets, cut into 4-ounce portions

TARTAR SAUCE:

⅔ cup fat-free mayonnaise

1 tablespoon sweet pickle relish

1 teaspoon fresh lemon juice

1 teaspoon minced parsley

pinch cayenne pepper

1. Preheat the oven to 450°F.

2. Lightly spray a baking sheet with non-stick cooking spray. Arrange the potato wedges on one side, leaving enough room for the fillets, and spray them with the cooking spray. Bake in the preheated oven for 25 minutes, or until golden brown and tender.

3. While the potatoes are baking, combine the flour, bread crumbs, and pepper in a shallow bowl.

4. In another shallow bowl lightly beat the egg white. Dip the fish fillets in the egg white, then coat both sides with the flour mixture. Transfer to the baking sheet, alongside the potatoes, and continue to cook for 10 minutes more, or until the fillets are crisp and browned.

5. Combine all the ingredients for the tartar sauce in a small bowl and mix well. Serve 1 tablespoon on each fish fillet.

MAKES 4 SERVINGS

208

• EACH 3-OUNCE SERVING OF COOKED FISH WITH POTATOES AND 1 TABLESPOON OF SAUCE CONTAINS APPROXIMATELY:

CALORIES: 250 | FAT: 2 g | CHOLESTEROL: 47 mg | SODIUM: 398 mg | CARBOHYDRATES: 33 g | PROTEIN: 23 g

fish tacos

This easy-to-make Mexican dish is always a big hit with guests. To complete your south-of-the-border menu, start with Gazpacho (see page 58) and serve Caramelized Custard (see page 394) for dessert.

2/3 cup fat-free mayonnaise

1 cup tomato salsa
(see page 324)

1 pound sole fillets

8 corn tortillas, warmed

2 cups shredded cabbage or packaged coleslaw mix

3/4 cup chopped cilantro leaves

4 limes, quartered

1. Combine the mayonnaise and salsa in a bowl, mix well, and set aside.

2. Prepare the grill or preheat the broiler.

3. Spray the grill rack or broiler pan with non-stick cooking spray. Place the sole on the rack or pan and grill or broil for about 3 minutes per side, or until the fish flakes easily.

4. Cut the sole into 8 pieces and place a piece in the center of each warm tortilla. Top the fish with 1/4 cup of the cabbage or coleslaw mix and a sprinkle of cilantro. Spoon about 3 tablespoons of the mayonnaise and salsa sauce over the top. Fold each taco in half and serve with 2 lime quarters to squeeze on it.

209

MAKES 8 SERVINGS

• EACH FILLED TACO CONTAINS APPROXIMATELY:

CALORIES: 147 | FAT: 2 g | CHOLESTEROL: 0 | SODIUM: 249 mg | CARBOHYDRATES: 22 g | PROTEIN: 11 g

saffron potato-crusted grouper fillets

For even more flavor in this already tasty dish use the recipe for Garlic Mashed Potatoes (see page 304) and add a pinch of saffron.

(see page 304)

DRESSING:

1 tablespoon balsamic vinegar

2 tablespoons extra-virgin olive oil

¼ teaspoon salt

¼ teaspoon freshly ground black pepper

4 plum tomatoes, quartered

6 basil leaves, cut into thin strips

1½ pounds russet potatoes, peeled and cubed (4½ cups)

¼ cup warmed skim milk

pinch saffron

¼ teaspoon salt

¼ teaspoon freshly ground black pepper

4 grouper fillets (4 ounces each)

2 pounds fresh pea pods, lightly steamed (2 cups)

1. Combine all the dressing ingredients in a bowl and mix well. Add the quartered tomatoes and basil and stir to coat. Set aside.

2. Preheat the oven to 350°F.

3. Put the cubed potatoes in a saucepan and cover with water. Bring to a boil over medium heat and cook for about 15 minutes, or until the potatoes can be pierced easily with a fork. Put the cooked potatoes in a bowl and mash.

4. Combine the warm milk, saffron, salt, and pepper in a small bowl and mix well. Add to the mashed potatoes and continue mashing until thoroughly mixed. Spoon the mixture into a pastry bag.

5. Spray a baking dish with non-stick cooking spray and put the fish fillets in the dish. Pipe the potato mixture onto the fish fillets. Bake in the preheated oven for 8 minutes, or until the fish is completely opaque when tested with the tip of a knife.

6. Place each potato-crusted fish fillet on a plate. Arrange 4 tomato quarters and ½ cup of pea pods on each plate. Drizzle any remaining dressing over the top of each serving.

MAKES 4 SERVINGS

210

• EACH SERVING CONTAINS APPROXIMATELY:

CALORIES: 496 | FAT: 10 g | CHOLESTEROL: 96 mg | SODIUM: 436 mg | CARBOHYDRATES: 43 g | PROTEIN: 57 g

lemon rosemary marinated halibut

This marinade is also wonderful for chicken as well as other types of fish and shellfish.

MARINADE:

2 tablespoons dry white wine

2 tablespoons fresh lemon juice

2 teaspoons extra-virgin olive oil

2 teaspoons chopped fresh rosemary

1/4 teaspoon salt

1/4 teaspoon freshly ground black pepper

1 pound halibut fillets, or any firm white fish, cut into 4- ounce portions

1. To make the marinade combine the wine, lemon juice, olive oil, rosemary, salt, and pepper in a shallow dish large enough to hold the fish in 1 layer. Place the fish fillets in the marinade, turning to coat both sides. Cover tightly and allow to marinate in the refrigerator for several hours, turning the fillets over several times.

2. Prepare a grill or preheat the broiler.

3. Coat a piece of foil large enough to hold the fish with non-stick cooking spray. With a skewer, poke holes in the foil every few inches. Place the foil on a grill or broiler pan, 4 to 6 inches from the hot coals or heat. Remove the fillets from the marinade and place on the foil and grill or broil for about 6 to 8 minutes, turning once, or until the desired amount of doneness when cut.

MAKES 4 SERVINGS

• EACH SERVING CONTAINS APPROXIMATELY:

CALORIES: **154** | FAT: **4 g** | CHOLESTEROL: **36 mg** | SODIUM: **195 mg** | CARBOHYDRATES: **1 g** | PROTEIN: **24 g**

mahimahi with citrus balsamic vinaigrette

Mahimahi is a mild-flavored fish that pairs beautifully with this zesty combination of sauces. If you are unable to get mahimahi, any mild-tasting white fish, such as bass or halibut, can be substituted in the recipe.

1 cup roasted red peppers (see page 49)

1 roasted garlic clove (see page 332)

1/4 cup sliced red onion

1/4 teaspoon cayenne pepper

1/4 cup vegetable stock (see page 56)

CITRUS BALSAMIC VINAIGRETTE:

1/2 tablespoon butter

2 tablespoons balsamic vinegar

2 tablespoons frozen orange juice concentrate, undiluted

1 tablespoon flour

pinch kosher salt

1 pound mahimahi, cut into 4-ounce portions

4 teaspoons chopped chives for garnish

2 teaspoons grated or finely chopped orange zest for garnish

1. Preheat the oven to 350°F.

2. In a blender combine the peppers, garlic, onion, cayenne, and only enough of the vegetable stock to thin, and blend until smooth. Set aside.

3. Brown the butter in a skillet over medium heat. Whisk in the vinegar, orange juice concentrate, and the remaining vegetable stock and bring to a boil. Remove from the heat and stir in the flour and salt. Return to the heat and simmer for 3 minutes, or until slightly thickened. Remove from the heat and set aside.

4. Spray a baking dish with non-stick cooking spray. Place the fish in the dish and bake in the preheated oven for about 10 to 12 minutes, or until the fish flakes easily.

5. To serve, place each portion of fish on a plate and top with 1/4 cup of the red pepper puree and 2 tablespoons of the warm vinaigrette sauce. Garnish each serving with a teaspoon of chives and 1/2 teaspoon of orange zest.

MAKES 4 SERVINGS

212

• EACH 4-OUNCE GARNISHED FISH SERVING CONTAINS APPROXIMATELY::

CALORIES: **140** | FAT: **3 g** | CHOLESTEROL: **84 mg** | SODIUM: **138 mg** | CARBOHYDRATES: **8 g** | PROTEIN: **21 g**

mahimahi with basmati rice cakes and napa cabbage slaw

When cooking the rice for the rice cakes here, add a bit more liquid than is called for in the directions for Boiled Rice and overcook the rice until it's mushy. This will make the rice cakes stick together better.

RICE CAKES:

2 cups cooked basmati rice
(see page 171)

¼ cup corn kernels

¼ cup blanched pea pods or snow peas, thinly sliced

1 tablespoon fresh thyme leaves

¼ teaspoon salt

¼ teaspoon freshly ground black pepper

NAPA CABBAGE SLAW:

2 cups shredded napa cabbage

½ red bell pepper, seeded and thinly sliced

½ green bell pepper, seeded and thinly sliced

¼ cup thinly sliced pickled ginger

3 tablespoons rice vinegar

4 mahimahi fillets (4 ounces each)

1 cup mango or papaya salsa
(see page 321)

1. Combine all the rice cake ingredients in a bowl and mix well. Cover tightly and refrigerate for at least 1 hour.

2. While the rice mixture is chilling make the slaw. Combine all slaw ingredients in a bowl and mix well. Cover tightly and refrigerate until cold.

3. Mold the cold rice mixture into 8 cakes. Spray a large skillet with non-stick cooking spray and place over medium-low heat. Arrange the rice cakes in the hot skillet and cook until heated through and lightly browned on both sides. Remove the rice cakes from the pan and cover to keep warm.

4. In the same pan cook the fish over medium heat for about 3 minutes per side, or until desired doneness.

5. To serve, place 2 rice cakes in the center of each plate. Spoon one-fourth of the slaw over the top of the cakes. Place the fish on top of the slaw and spoon the salsa around the plate.

MAKES 4 SERVINGS

213

• EACH SERVING, INCLUDING ¼ CUP OF SALSA, CONTAINS APPROXIMATELY:

CALORIES: 554 | FAT: 2 g | CHOLESTEROL: 31 mg | SODIUM: 204 mg | CARBOHYDRATES: 107 g | PROTEIN: 27 g

party salmon plate

This tasty low-fat marinade was created by Chef Joe D. Cochran, Jr., while he was the visiting chef at Canyon Ranch in the Berkshires.

MARINADE:

½ cup reduced-sodium soy sauce

¼ cup rice vinegar

¼ cup water

1 teaspoon dark sesame oil

1 tablespoon chopped fresh ginger

¼ cup cilantro leaves

1 tablespoon fresh lime juice

1 tablespoon hoisin sauce, optional

1 pound salmon fillets, skin removed

½ cup chopped scallions for garnish

lime slices and cilantro sprigs
  for garnish

The recipe makes about 1 cup of the marinade, which is more than you need for the salmon, but it keeps well in the refrigerator and is great to have on hand. It is not only good for all types of fish and shelfish, but it is excellent for marinating chicken and meat as well. It even makes a terrific salad dressing!

I call it a "party" salmon plate because it is ideal for entertaining. You can prepare the salmon in the morning, cover it with plastic wrap, and refrigerate it. When it's time to cook it, all you have to do is spoon a little of the marinade on each plate and put it under a broiler for 1 minute. This recipe is a good example of how pounding fish very thin can change the perception of the amount. However, if you don't want to take the time to pound the salmon, you can cut the fillets into 4-ounce pieces and simply cook it a little longer.

1. Combine all the marinade ingredients in the blender and blend on high speed for 2 minutes. Set aside.

2. Cut the salmon into 4 thin slices. Place the slices between pieces of plastic wrap and pound them paper thin. Arrange the slices on 4 ovenproof serving plates and spoon a small amount of the marinade over the top of each portion. Allow to stand for 15 minutes.

3. Meanwhile, heat the broiler. Place each plate of salmon under the broiler for 1 minute.

4. To serve, garnish each plate with chopped scallions, slices of lime, and sprigs of cilantro. Serve the remaining marinade on the side to use as a sauce.

MAKES 4 SERVINGS

214

• **EACH SERVING CONTAINS APPROXIMATELY:**

CALORIES: **147** | FAT: **4 g** | CHOLESTEROL: **59 mg** | SODIUM: **321 mg** | CARBOHYDRATES: **3 g** | PROTEIN: **23 g**

escallopes of salmon with horseradish sauce

Salmon, though a high-fat fish, is still a very healthy choice because the fats in it are primarily unsaturated, and they are the best source of omega−3 fatty acids, considered helpful in preventing heart attacks and in controlling high blood pressure. Salmon is perhaps the most popular of all fish served at Canyon Ranch and this is a very pretty plate as well as a delicious and tangy cold entree. It is good served with toasted rye bread triangles.

1 pound salmon fillets

HORSERADISH SAUCE:

1/3 cup chopped red onion

1/3 cup chopped scallions

1 cup chopped spinach

2 1/2 tablespoons prepared horseradish

1/2 cup plain non-fat yogurt

1 teaspoon chopped parsley

1 teaspoon chopped chives

pinch freshly ground white pepper

pinch cayenne pepper

1/4 cup diced tomato for garnish

1. Preheat the broiler.

2. Divide the salmon into 4 fillets, 4 ounces each. Place the salmon between 2 pieces of wax paper or plastic wrap and flatten to 1/4-inch thickness with the flat side of a mallet.

3. Place the salmon under the broiler for about 2 minutes per side. Remove from the broiler and allow to cool. Place in refrigerator, tightly covered, for about 2 hours, or until cold.

4. Make the horseradish sauce: Spray a skillet with non-stick vegetable spray and place over medium heat. Add the onion, scallions, and spinach and cook until wilted. Place them in a covered bowl and refrigerate for about 1 hour. When the vegetables are chilled, add the horseradish, yogurt, parsley, chives, and peppers and mix well.

5. Spoon 1/4 cup of the horseradish sauce on each serving plate and place the chilled salmon on top of the sauce. Garnish with diced tomatoes.

MAKES 4 SERVINGS

216

• EACH SERVING CONTAINS APPROXIMATELY:

CALORIES: **205** | FAT: **7 g** | CHOLESTEROL: **62 mg** | SODIUM: **155 mg** | CARBOHYDRATES: **10 g** | PROTEIN: **27 g**

salmon teriyaki

Salmon Teriyaki has been one of the most popular fish dishes on our menu since the day we opened in December 1979, and it continues to be one of our most frequently requested recipes.

TERIYAKI MARINADE:

1/2 cup reduced-sodium soy sauce

2 tablespoons rice vinegar

3 garlic cloves, halved

1 tablespoon finely chopped fresh
   gingerroot

1 1/2 cups frozen unsweetened
   apple juice concentrate (12 ounces),
   undiluted and thawed

1/2 cup finely chopped scallions

6 salmon steaks (4 ounces each)

1. Combine all the ingredients, except the scallions and salmon, in a blender and blend until smooth. Stir in the scallions.

2. Place the salmon in a glass baking dish and pour the marinade over it. Cover tightly and refrigerate for 8 to 10 hours, turning the salmon occasionally so that the marinade is absorbed evenly.

3. Preheat the oven to 350°F.

4. Bake the salmon, in the marinade, in the preheated oven for 8 to 10 minutes, or until the fish flakes easily.

MAKES 6 SERVINGS

217

• EACH SERVING CONTAINS APPROXIMATELY:

CALORIES: 175 | FAT: 7 g | CHOLESTEROL: 62 mg | SODIUM: 132 mg | CARBOHYDRATES: 3 g | PROTEIN: 23 g

salmon with sorrel sauce

Sorrel is a hardy perennial herb with leaves similar to spinach and a sourness that is often used for balance in recipes. When it is not available, spinach can be used as a substitute in many recipes.

1 pound salmon fillet, cut into 4-ounce pieces

SORREL SAUCE:

1 large shallot, minced

1/4 teaspoon butter

2 tablespoons champagne vinegar

2 tablespoons non-alcoholic white wine

3/4 cup fish stock (see page 55) or bottled clam juice, diluted, if desired, with water for a milder flavor

5 tablespoons canned evaporated skim milk

1/4 teaspoon arrowroot

1 teaspoon fresh lemon juice

1/4 teaspoon dijon mustard

2 tablespoons finely diced tomatoes

2 tablespoons chopped fresh sorrel

pinch salt

pinch freshly ground black pepper

1. Preheat the oven to 200°F.

2. Spray a large ovenproof skillet with non-stick cooking spray and place over medium heat. When the skillet is hot, add the salmon fillets and cook about 4 minutes per side, or until medium-rare. Remove the skillet from the heat and keep warm in the preheated oven.

3. In another pan, combine the shallot and butter and cook over medium heat, stirring constantly, until the shallot is translucent. Add the vinegar and continue to cook until almost dry.

4. Add the wine and reduce the mixture by one-third. Add the stock and simmer for 10 minutes, skimming off with a large spoon any fat that forms on the top. Remove the pan from the heat.

5. Combine the milk and arrowroot in a small bowl and stir until the arrowroot is completely dissolved. Stir in the lemon juice. Add the milk mixture to the pan and mix well.

6. Return the sauce to the heat and simmer for 5 more minutes. Again remove from the heat and finish the sauce by stirring in the mustard, tomatoes, sorrel, salt, and pepper.

7. To serve, arrange a piece of salmon on each serving plate and spoon 2 tablespoons of sauce over it. Serve immediately.

MAKES 4 SERVINGS

• EACH SERVING CONTAINS APPROXIMATELY:

CALORIES: 185 | FAT: 7 g | CHOLESTEROL: 63 mg | SODIUM: 153 mg | CARBOHYDRATES: 3 g | PROTEIN: 23 g

218

ahi tuna in pepper crust with ponzu sauce

Classic Ponzu is a Japanese sauce made with lemon juice or rice vinegar, soy sauce, mirin (a low-alcohol sweet wine made from glutinous rice), and/or sake, kombu (seaweed), and dried bonito (fish) flakes. This Canyon Ranch adaptation is an excellent addition to this hot and spicy fish dish. It is good served with a side dish of boiled rice seasoned with just a dash of dark sesame oil. If you would prefer the tuna a little less hot, use less cracked pepper to coat the fish.

2 tablespoons cracked black pepper, or a bit more

1 pound ahi tuna, cut into 4-ounce portions

PONZU SAUCE:

2 tablespoons reduced-sodium soy sauce

2 tablespoons fresh lemon juice

1 teaspoon minced fresh gingerroot

2 tablespoons fat-free chicken stock (see page 54)

pinch freshly ground black pepper

2 tablespoons extra-virgin olive oil

1 finely chopped scallion

1 teaspoon minced garlic

1/2 cup diced tomato

4 whole scallions

1 small head bok choy, separated into leaves and lightly steamed

1. Place the cracked pepper in a shallow bowl. Press each piece of tuna in the pepper to form an outer crust, adding a little more cracked pepper if necessary. Set aside.

2. Prepare the coals for grilling or preheat the broiler.

3. Combine all the Ponzu sauce ingredients in a saucepan and heat just to boiling. Remove from the heat. Add the chopped scallion, garlic, and diced tomato to the sauce and set aside, covered, to keep warm.

4. Place the tuna and whole scallions over the hot coals or under the hot broiler and cook for about 3 minutes per side, or until desired doneness. Remove the scallions when they are just browned and set aside.

5. Divide the steamed bok choy among 4 plates and top each serving with a piece of the tuna. Spoon 2 tablespoons of the sauce over each portion. Garnish each serving with a grilled scallion.

MAKES 4 SERVINGS

219

• EACH SERVING CONTAINS APPROXIMATELY:

CALORIES: 185 | FAT: 8 g | CHOLESTEROL: 98 mg | SODIUM: 458 mg | CARBOHYDRATES: 5 g | PROTEIN: 23 g

seared ahi tuna on warm potato and leek salad with sun-dried tomato dressing

This colorful and delicious dish certainly offers an unusual presentation of a tuna salad. It is a perfect one-dish Canyon Ranch meal for a luncheon or light dinner.

SUN-DRIED TOMATO DRESSING:

2 ounces sun-dried tomatoes (1 cup), soaked in hot water for 10 minutes and drained

1/2 cup reduced vegetable stock
(see page 56)

1/2 teaspoon chopped Italian parsley

1 tablespoon canola oil

1 garlic clove, minced or pressed

1 pound ahi tuna, cut into 4 portions

1/4 teaspoon salt

1/2 teaspoon freshly ground black pepper

1/4 cup fat-free chicken stock
(see page 54)

2 leeks, white part only, sliced into thin rings

1 russet potato, peeled, sliced into finger-size pieces, and blanched

1/2 teaspoon chopped fresh chervil

1 head radicchio, cut into thin strips

1/2 cup baby arugula, any tough stems removed

12 golden baby beets, peeled and blanched

1. Combine all the dressing ingredients in a blender and puree. Pour into a saucepan and heat until hot. Do not allow to boil.

2. Wash the fish and pat it dry. Sprinkle both sides of the fish with the salt and pepper. Spray a skillet with non-stick cooking spray and place over medium-high heat. Place the tuna in the hot skillet and spray the tuna. Cook, turning once, until medium-rare, about 5 minutes.

3. Pour the chicken stock into a saucepan and cook the leeks over medium heat for 20 minutes. Add the potatoes and chervil and heat through. Add the bitter greens and cook just until wilted.

4. Place the hot salad mixture in the center of the plate. Slice each portion of the tuna in half and arrange on the top. Place the heated beets around each serving and drizzle the warm dressing around the plate.

MAKES 4 SERVINGS

220

• EACH SERVING CONTAINS APPROXIMATELY:

CALORIES: 310 | FAT: 5 g | CHOLESTEROL: 49 mg | SODIUM: 448 mg | CARBOHYDRATES: 35 g | PROTEIN: 33 g

teriyaki marinade

This is an excellent marinade for fish, poultry, and meat. Marinate fish steaks or thick fillets, such as salmon, swordfish, or bass, for about 30 minutes, and steak or chicken, 1½ to 2 hours, all tightly covered, in the refrigerator. Most marinades, this one included, improve in flavor and are better if made at least 24 hours prior to using them. This allows the flavors to marry.

3/4 cup reduced-sodium soy sauce

1/2 cup sugar

3 garlic cloves, crushed

3 slices fresh ginger, unpeeled and crushed

2 tablespoons sake

1. Combine the soy sauce and sugar in a small bowl and stir until the sugar is completely dissolved. Add the garlic, ginger, and sake and mix well.
2. Store, tightly covered, in the refrigerator. It will keep for a couple of weeks.

221

MAKES 1 CUP

• EACH 1-TABLESPOON SERVING CONTAINS APPROXIMATELY:

CALORIES: 37 | FAT: negligible | CHOLESTEROL: 0 | SODIUM: 363 mg | CARBOHYDRATES: 8.2 g | PROTEIN: negligible

polenta-crusted sea bass with corn salsa

The buttermilk marination imparts a fabulous flavor to this spicy fish dish and the polenta crust gives it a slightly crunchy texture that pairs perfectly with the salsa.

1 pound sea bass, cut into 4-ounce servings

1/2 cup buttermilk

CORN SALSA:

1 1/2 cups corn kernels

1 tablespoon fresh lime juice

1/4 teaspoon salt

1/4 teaspoon freshly ground black pepper

2 medium tomatillos (3 ounces), blanched and diced (1/3 cup)

1/2 pound tomatoes, diced (3/4 cup)

1 small jalapeño pepper, seeded and finely chopped

1/2 small cucumber, diced

1/2 small red pepper, diced

2 tablespoons chopped cilantro leaves

1/2 cup cornmeal

1 tablespoon extra-virgin olive oil

sprigs cilantro for garnish, optional

1. Place the sea bass in a glass baking dish. Pour the buttermilk over the fish and turn over to coat both sides. Cover tightly and refrigerate all day or overnight.

2. Preheat the broiler. Spray a flat pan with non-stick cooking spray and spread the corn kernels out evenly in it. Place under the broiler and toast the corn, stirring to brown evenly. Set aside.

3. Combine the lime juice and salt in a bowl and mix until the salt is completely dissolved. Add the pepper and mix well. Add the browned corn, blanched tomatillos, tomatoes, jalapeño, cucumber, red pepper, and cilantro and mix well. Reserve the salsa at room temperature.

4. Preheat the oven to 350°F.

5. Put the cornmeal in a shallow bowl. Remove the fish from the buttermilk and press it into the cornmeal, coating each side evenly. Heat the oil in an ovenproof skillet. Place the coated fish in the hot skillet and cook for 2 minutes on one side and 1 minute on the other. Place in the preheated oven for 15 minutes.

6. To serve, place each piece of fish on a plate and arrange the salsa around it. Garnish with cilantro sprigs, if desired.

MAKES 4 SERVINGS

• EACH SERVING CONTAINS APPROXIMATELY:

CALORIES: **287** | FAT: **7 g** | CHOLESTEROL: **48 mg** | SODIUM: **267 mg** | CARBOHYDRATES: **31 g** | PROTEIN: **26 g**

swordfish and peruvian blue potatoes with papaya seed dressing

If possible, sprinkle the swordfish with lime juice several hours before grilling it so that it will absorb more of the lime flavor. Also the fact that the papaya seeds are part of the dressing is novel and they contribute to both the flavor and the great look of the plate. This is a marvelous entree for entertaining because it is sure to arouse interest among your guests and you can tell them that it is a Canyon Ranch recipe.

PAPAYA SEED DRESSING:

1 papaya, peeled, flesh chopped, and seeds reserved

2 tablespoons fresh lime juice

1 teaspoon honey

1/4 teaspoon salt

1/8 teaspoon cayenne pepper

1/2 tablespoon extra-virgin olive oil

VEGETABLE SALAD:

1 teaspoon extra-virgin olive oil

1 small zucchini, diced

1 small bell pepper, seeded and diced

1 small carrot, diced

1 cup pea pods or snow peas, thinly sliced

1 tablespoon chopped fresh herbs, such as thyme or tarragon

1 tablespoon diced tomato

1 pound small blue potatoes, unpeeled and cooked

4 swordfish steaks (4 ounces each)

1/2 teaspoon salt

2 tablespoons fresh lime juice

1. To make the papaya seed dressing, combine the papaya flesh and seeds, lime juice, honey, salt, and cayenne pepper in a blender and puree. Slowly add the oil and blend until emulsified. Set aside.

2. To make the vegetable salad, spray a skillet with non-stick cooking spray and place over medium heat. Add the olive oil, zucchini, pepper, carrot, and pea pods and cook, stirring frequently, until crisp-tender. Add the herbs and tomato and mix well. Spoon into a bowl and keep warm. Do not wash the skillet.

3. Cut the cooked potatoes into 1/4-inch slices, put them in the same skillet used for the vegetables, and cook over medium-high heat until lightly browned.

blue potatoes

Blue potatoes are small and the flesh ranges in color from bluish purple to purple-black. They have a dense texture and are best for boiling. There are also purple potatoes with skins that range in color from lavender to dark blue, but the flesh is white to beige with only a few purple streaks. The blue potatoes, many imported from Peru, are much more dramatic for plate presentation. They are available year round in most supermarkets.

4. Prepare the coals for grilling or preheat the broiler.

5. Sprinkle both sides of each swordfish steak with salt and lime juice. Place on a hot grill or under a broiler for about 3 to 4 minutes per side, or to the desired doneness.

6. Divide the warm vegetable salad evenly among 4 plates, arranging it in the center of each. Arrange the blue potatoes around the vegetable salads. Place a piece of fish on top of the vegetables and drizzle one-fourth of the papaya dressing over the top of each serving.

MAKES 4 SERVINGS

• **EACH SERVING CONTAINS APPROXIMATELY:**

CALORIES: **399** | FAT: **10 g** | CHOLESTEROL: **66 mg** | SODIUM: **661 mg** | CARBOHYDRATES: **38 g** | PROTEIN: **39 g**

southwestern swordfish en papillote

En papillote (pah-pee-yoht) is a French term describing food baked inside a sealed wrapping of either parchment paper or aluminum foil. This method of cooking holds in moisture and therefore allows cooking with less fat. As the food bakes and lets off steam, the paper or foil puffs up into a dome shape. Just before serving, the paper is slit open and folded back to display the food inside.

1 swordfish steak (1 pound), cut into 4 equal pieces

2 limes

1 medium onion, finely chopped (1¹/2 cups)

2 garlic cloves, pressed or minced

7 ounces canned diced green chiles

¹/4 teaspoon salt

¹/2 teaspoon freshly ground black pepper

¹/2 teaspoon ground cumin

2 teaspoons chili powder

2 cups cooked black beans, or 15 ounces canned black beans, rinsed and drained

4 sheets parchment paper (about 24 inches square)

1¹/3 cups fresh or frozen corn kernels

1¹/3 cups tomato salsa (see page 324)

¹/2 cup chopped cilantro

1 egg white (for sealing the parchment paper packages)

This is a perfect dish for entertaining because it can be made ahead of time and cleanup is so easy. For an even more dramatic presentation, allow your guests to open their own papillote packages at the table and get the full impact of the aroma as it is released as well as the visual impact of the colorful dish inside.

1. Wash the swordfish with cold water and pat dry. Squeeze the juice of both limes over the fish. Cover and refrigerate until ready to use.

2. Combine the onion and garlic in a heavy saucepan and cook, covered, over low heat for about 10 minutes, or until soft and translucent, adding a little water if necessary to prevent scorching. Add the diced chiles, salt, pepper, cumin, and chili powder and cook for 3 more minutes. Add the beans and mix well. Set aside.

3. Preheat the oven to 350°F.

4. Cut the parchment paper into large hearts by folding each piece of paper in half and then cutting the folded paper into a half-heart shape. Unfold hearts and spoon ¹/2 cup of the bean mixture onto the center of one side of each heart. Top the beans with ¹/3 cup of corn, a piece of fish, and ¹/3 cup of

salsa, in that order. Top each serving with 2 tablespoons of the chopped cilantro.

5. To close the parchment hearts, brush the edges with egg white. Then fold the empty half of the heart carefully over the contents, pressing the edges together.

6. To seal each "package," fold the edges over, starting at the top with a small fold and continuing all the way around with overlapping folds, crimping the edges tightly with your fingers.

7. Place the packages on baking sheets, 2 per sheet, and bake in the preheated oven for 13 minutes.

8. To serve, place each package on a plate and cut a large X on the top. Fold back the corners to dramatically display the contents.

MAKES 4 SERVINGS

• EACH SERVING CONTAINS APPROXIMATELY:

CALORIES: 389 | FAT: 9 g | CHOLESTEROL: 45 mg | SODIUM: 516 mg | CARBOHYDRATES: 41 g | PROTEIN: 35 g

pasta with clam sauce

If using canned clams for this recipe, you will have enough clam juice by just draining the clams. If you are using fresh clams, then you will need to purchase an 8-ounce bottle of the juice. My favorite cut of pasta for this recipe is fusilli, or any spiral-cut pasta, because the sauce adheres to it better than it does to any of the smooth-surfaced varieties. Many of my Italian friends shudder at the thought of putting Parmesan cheese on any fish dish. However, I like a little of it sprinkled over this clam pasta.

2 teaspoons extra-virgin olive oil

1/2 medium onion, finely chopped

2 garlic cloves, pressed or minced

1 cup clam juice

1/4 cup canned evaporated skim milk

1 1/2 tablespoons cornstarch

2 tablespoons water

1/8 teaspoon freshly ground white pepper

2 cups chopped clams

8 cups cooked pasta

2 tablespoons chopped parsley for garnish

6 tablespoons diced red peppers for garnish

3 tablespoons freshly grated parmesan cheese for garnish, optional

1. Heat the oil in a large skillet over medium heat. Add the onion and garlic and cook, stirring frequently, until soft and a rich caramel color.

2. Combine the clam juice and evaporated skim milk in a saucepan and cook over low heat for 10 minutes.

3. Dissolve the cornstarch in the 2 tablespoons of water and add it to the simmering clam juice mixture. Add the pepper, mix well, and continue cooking over low heat until slightly thickened, about 10 minutes.

4. When thickened, add the sauce to the caramelized onions. Add the chopped clams and heat through. Do not overcook or the clams will become tough.

5. To serve, arrange 1 1/3 cups pasta on each of 6 serving plates. Top with 1/2 cup of the sauce. Garnish each serving with 1 teaspoon of parsley, 1 tablespoon of red peppers, and 1/2 tablespoon of Parmesan cheese, if desired.

MAKES 6 SERVINGS

• EACH SERVING CONTAINS APPROXIMATELY:

CALORIES: 353 | FAT: 3 g | CHOLESTEROL: 19 mg | SODIUM: 106 mg | CARBOHYDRATES: 62 g | PROTEIN: 17 g

228

whole-wheat pasta with clams and tomatoes

All the ingredients for this delicious and nutritious pasta dish can be kept in your cupboard. However, it is also good with fresh vegetables added to it, making it a perfect dish for using up leftover bits and pieces of vegetables you may have accumulated in your refrigerator. Or you can buy a variety of already cut-up vegetables in the salad bar section of your supermarket and lightly steam them for your own shellfish variation of a pasta primavera.

8 ounces whole-wheat pasta

13 ounces canned chopped clams, undrained

1 tablespoon extra-virgin olive oil

3 garlic cloves, pressed or minced

28 ounces canned ready-cut tomatoes, drained

1/2 teaspoon freshly ground black pepper

1/2 teaspoon dried rosemary, crushed

1 teaspoon dried sage, crushed

freshly grated parmesan cheese to taste, optional

1. Cook the pasta in a large pot of boiling water until tender but still very firm, about 8 minutes. Drain thoroughly and return to the same pot. Add all the liquid from the cans of clams, reserving the drained clams to add later. Simmer until most of the clam juice has been absorbed, about 2 to 3 minutes.

2. While the pasta is cooking, heat the oil and garlic in a large skillet or saucepan just until the garlic starts to sizzle. Add the tomatoes, pepper, rosemary, and sage, mix well, and bring to a simmer. Remove from the heat and stir in the drained clams. Add the mixture to the pasta and toss thoroughly. Serve immediately. Top each serving with a sprinkle of Parmesan cheese, if desired.

MAKES 4 SERVINGS

229

• EACH 1 1/2 CUPS OF PASTA AND 1/2 CUP OF SAUCE CONTAIN APPROXIMATELY:

| CALORIES: 432 | FAT: 9 g | CHOLESTEROL: 62 mg | SODIUM: 440 mg | CARBOHYDRATES: 58 g | PROTEIN: 32 g |

asian scallop stir-fry

At Canyon Ranch we serve this stir-fried scallop mixture over pasta or rice. There are enough colorful vegetables for it to make a beautiful plate without any additional garnish. If you are using frozen scallops for this recipe, allow them to completely thaw in the refrigerator before adding them. Force-thawing of any seafood causes either toughness or a mushy texture.

1 pound sea scallops

6 tablespoons cornstarch, divided use

1 teaspoon dark sesame oil

4 teaspoons tamari soy sauce

1 teaspoon peanut oil

4 teaspoons minced garlic

2 teaspoons minced ginger

1 cup sliced carrots

2 cups broccoli florets

2 cups shredded cabbage

½ cup pea pods

2 tablespoons plus 2 teaspoons ketchup

4 teaspoons sugar

4 ounces sake or dry sherry

2 tablespoons dried chipotle peppers

1½ cups fat-free chicken stock
(see page 54)

1. Lightly dust the scallops with 3 tablespoons of the cornstarch. Combine the sesame oil and tamari in a small bowl, mix well, and sprinkle over the scallops. Cover them tightly and allow to marinate in the refrigerator for at least 2 hours.

2. Heat a wok or large skillet over medium-high heat. Add the peanut oil and cook the garlic and ginger until soft. Add the scallops and stir-fry until golden brown, about 3 minutes. Remove the scallops from the wok or skillet and set aside. Stir-fry the vegetables until tender but crisp, about 5 minutes. Add the remaining ingredients except for the remaining cornstarch.

3. Add enough water to the remaining cornstarch to make a thin paste. Return the scallops to the wok or skillet. Quickly bring the vegetables and scallops to a simmer and add the cornstarch mixture as needed to thicken the sauce. Serve immediately.

MAKES 4 SERVINGS

230

• EACH SERVING CONTAINS APPROXIMATELY:

CALORIES: **286** | FAT: **2 g** | CHOLESTEROL: **37 mg** | SODIUM: **664 mg** | CARBOHYDRATES: **35 g** | PROTEIN: **23 g**

shrimp gumbo

Gumbo is a Creole dish and is traditionally made with a dark roux — a cooked paste of flour and butter — that thickens it and gives it its rich dark color. To lighten this New Orleans specialty we have relied on the addition of cooked brown rice, okra, and filé powder for both color and thickening. For more information on filé powder, see the box below.

1/4 cup diced onion

1/4 cup diced celery

3 garlic cloves, pressed or minced

2 cups cooked brown rice (see page 171), **divided use**

4 cups fish stock (see page 55)

1 teaspoon paprika

1/8 teaspoon cayenne pepper

1/2 pound okra, trimmed and sliced (1 1/2 cups)

1/4 cup diced red pepper

1/4 cup diced green bell pepper

1/4 cup diced tomato

1/2 teaspoon freshly ground black pepper

1 pound cleaned, sliced shrimp

1 teaspoon gumbo filé powder

1. Lightly spray a pot or large saucepan with non-stick cooking spray and place over medium heat. Add the onion, celery, and garlic and cook until the onion is translucent, adding a little fish stock if necessary to prevent scorching.

2. Add 2/3 cup of the cooked brown rice and all the remaining ingredients, except the shrimp, filé powder, and remaining rice, and continue to cook, uncovered, over medium heat for 10 minutes, or until the vegetables are cooked. Add the shrimp and continue to cook just until the shrimp turn from translucent to opaque and pink in color, about 2 minutes. Remove from the heat and stir in the filé powder.

3. Spoon 1/3 cup of the remaining rice in the bottom of each of 4 gumbo bowls or large soup plates and ladle about 1 1/2 cups of the gumbo over the rice.

231

MAKES 4 SERVINGS

filé powder

Filé powder is made from dried ground leaves of the sassafras tree and is an integral part of Creole cooking. It has a woodsy flavor reminiscent of root beer and is used to flavor and thicken gumbos and other Creole dishes. Filé should never be added until the dish is removed from the heat. Cooking will toughen filé and make it stringy.

• EACH 3/4-CUP SERVING CONTAINS APPROXIMATELY:

CALORIES: **200** | FAT: **2 g** | CHOLESTEROL: **114 mg** | SODIUM: **180 mg** | CARBOHYDRATES: **26 g** | PROTEIN: **18 g**

smoked shrimp and carrots

This unusual dish can be served as an hors d'oeuvre, a salad, or an entree. It is a perfect example of how the smoking technique can be incorporated into the method of preparing a dish and can give the ingredients a totally different personality. If you are considering it as an entree, either rice or pasta makes a fine accompaniment. Before starting to smoke be certain that the ventilation fan is turned on.

2 tablespoons white rice

2 spice tea bags

1 teaspoon freshly grated lemon zest

1/4 teaspoon ground coriander

1 pound medium shrimp, peeled and deveined

4 medium carrots (1/2 pound), sliced and steamed until crisp-tender

2 tablespoons freshly chopped parsley for garnish

1. Line a 3-quart saucepan with aluminum foil. Tear a separate piece, 12 by 12 inches, and roll up the edges to form a bowl about 4 inches in diameter. In the center of the foil bowl, place the rice, tea from the bags, lemon zest, and coriander. Place the bowl in a saucepan and cover with a tight-fitting lid.

2. Place the saucepan over low heat for 10 minutes, or until it begins to smoke. Meanwhile, coat a steamer basket with non-stick cooking spray. Place the shrimp in the center of the basket and the steamed carrots around the edge. Carefully insert the basket into the smoking pan and smoke, tightly covered, over low heat for about 20 minutes, or until the shrimp has turned from translucent to opaque and is pink in color.

3. Divide the shrimp and carrots among 4 plates and sprinkle with parsley for garnish.

MAKES 4 SERVINGS

• EACH SERVING CONTAINS APPROXIMATELY:

CALORIES: **181** | FAT: **2 g** | CHOLESTEROL: **173 mg** | SODIUM: **205 mg** | CARBOHYDRATES: **15 g** | PROTEIN: **25 g**

spicy shrimp with cucumber-papaya salsa

You can serve this spicy shrimp over pasta instead of rice if you prefer, or you can serve it on greens as a salad.

CUCUMBER-PAPAYA SALSA:

1 medium cucumber, peeled

2 cups mango or papaya salsa
(see page 321)

1/2 tablespoon canola oil

1/2 medium onion, chopped (3/4 cup)

4 garlic cloves, chopped

1 pound peeled and deveined medium raw shrimp

3/4 cup chopped scallions

1/2 teaspoon crushed red pepper

2 tablespoons chopped cilantro

3 tablespoons reduced-sodium soy sauce

2 teaspoons fresh lemon juice

8 large bok choy leaves, lightly blanched

2 cups cooked brown rice
(see page 171)

1. Cut the cucumber in half lengthwise. Remove the seeds from the cucumber by pulling a teaspoon down the center of each half. Discard the seeds and dice the cucumber. Combine the mango or papaya salsa and diced cucumber in a bowl and mix well. Set aside.

2. Heat the oil in a skillet over medium heat. Add the onion and garlic and cook, stirring frequently, for about 5 minutes, or until translucent. Add the shrimp, scallions, crushed red pepper, and cilantro and cook until the shrimp turns from translucent to opaque and is pink in color, about 2 minutes. Add the soy sauce and lemon juice to the pan, mix well, and remove from the heat.

3. To serve, place 2 blanched bok choy leaves on each plate. Spoon 1/2 cup of brown rice on top of the bok choy leaves. Spoon 1/4 of the shrimp mixture on the rice and top with 1/2 cup of the papaya salsa.

MAKES 4 SERVINGS

234

• **EACH SERVING WITH PAPAYA SALSA CONTAINS APPROXIMATELY:**

CALORIES: **299** | FAT: **5 g** | CHOLESTEROL: **173 mg** | SODIUM: **621 mg** | CARBOHYDRATES: **37 g** | PROTEIN: **27 g**

poultry

Unlike the fat in red meat, which is spread throughout the red muscle of the meat, the fat in poultry is concentrated in or just below the skin. Therefore, just by removing the skin and all visible fat from poultry, you dispose of over half of its total fat.

White meat is always lower in fat and calories than dark meat, but dark meat is still preferable in some recipes because it does not dry out as easily when cooked. The white meat of turkey has about the same amount of fat as the white meat of chicken, but the dark meat is higher in fat than that of chicken. Farm-raised duck and goose have about 50 percent more fat than chicken, but wild duck and other game birds, such as pheasant and quail, are comparably low in fat.

When buying chicken or turkey ask for free-range or cage free birds that have been allowed to grow up naturally without being confined. They are available in many supermarkets and almost all poultry stores. They are more expensive but well worth the price because the meat is firmer and better tasting. Look for chickens with moist skin, free of blemishes. When packaged there should not be any red liquid in the bottom of the container because this is a sign that it has been frozen and defrosted.

All poultry is extremely perishable and should be refrigerated as soon after purchase as possible. You can leave it in its original package if you will be using it within 24 hours; if not, rewrap it in plastic wrap. Salmonella can be a serious problem associated with poultry; therefore, you should be careful to wash your hands both before and after handling raw poultry and you should wash the cutting board, knife, or any other utensil used with poultry in the dishwasher or in hot, soapy water. (Salmonella is a strain of bacteria that can enter the human system through contaminated water or food, such as meat or poultry and eggs with cracked shells, and cause serious illness.) Also, never defrost poultry at room temperature because the bacteria multiply more rapidly. Let it thaw in the refrigerator or in several changes of cold water. And when it comes to stuffing fowl, it is safer to cook the dressing in a baking dish rather than stuffing it into the cavity of the bird because the moisture in the cavity can also encourage bacterial growth.

Before cooking poultry it should be rinsed under cold running water. If washing a whole chicken, be sure to rinse inside the cavity as well. Also, there is often a package of giblets inside the bird; it should, of course, be removed before cooking the bird. If desired, wash the giblets and either cook them with the bird or prepare them separately for use in a dressing or gravy.

When cooking poultry, the most important thing to remember is not to overcook it. When roasting chicken, it is done as soon as the liquid runs clear when the chicken is pierced with a knife. When cooking a chicken breast, it takes only a few minutes per side for the color of the meat to turn from translucent to opaque and spring back when touched with your finger. At this point the chicken is done, yet still moist and tender. Further cooking will only serve to toughen it.

When not otherwise specified, all chicken breast halves in this chapter described as "boned and skinless" are 4 ounces raw weight and 3 ounces when cooked. We use a great many chicken breasts at Canyon Ranch because they are so easily portioned, are low in fat, and are quick to prepare. For all the same reasons they are wonderful to use at home.

barbecued chicken

I usually double the barbecue sauce in this recipe because it is good on so many other dishes and it's a great fat-free spread for sandwiches. If tightly covered, it keeps well in the refrigerator for at least 2 weeks.

BARBECUE SAUCE:

1 large onion, minced

8 ounces low-sodium canned tomato sauce

1/4 cup freshly squeezed lemon juice

3 tablespoons worcestershire sauce

2 tablespoons white vinegar

2 tablespoons sugar

1 1/2 teaspoons dry mustard

1/4 teaspoon salt

1 cup water

1/2 teaspoon liquid smoke

2 teaspoons canola oil

2 garlic cloves, pressed or minced

6 boned and skinless chicken breast halves, all visible fat removed (1 1/2 pounds)

1. To make the sauce, put the onion in a saucepan and cook, covered, over low heat until it is soft and translucent, adding a little water if necessary to prevent scorching. Add all the remaining sauce ingredients, except the liquid smoke, and bring to a boil. Reduce the heat to low and cook, covered, for 30 minutes. Remove from the heat, stir in the liquid smoke, and set aside.

2. Preheat the oven to 350°F.

3. Heat the oil and garlic in a large ovenproof skillet over medium heat just until the garlic starts to sizzle. Add the chicken breasts and cook, turning, until both sides are browned. Spoon the sauce over the browned chicken breasts, cover, and bake for 30 minutes, or until done.

MAKES 6 SERVINGS

239

• EACH 3-OUNCE SERVING CONTAINS APPROXIMATELY:

CALORIES: 208 | FAT: 3 g | CHOLESTEROL: 81 mg | SODIUM: 363 mg | CARBOHYDRATES: 9 g | PROTEIN: 33 g

chicken burger with three mustard sauce

These spicy chicken burgers are a delightful departure from the more usual beef burgers and are about 50 percent lower in fat. You can also make them with ground turkey breast, but be sure it is ground without the skin.

THREE MUSTARD SAUCE:

1½ tablespoons diced onion

1½ tablespoons diced celery

1 tablespoon non-alcoholic white wine

1 teaspoon dry mustard

1 tablespoon dijon mustard

1 tablespoon green peppercorn mustard

½ cup fat-free chicken stock (see page 54)

2 teaspoons chopped parsley

3 tablespoons finely chopped onion

pinch dried thyme, crushed

1 tablespoon chopped parsley

½ pound ground skinless chicken breast

½ pound ground skinless chicken dark meat

¼ teaspoon freshly ground black pepper

¼ teaspoon worcestershire sauce

2 drops tabasco sauce

4 small whole-grain hamburger buns

4 tomato slices

4 lettuce leaves

1. To make the mustard sauce, combine the onion and celery in a small saucepan and cook, covered, over low heat until the onion is translucent, adding a little water if necessary to prevent scorching. Add the white wine and mustards and mix well. Add the chicken stock and cook over medium heat for 2 minutes. Stir in the parsley and remove from heat. Pour the sauce into a bowl and set aside to cool.

2. Combine the onion, thyme, and parsley in a skillet and cook, covered, over very low heat until the onion is translucent, adding a little water if necessary to prevent scorching. Remove from the heat and spoon the onion mixture into a bowl. Add the ground chicken, pepper, Worcestershire sauce, and Tabasco and mix well. Divide the chicken mixture into 4 patties.

3. Prepare the coals for grilling or preheat the broiler and grill or broil the patties about 4 minutes per side, or until done.

4. To serve, place each chicken burger on a bun with a slice of tomato and a lettuce leaf. Serve 2 tablespoons of mustard sauce per serving on the side.

MAKES 4 SERVINGS

240

• **EACH BURGER ON A BUN WITH 2 TABLESPOONS OF MUSTARD SAUCE CONTAINS APPROXIMATELY:**

CALORIES: **245** | FAT: **4 g** | CHOLESTEROL: **77 mg** | SODIUM: **521 mg** | CARBOHYDRATES: **11 g** | PROTEIN: **29 g**

chicken cacciatore

Cacciatore is the Italian word for hunter. In culinary terms it identifies food that has been prepared "hunter-style," with onions, tomatoes, mushrooms, herbs, and wine. Wonderful for entertaining, it can be made ahead of time and then baked just before serving. All you need to accompany it is a tossed green salad and crusty Italian bread. To complete the menu Lemon Panna Cotta (see page 391) is a perfect light dessert.

½ tablespoon extra-virgin olive oil

2 medium onions, finely chopped
(3 cups)

2 garlic cloves, pressed or minced

2 cups sliced mushrooms

3 plum tomatoes, peeled and diced
(1½ cups)

2 teaspoons dried rosemary, crushed

2 teaspoons dried oregano, crushed

8 boned and skinless chicken breast
halves, all visible fat removed
(2 pounds)

freshly ground black pepper

6 ounces canned tomato paste

1 cup dry white wine

1 cup dry marsala wine

1. Preheat the oven to 350°F.

2. Heat the oil in a large skillet. Add the onions, garlic, and mushrooms and cook over medium heat, stirring frequently, until the onions are translucent. Stir in the tomatoes, rosemary, and oregano and spread the mixture evenly in a 9 x 11-inch baking dish.

3. Spray a skillet with non-stick cooking spray and place over medium heat. Lightly sprinkle both sides of the chicken breasts with pepper and place them in the hot skillet. Cook until browned on both sides.

4. Arrange the chicken breasts on top of the tomato-onion mixture in the baking dish and bake, covered, for 10 minutes.

5. Combine the tomato paste, white wine, and Marsala and mix well. Pour over the chicken breast halves and continue to bake, covered, for 20 more minutes.

6. To serve, place each chicken breast half on a plate. Stir the sauce well and spoon equally over each serving.

MAKES 8 SERVINGS

• EACH SERVING CONTAINS APPROXIMATELY:

CALORIES: 159 | FAT: 1 g | CHOLESTEROL: 41 mg | SODIUM: 205 mg | CARBOHYDRATES: 9 g | PROTEIN: 18 g

poultry gravy

Just a small amount of this delicious, rich-tasting gravy will add to the opulence of any dish. Plan to serve it over roast turkey breast for your next holiday party and tell your guests that you learned how to make it at Canyon Ranch. Rather than relying on high-fat pan drippings for a rich-tasting gravy, this recipe includes other ingredients for flavor and just a touch of cream for richness and a creamier texture.

1 cup fat-free chicken stock
(see page 54), **divided use**

2 teaspoons reduced-sodium soy sauce

pinch salt

2 teaspoons white pepper

2 teaspoons minced fresh rosemary

2½ tablespoons arrowroot

2½ tablespoons whipping cream

1. Pour 3/4 cup of the chicken stock into a small saucepan, reserving the remaining 1/4 cup to add later. Add the soy sauce, salt, pepper, and rosemary and bring to a boil over medium heat.

2. Whisk the arrowroot into the remaining 1/4 cup of chicken stock and slowly add it to the boiling stock mixture. Stir in the cream. Reduce the heat to low and simmer until thickened, about 3 to 5 minutes.

MAKES 1 CUP

242

• EACH 1/4-CUP SERVING CONTAINS APPROXIMATELY:

CALORIES: 65 | FAT: 4 g | CHOLESTEROL: 4 mg | SODIUM: 217 mg | CARBOHYDRATES: 7 g | PROTEIN: 1 g

chicken fajitas

Canyon Ranch fajitas are a fun party dish because each guest literally makes his or her own entree by combining the component parts served on the plate and at the same time enjoys a delicious low-fat meal.

MARINADE:

2 tablespoons reduced-sodium soy sauce

1/4 teaspoon minced fresh gingerroot

1 garlic clove, pressed or minced

2 tablespoons canola or olive oil

1/3 cup chopped cilantro

pinch chili powder

3 tablespoons beer

1/2 teaspoon tabasco sauce

1/2 orange, thinly sliced

1/2 lemon, thinly sliced

1/2 lime, thinly sliced

1 tablespoon chopped parsley

4 boned and skinless chicken breast halves, all visible fat removed (1 pound)

4 large whole-wheat flour tortillas, 9 inches in diameter

1 cup tomato salsa (see page 324)

1 1/3 cups canyon ranch guacamole (see page 36)

1/2 cup light sour cream

1. Combine all the marinade ingredients in a shallow baking dish and mix well.

2. Place the chicken breasts in the marinade, turning to coat evenly. Cover and refrigerate for at least 2 hours or as long as overnight.

3. Prepare the coals for grilling or preheat the broiler.

4. Remove the chicken from the marinade and grill or broil for about 3 to 4 minutes per side, or until desired degree of doneness.

5. Cut the chicken into strips and serve with whole-wheat tortillas, salsa, guacamole, and light sour cream.

243

MAKES 4 SERVINGS

• EACH SERVING CONTAINS APPROXIMATELY:

CALORIES: 340 | FAT: 11 g | CHOLESTEROL: 86 mg | SODIUM: 508 mg | CARBOHYDRATES: 27 g | PROTEIN: 34 g

chicken saté

Saté, or satay, is an Indonesian specialty, the favorite snack food there. At Canyon Ranch we serve these for lunch with seasoned rice and stir-fried Asian vegetables, but they are also wonderful as appetizers. If using wooden skewers, soak them in water so they don't burn.

MARINADE:

1 tablespoon reduced-sodium soy sauce

¼ cup water

¾ teaspoon turbinado sugar

1 tablespoon fresh lime juice

½ garlic clove, pressed or minced

½ teaspoon curry powder

¼ teaspoon unhomogenized peanut butter

pinch crushed red pepper flakes

4 boned and skinless chicken breast halves, all visible fat removed (1 pound)

12 skewers

PEANUT SAUCE:

1 tablespoon unhomogenized peanut butter

1 tablespoon lemon juice

¼ teaspoon coconut extract

¼ teaspoon minced garlic

6 tablespoons soy milk

¾ teaspoon crushed red pepper flakes

2 teaspoons grated lemon zest for garnish

1. Combine all the marinade ingredients in a blender and blend until smooth. Set aside.

2. Cut each chicken breast into 3 strips lengthwise and thread each strip on a skewer.

3. Place the skewers in a shallow baking dish and pour the marinade over them. Cover and marinate in the refrigerator for 8 hours or overnight.

4. To make the peanut sauce, combine all the sauce ingredients, except the red pepper flakes, in a blender and blend until smooth. Stir in the red pepper flakes and set aside.

5. Prepare the coals for grilling or preheat the broiler. Place the skewers on the hot grill or under the preheated broiler and cook until desired doneness, turning once to ensure even cooking.

6. To serve, place 3 skewers on each of 4 plates. Spoon 2 tablespoons of the peanut sauce for dipping onto each plate and garnish with ½ teaspoon of lemon zest.

MAKES 4 SERVINGS

244

• EACH 3-SKEWER SERVING WITH 2 TABLESPOONS OF SAUCE CONTAINS APPROXIMATELY:

CALORIES: **186** | FAT: **4 g** | CHOLESTEROL: **81 mg** | SODIUM: **124 mg** | CARBOHYDRATES: **2 g** | PROTEIN: **34 g**

chicken roulade with lobster

Roulade is the French term describing a thin slice of fish, poultry, or meat rolled around a filling. A roulade can be browned and baked, braised, or wrapped and steamed as it is in this recipe. Steaming is a wonderful technique for light cooking because lean and healthy ingredients can be used and the preparation requires no added fat.

4 boned and skinless chicken breast halves, all visible fat removed (16 ounces total weight)

1/2 tablespoon mrs. dash seasoning

2 garlic cloves, pressed or minced

2 tablespoons chopped fresh dill

1 cup thoroughly washed and drained spinach leaves

1/4 pound cooked lobster meat (1 cup)

1 cup provençal vinaigrette (see page 146)

You can serve these roulades hot or leave them wrapped and refrigerate them until cold before cutting and serving them. Either way, diced tomato sprinkled over the top makes a lovely plate garnish. You can also substitute crabmeat for the lobster.

1. Place each chicken breast between sheets of plastic wrap and pound with the flat side of a meat mallet until very thin, about 1/4 inch. Sprinkle each pounded breast with Mrs. Dash, garlic, and dill.

2. Place 1/4 cup of spinach leaves on each breast. Place 1/4 cup of cooked lobster on top of the spinach and carefully roll up the chicken breast around the filling. Wrap each breast individually in foil, twisting tightly at each end to seal.

3. Bring water to a boil in a saucepan with a steamer basket. Place the chicken roulades in the basket and steam, covered, for about 7 minutes, or until done.

4. Remove from the steamer and unwrap the roulades. Using a very sharp knife, slice each roulade into 4 pieces.

5. Serve 4 roulade pieces on each plate and top with 1/4 cup of Provençal vinaigrette.

MAKES 4 SERVINGS

. **EACH SERVING CONTAINS APPROXIMATELY:**

CALORIES: **208** | FAT: **3 g** | CHOLESTEROL: **102 mg** | SODIUM: **245 mg** | CARBOHYDRATES: **5 g** | PROTEIN: **39 g**

barley risotto with shredded chicken and parmesan cheese

This high-carbohydrate, low-fat dish is good hot or cold and can be served in a number of ways. At Canyon Ranch we usually serve it hot accompanied by a variety of colorful steamed vegetables. When serving it cold I like to pack it into molds or press it into rings so that it has a definite form, then surround it with greens and cold marinated vegetables for a uniquely different salad.

2/3 cup pearl barley

2 tablespoons chopped onion

3/4 cup diced carrot

3/4 cup diced celery

3/4 cup diced leeks, white parts only

1/2 cup fat-free chicken stock (see page 54), **divided use**

2 boned and skinless chicken breast halves, all visible fat removed (8 ounces)

6 tablespoons freshly grated parmesan cheese

1/2 cup chopped parsley

1/4 teaspoon cracked black pepper

1. Place the barley in a small saucepan with enough water to cover and bring to a boil. Lower the heat and simmer for about 20 minutes, or until the barley is tender. Drain and set aside.

2. While the barley is cooking, prepare the coals for grilling or preheat the broiler.

3. Combine the onion, carrot, celery, and leeks in a large saucepan. Add 1/4 cup of the chicken stock and cook, covered, over low heat for about 10 minutes, or until the vegetables are tender. Remove from the heat and then remove half of the vegetables from the pan and set aside. Add the remaining 1/4 cup of chicken stock to the vegetables in the pan and cook over medium-high heat until the stock is reduced by half. Set aside and keep warm.

4. Grill or broil the chicken breasts for 3 to 5 minutes on each side, or until done. Remove from the heat and cool. When cool enough to handle, shred the chicken by pulling it apart with the tines of 2 forks into long strands. In a bowl combine all the ingredients including the barley and toss gently.

5. Serve hot or cold. To serve, divide equally among 4 plates.

247

MAKES 4 SERVINGS

• EACH SERVING CONTAINS APPROXIMATELY:

CALORIES: 260 | FAT: 4 g | CHOLESTEROL: 53 mg | SODIUM: 205 mg | CARBOHYDRATES: 30 g | PROTEIN: 24 g

stuffed chicken breasts with paprika sauce

At Canyon Ranch we serve these stuffed chicken breasts on a mound of Celery Root and Potato Puree (see page 295) and then spoon the chunky paprika sauce over the top. A bright green vegetable, such as steamed asparagus or broccoli, is also good served with it and makes a very pretty plate.

STUFFING:

1/2 cup finely chopped onion

1/4 cup finely chopped carrot

2 tablespoons finely chopped celery

2 tablespoons finely chopped scallions

1 tablespoon fresh tarragon, chopped, or 1 teaspoon dried, crushed

1 tablespoon finely chopped fresh chervil, or 1 teaspoon dried, crushed

1 tablespoon finely chopped parsley

pinch dried sage

2 slices whole-wheat bread, crumbled

2/3 cup fat-free chicken stock
(see page 54)

1/2 teaspoon seasoned salt

PAPRIKA SAUCE:

2 tablespoons finely chopped shallots

2 tablespoons finely chopped onion

3 cups diced red bell peppers

1 teaspoon paprika

1 1/2 cups fat-free chicken stock

1 tablespoon light sour cream

pinch freshly ground black pepper

4 boned and skinless chicken breast halves, all visible fat removed (1 pound)

1. To make the stuffing, combine the onion, carrot, celery, and scallions in a saucepan and cook over low heat, covered, for 10 minutes, or until the onion is translucent, adding a little water if necessary to prevent scorching. Remove from the heat, add all the remaining ingredients for the stuffing, and mix well. Set aside.

2. Preheat the oven to 450°F.

3. To make the sauce, spray a saucepan with non-stick cooking spray and place it over medium-low heat. Add the shallots, onion, and red peppers and cook, stirring frequently, for about 10 minutes, or until tender. Add the paprika and stock and continue cooking until reduced by half. Cover to keep warm and set aside.

4. Cut an incision in the thickest part of each chicken breast to form a pocket. Spoon one-fourth of the stuffing into the pocket of each chicken breast and place in a baking dish. Bake the chicken breasts for 8 to 10 minutes, or until done.

5. Just before serving, stir the sour cream and pepper into the paprika sauce and spoon about 1/3 cup of the sauce over each serving.

MAKES 4 SERVINGS

• EACH SERVING OF 1 CHICKEN BREAST TOPPED WITH 1/3 CUP OF SAUCE CONTAINS APPROXIMATELY:

CALORIES: **261** | FAT: **3 g** | CHOLESTEROL: **81 mg** | SODIUM: **662 mg** | CARBOHYDRATES: **20 g** | PROTEIN: **37 g**

chicken with potatoes and oven-roasted vegetables

This simple country dish is a healthy and hearty meal that can be served any time of the year. If some of the vegetables called for are not available, either use more of the ones that are, or substitute other fresh vegetables for them.

FOR ROASTED VEGETABLES:

½ tablespoon extra-virgin olive oil

3 garlic cloves, pressed or minced

1 pound diced russet potatoes (2 cups), blanched

2 cups young green beans

1 cup diced red peppers

1 cup thinly sliced fennel bulb

4 shallots, peeled and cut lengthwise

1 tablespoon chopped fresh sage

2 teaspoons chopped fresh rosemary

½ teaspoon freshly ground black pepper

½ teaspoon kosher salt

½ teaspoon paprika

2 cups fat-free chicken stock
(see page 54)

4 boned and skinless chicken breast halves, all visible fat removed (1 pound)

sprigs fresh herbs for garnish

1. Preheat the oven to 375°F.

2. To make the roasted vegetables, combine the oil and garlic in a roasting pan and heat in the preheated oven just until the garlic starts to sizzle. Remove the pan from the oven and add all the ingredients for the roasted vegetables. Combine well and return the pan to the oven. Bake for about 1 hour, stirring every 15 minutes, or until the vegetables are browned. Remove the vegetables from the oven and preheat the broiler.

3. While the vegetables roast, in a saucepan reduce the chicken stock over medium-high heat until only about ¼ cup remains.

4. Add the reduced chicken stock to the pan of roasted vegetables, tossing gently and scraping up all the bits on the bottom of the pan. Keep warm, covered, while broiling the chicken.

5. In a roasting pan broil the chicken breasts for 3 to 4 minutes per side, or until done.

6. Divide the roasted vegetables among 4 plates, top each serving with a broiled chicken breast, and garnish with fresh herb sprigs of your choice.

MAKES 4 SERVINGS

249

• EACH SERVING CONTAINS APPROXIMATELY:

CALORIES: 264 | FAT: 3 g | CHOLESTEROL: 81 mg | SODIUM: 507 mg | CARBOHYDRATES: 20 g | PROTEIN: 36 g

coq au vin

This is a light variation of the classic French dish. For a cross-cultural presentation, which happens to be delicious, serve this over pasta.

4 boned and skinless chicken breast halves, all visible fat removed (1 pound)

freshly ground black pepper

1 teaspoon corn oil margarine or butter

1 garlic clove, pressed or minced

8 large fresh mushrooms, cleaned and trimmed

8 small boiling onions, peeled, cooked in boiling water until tender, and drained

SAUCE:

2 tablespoons finely chopped shallots

1/2 cup dry sherry

1/2 cup dry red wine

4 cups fat-free chicken stock (see page 54), boiling

1/3 cup cornstarch

1/3 cup cold water

1/4 teaspoon freshly ground black pepper

1 tablespoon kitchen bouquet

1. Lightly sprinkle both sides of the chicken breasts with pepper.

2. Melt the margarine or butter in a large skillet. Add the garlic and cook just until it starts to sizzle. Place the chicken in the hot skillet and brown on both sides. Do not overcook.

3. Remove the chicken from the skillet and arrange in a 7 x 11-inch baking dish. Add the mushrooms to the skillet and brown. Add the browned mushrooms and cooked onions to the baking dish with the chicken.

4. Preheat the oven to 350°F.

5. To make the sauce, combine the shallots, sherry, and red wine in the skillet in which you have cooked the chicken and bring to a boil. Continue cooking until the volume has been reduced by one-third.

6. Add the boiling chicken stock and reduce the heat to low so that the mixture is just simmering. Dissolve the cornstarch in the cold water and pour into the sauce, stirring constantly with a wire whisk. Add the pepper and Kitchen Bouquet and continue stirring until the mixture has thickened slightly.

7. Pour the sauce evenly over the chicken and vegetables. Cover and bake for 20 minutes, or until the chicken is done.

8. Divide the chicken breasts among 4 plates and top each serving with 1/2 cup of sauce.

MAKES 4 SERVINGS

• EACH SERVING CONTAINS APPROXIMATELY:

CALORIES: **278** | FAT: **4 g** | CHOLESTEROL: **75 mg** | SODIUM: **263 mg** | CARBOHYDRATES: **20 g** | PROTEIN: **28 g**

250

indonesian chicken with grilled bananas

To turn this spicy Indonesian dish into a meal, accompany it with hot cooked rice and stir-fried Asian vegetables and serve Spiced Guava-Strawberry Sorbet (see page 399) for dessert.

DRY RUB MIX:

1/2 teaspoon ground ginger

1 teaspoon ground cayenne pepper

1/2 teaspoon ground allspice

1/2 teaspoon ground cinnamon

1 teaspoon ground curry powder

1 teaspoon ground paprika

1/2 teaspoon ground turmeric

1/4 teaspoon kosher salt

4 skinless chicken breast halves, all visible fat removed

2 bananas, skin on

1 tablespoon light brown sugar

1. Combine all the dry rub mix ingredients and mix well. Lightly coat each chicken breast with the spice mixture. Place on a plate and cover tightly. Refrigerate for at least 1 hour before grilling.

2. Prepare the coals for grilling.

3. Slice the bananas into halves lengthwise with the peel left on. Sprinkle the brown sugar on the bananas and rub it in as much as possible. Grill the bananas lightly, cut side down. Remove from the heat and set aside.

4. Remove the chicken from the refrigerator and place on the grill. Grill for about 5 minutes per side, or until done.

5. Serve each grilled chicken breast with a grilled banana half still in the peel.

MAKES 4 SERVINGS

251

• EACH SERVING CONTAINS APPROXIMATELY:

CALORIES: **223** | FAT: **2 g** | CHOLESTEROL: **81 mg** | SODIUM: **211 mg** | CARBOHYDRATES: **17 g** | PROTEIN: **33 g**

curried chicken

Curried dishes are great for buffets because you can offer a large array of condiments from which to choose. Popular light selections include chutney, raisins, diced bell peppers of all colors, cucumber, tomato, pineapple, papaya, mango, banana, kiwi, chopped scallions, and hard-boiled egg whites. Also, if you're serving buffet style, rather than sprinkling the toasted almonds over the top of the curried chicken, the nuts would be included with the other condiments, and you might want to offer peanuts as well as toasted almonds.

CURRY SAUCE:

1 tablespoon corn oil margarine or butter

$1/2$ medium onion, finely chopped

1 small green apple, peeled, cored, and finely chopped

$1/2$ garlic clove, finely chopped

1 tablespoon flour

$1^1/2$ tablespoons curry powder

1 cup fat-free chicken stock (see page 54), **boiling**

$1/4$ cup non-fat milk

1 tablespoon non-fat dry milk powder

1 teaspoon fresh lemon juice

$1^1/2$ teaspoons grated lemon zest

4 boned and skinless chicken breast halves (1 pound), all visible fat removed and butterflied

2 tablespoons fresh lemon juice

$1/4$ cup fat-free chicken stock

2 cups cooked brown rice (see page 171)

$1/4$ cup chopped raw almonds, toasted

$1/2$ cup apple and fig chutney (see page 362), **optional**

1. To make the curry sauce, heat the margarine or butter in a large skillet over medium-low heat. Add the onion, apple, and garlic and cook until the onion is tender and translucent, about 10 minutes.

2. Combine the flour and curry powder and mix well. Add it to the onion mixture, stirring constantly for 3 minutes. Add the boiling chicken stock all at once and mix thoroughly using a whisk. Combine the milk with the non-fat dry milk and add to the mixture along with the lemon juice and zest. Reduce the heat to low and allow the sauce to simmer slowly, partially covered, for 1 hour, or until slightly thickened. This makes 1 cup of sauce.

3. Sprinkle the butterflied chicken breasts with the lemon

juice. Heat the $1/4$ cup of chicken stock in a large skillet and reduce until almost dry. Cook the chicken breasts until just done, turning for even browning and adding a little more stock as needed to prevent scorching.

4. To serve, place $1/2$ cup of cooked rice on each plate and place a butterflied chicken breast half on top of the rice. Spoon $1/4$ cup of sauce over each chicken breast and sprinkle 1 tablespoon of toasted almonds over the top. Serve with 2 tablespoons of apple and fig chutney on the side, if desired.

MAKES 4 SERVINGS

• **EACH SERVING CONTAINS APPROXIMATELY:**

CALORIES: **569** | FAT: **13 g** | CHOLESTEROL: **81 mg** | SODIUM: **196 mg** | CARBOHYDRATES: **82 g** | PROTEIN: **34 g**

roasted lemon chicken

This is a wonderful way to cook chicken you plan to use for salads and sandwiches. The light lemon flavor greatly enhances almost anything it accompanies.

1 whole 3-pound chicken, rinsed inside and out and all visible fat removed

¼ cup fat-free chicken stock
(see page 54)

1 tablespoon fresh lemon juice

1 tablespoon dried oregano, crushed

1 teaspoon grated lemon zest

1 teaspoon salt

1 teaspoon freshly ground black pepper

1. Preheat oven to 400°F.

2. Place the chicken on a rack in a roasting pan. Combine the stock and lemon juice and pour over the chicken. Combine the oregano, lemon zest, salt, and pepper and spread the chicken with the mixture. Cover tightly with aluminum foil and bake in the preheated oven for 1 hour. Uncover and bake an additional 25 minutes, or until the chicken is golden brown and the juices run clear when pierced in the thick part of the leg. Remove the skin before serving.

MAKES 4 SERVINGS

254

• EACH 3-OUNCE SERVING CONTAINS APPROXIMATELY:

CALORIES: **381** | FAT: **4 g** | CHOLESTEROL: **197 mg** | SODIUM: **242 mg** | CARBOHYDRATES: **1 g** | PROTEIN: **79 g**

grilled mediterranean chicken

This is truly a fabulous marinade and it can be used for fish and meat as well as all other types of poultry. For a Canyon Ranch menu serve this flavorful chicken with Creamy Polenta (see page 315) and Grilled Vegetables (see page 310). For dessert serve Lemon Panna Cotta (see page 391) with fresh fruit.

MARINADE:

1 cup coarsely chopped and tightly packed cilantro

4 scallions, thinly sliced, including greens

4 cloves garlic, finely chopped

2 tablespoons fennel seeds, toasted and crushed

1 tablespoon grated fresh ginger

1 tablespoon hot Hungarian paprika

1 teaspoon cayenne pepper

1 teaspoon ground cumin

1/4 teaspoon saffron threads, finely chopped

1/2 teaspoon salt

1/2 cup water

1/4 cup fresh lemon juice

1 tablespoon extra-virgin olive oil

6 skinless chicken breast halves, all visible fat removed (1 pound)

1. Mix all the marinade ingredients in a large, non-aluminum bowl. Add the chicken to the marinade and toss gently to coat well. Cover tightly and refrigerate all day or overnight.

2. Preheat a barbecue grill until the coals are white hot. Spray the grill with non-stick cooking spray. Remove the chicken pieces from the marinade and place on the grill. If you wish to use the marinade as a sauce on the cooked chicken, pour it into a saucepan and bring to a boil before serving. Cook the chicken until the juices run clear when the large part of the breast halves is pierced, about 4 to 5 minutes per side depending on the heat of the grill and the thickness of the pieces.

MAKES 6 SERVINGS

255

• EACH SERVING CONTAINS APPROXIMATELY:

CALORIES: **212** | FAT: **4 g** | CHOLESTEROL: **81 mg** | SODIUM: **285 mg** | CARBOHYDRATES: **8 g** | PROTEIN: **34 g**

szechuan chicken

Chinese chili paste is the ingredient that gives this Asian chicken its interesting, piquant flavor. It is a paste made of fermented fava beans, flour, red chiles, and sometimes garlic and it is available in all Chinese markets and many supermarkets. The Szechuan province in western China is known for its hot spicy dishes and they are always popular with our guests. You can serve this chicken over rice or noodles accompanied by stir-fried vegetables for a complete one-dish meal.

MARINADE:

3 tablespoons reduced-sodium soy sauce

1¹/₂ tablespoons rice wine or dry sherry

1 teaspoon rice vinegar

1 teaspoon minced fresh gingerroot

1 garlic clove, pressed or minced

1 tablespoon chinese chili paste

pinch freshly grated white pepper

1 tablespoon dark sesame oil

4 boned and skinless chicken breast halves, all visible fat removed (1 pound)

1. Combine all the marinade ingredients in a baking dish and mix well.

2. Place the chicken breasts in the marinade and turn to coat evenly. Cover tightly and refrigerate for at least 2 hours or as long as overnight.

3. Prepare the coals for grilling or preheat the broiler.

4. Remove the chicken from the marinade and discard the marinade. Grill or broil the marinated chicken for about 3 to 4 minutes per side, or until cooked to the desired degree of doneness.

MAKES 4 SERVINGS

256

• EACH SERVING CONTAINS APPROXIMATELY:

CALORIES: **165** | FAT: **5 g** | CHOLESTEROL: **72 mg** | SODIUM: **364 mg** | CARBOHYDRATES: **2 g** | PROTEIN: **27 g**

tandoori chicken

The tandoor oven used throughout India is made of brick and clay. The intense heat is produced by a smoky fire that also imparts a wonderful flavor to the foods cooked in it. A standard oven can give us the 525°F. heat, but it can't produce the smoky flavor. For the crustiness associated with tandoori chicken you may prefer to grill the chicken and onions over a charcoal fire. Serve this Indian-inspired chicken with Curried Basmati Rice (see page 314) and Naan Bread (see page 298).

MARINADE:

1/2 cup minced onion

2 garlic cloves, pressed or minced

1 cup non-fat plain yogurt

1 1/2 tablespoons fresh lemon juice

1/2 tablespoon paprika

1/4 teaspoon ground cinnamon

Pinch ground cloves

1/4 teaspoon freshly ground black pepper

1/2 teaspoon ground cumin

1/2 teaspoon ground turmeric

1/2 teaspoon ground ginger

1/2 teaspoon kosher salt

1 teaspoon chopped cilantro

4 large chicken thighs (1 pound), skin and all visible fat removed

1 large onion, thinly sliced

1. Combine all the marinade ingredients in a flat dish and mix well. Place the chicken in the marinade, turning to coat evenly. Cover tightly and refrigerate all day or overnight.

2. Preheat the oven to 525°F.

3. Remove the chicken from the marinade and place on a broiler pan or in a pan with a rack. Arrange the sliced onion around the chicken. Place the chicken in the hot oven and bake for about 15 minutes, or until done and the onions are browned.

4. Divide the chicken among 4 heated dinner plates.

MAKES 4 SERVINGS

257

• EACH SERVING CONTAINS APPROXIMATELY:

CALORIES: **130** | FAT: **4 g** | CHOLESTEROL: **78 mg** | SODIUM: **307 mg** | CARBOHYDRATES: **3 g** | PROTEIN: **20 g**

raspberry cornish hens

In order to remove the skin more easily and also keep the surface smoother and more moist, we partially roast the birds prior to removing the skin and all visible fat. These flavorful game hens make an attractive presentation and are ideal for dinner parties. They are good served on wild rice and garnished with fresh raspberries.

4 cornish game hens, about 1 pound each

1/2 cup raspberries

2 garlic cloves, halved

1 tablespoon extra-virgin olive oil

1 tablespoon reduced-sodium soy sauce

1/4 cup raspberry vinegar

1/4 cup plum vinegar

2 tablespoons fructose

2 tablespoons chopped fresh mint

1. Preheat the oven to 375°F.

2. Wash the game hens, inside and out, and pat dry. Place them on a rack in a baking pan with deep sides and salt lightly all over. Place them in the preheated oven for 30 minutes.

3. While the game hens are roasting, make the sauce. Put the raspberries, garlic, olive oil, soy sauce, vinegars, fructose, and mint in a blender and blend until smooth.

4. Remove the game hens from the oven and reduce the temperature to 300°F. Allow them to cool until safe to handle, then remove all the skin and any visible fat, being careful not to cut the flesh.

5. Place the hens back on the rack in the pan and brush generously with the raspberry sauce. Place them back in the oven and roast for 25 more minutes, brushing them with the sauce every 10 minutes to glaze them evenly.

6. Just before serving top each hen with any of the remaining sauce.

MAKES 4 SERVINGS

• EACH SERVING CONTAINS APPROXIMATELY:

CALORIES: 144 | FAT: 4 g | CHOLESTEROL: 41 mg | SODIUM: 169 mg | CARBOHYDRATES: 9 g | PROTEIN: 17 g

258

marinated duck with blueberry-madeira sauce

Duck breasts are sold individually packaged at most supermarkets. Cooking them before removing the skin keeps the meat moist. At Canyon Ranch we serve these tasty, sauced duck breasts with Braised Red Cabbage (see page 294) and Whole-Wheat Spaetzle (see page 317).

MARINADE:

1/3 cup fresh blueberries

1 cup dry red wine

1/4 cup red wine vinegar

1/4 cup diced carrot

1/4 cup celery

1 teaspoon chopped fresh parsley

1 teaspoon chopped fresh rosemary

1/3 cup diced onion

1/4 teaspoon cracked black pepper

4 duck breasts (1 pound), skin on

BLUEBERRY-MADEIRA SAUCE:

1 1/2 cups fat-free duck or chicken stock (see page 54)

1/4 teaspoon extra-virgin olive oil

1 tablespoon chopped shallot

1 garlic clove, pressed or minced

2 tablespoons madeira wine

1/4 cup fresh blueberries

1/4 teaspoon salt

1/4 teaspoon freshly ground black pepper

1. Combine all the marinade ingredients in a bowl. Put the duck in the marinade, turning to coat completely. Cover tightly and marinate in the refrigerator all day or overnight.

2. To make the sauce, pour the stock in a small saucepan and bring to a boil. Continue to boil until reduced by two-thirds. Set aside.

3. Heat the olive oil in a small saucepan. Add the shallot and garlic and cook until just golden. Add the Madeira and simmer until reduced by half.

4. Add the blueberries and stock and simmer for 5 minutes. Add the salt and pepper, spoon into a blender, and blend until smooth. Pour through a strainer. Set aside.

5. Preheat the oven to 375°F.

6. Spray an ovenproof skillet with non-stick cooking spray and place over medium heat. Remove the duck breasts from the marinade, discarding the marinade, and place in the hot skillet. Brown on both sides, then transfer the pan to the oven and cook an additional 5 to 6 minutes for medium-rare, or until the desired degree of doneness.

7. To serve, remove the skin from the duck and spoon 2 tablespoons of the sauce over each duck breast.

MAKES 4 SERVINGS

260

• **EACH SERVING OF 1 DUCK BREAST WITH 2 TABLESPOONS OF SAUCE CONTAINS APPROXIMATELY:**

CALORIES: **185** | FAT: **7 g** | CHOLESTEROL: **87 mg** | SODIUM: **196 mg** | CARBOHYDRATES: **3 g** | PROTEIN: **21 g**

turkey meat loaf

The secret ingredient in this flavorful and succulent meat loaf is the cottage cheese because it retains moisture during baking. It is a wonderful summer recipe in that it pairs perfectly with all the fabulous fresh fruits available that time of the year, and it is delicious served hot or cold. Leftover meat loaf is great for sandwiches and a tasty addition to cold salads or hot casserole dishes. It can also be used in pasta sauces, pizza toppings, and omelets.

1 pound ground turkey breast

1/2 large onion, finely chopped (2/3 cup)

3 pieces white bread made into soft crumbs in blender (1 1/2 cups)

1/3 cup non-fat egg substitute

1/4 cup white wine or apple juice

2 teaspoons extra-virgin olive oil

1 1/4 teaspoons dried thyme, crushed, divided use

1 garlic clove, pressed

2 teaspoons minced fresh lemon zest, divided use

1/2 teaspoon salt

1/2 cup low-fat (1 percent) cottage cheese

1. Preheat the oven to 350°F.

2. Coat a 9 x 5-inch loaf pan with non-stick vegetable cooking spray and set aside.

3. Combine the ground turkey breast, onion, bread crumbs, egg substitute, wine or apple juice, olive oil, 1 teaspoon of the thyme, garlic, 1 teaspoon of the minced lemon zest, and the salt in a large mixing bowl and mix well. In another bowl combine the cottage cheese, the remaining 1/4 teaspoon of thyme, and the remaining 1 teaspoon of minced lemon zest and mix well.

4. Place half of the turkey mixture in the bottom of the loaf pan and press out evenly. Spoon the cottage cheese mixture on top of the turkey and spread out evenly. Cover with the remaining turkey mixture.

5. Place the meat loaf in the preheated oven and bake for 1 hour. Allow to rest for 10 minutes before cutting into six 1 1/2-inch slices.

261

MAKES 6 SERVINGS

• EACH SLICE CONTAINS APPROXIMATELY:

CALORIES: **194** | FAT: **8 g** | CHOLESTEROL: **61 mg** | SODIUM: **464 mg** | CARBOHYDRATES: **9 g** | PROTEIN: **18 g**

turkey mole

Mole (MOH-lay) literally means concoction in Spanish, and indeed it is. There are many variations of this spicy Mexican sauce that are usually served with poultry. Most of them contain ground nuts or seeds and Mexican bar chocolate. This spa version does contain ground peanuts, but cocoa powder has been added to replace the bar chocolate because it is lower in calories and fat.

1 medium onion, finely chopped

1 garlic clove, pressed or minced

1 large tomato or 2 small ones, peeled and chopped

2 tablespoons finely chopped raisins

1/4 cup chopped cilantro

3 tablespoons chili powder

3 tablespoons unsweetened cocoa powder

1/2 teaspoon salt (omit if using salted stock)

1/2 teaspoon fructose

1/2 teaspoon ground cinnamon

1/4 teaspoon ground anise seed

2 tablespoons unhomogenized smooth peanut butter

1 1/2 cups fat-free chicken stock (see page 54)

2 pounds sliced cooked turkey breast

Serve this spicy and extremely flavorful Mexican dish with hot corn tortillas. I usually double the recipe for the sauce because it keeps well, tightly covered, in the freezer for several months, and it's a wonderful emergency meal to have on hand.

1. Put the onion in a large saucepan and cook, covered, over low heat until soft and translucent, adding a little water if necessary to prevent scorching. Add the other ingredients, except the chicken stock and turkey, and mix well.

2. Bring the chicken stock to a boil and add it to the mole sauce. Cook, uncovered, over very low heat, stirring occasionally, for 45 minutes.

3. To serve, heat the sliced turkey and pour 1/4 cup of sauce over the top of each 4-ounce serving of cooked turkey, or chop the turkey and add it to the sauce and serve like a stew.

MAKES 8 SERVINGS

• EACH SERVING CONTAINS APPROXIMATELY:

CALORIES: **202** | FAT: **5 g** | CHOLESTEROL: **66 mg** | SODIUM: **316 mg** | CARBOHYDRATES: **9 g** | PROTEIN: **28 g**

white russian stroganoff

Stroganoff, a Russian-derived dish named for the nineteenth-century diplomat Count Paul Stroganov, is classically made with thin slices of beef, onions, and mushrooms in a sour cream sauce. In this lighter, whiter version, we are substituting chicken or turkey for the beef and yogurt for the sour cream. When using non-fat yogurt in hot dishes, it is necessary to combine it with a small amount of a starch, such as flour or cornstarch, to prevent it from separating, as we do in this recipe. Not only is this a truly delicious dish, but it's a real conversation piece for a dinner party. Serve it over rice or noodles with a bright green vegetable to brighten up the plate.

2 large onions, thinly sliced

3 cups sliced mushrooms

1 cup fat-free chicken stock
(see page 54)

1¼ cups low-fat white sauce
(see page 325)

2 tablespoons low-sodium tomato
paste

1 teaspoon dried basil, crushed

½ teaspoon paprika

¼ teaspoon ground nutmeg

¼ cup dry sherry

4 cups chopped cooked chicken or
turkey

½ cup non-fat plain yogurt

½ tablespoon cornstarch

1. Cook the onions in a pan, covered, over very low heat until soft, stirring frequently to prevent scorching. Add the mushrooms and continue cooking, covered, until soft.

2. Add all the other ingredients, except the chicken or turkey, yogurt, and cornstarch, and simmer, uncovered, for 10 minutes.

3. Add the chicken or turkey and cook until thoroughly heated. Combine the yogurt and cornstarch in a small bowl and mix well. Remove the pan from the heat and stir in the yogurt mixture.

MAKES 8 SERVINGS

266

• EACH 3/4-CUP SERVING CONTAINS APPROXIMATELY:

CALORIES: **177** | FAT: **2 g** | CHOLESTEROL: **70 mg** | SODIUM: **299 mg** | CARBOHYDRATES: **6 g** | PROTEIN: **30 g**

meat

Although red meat does contribute protein, iron, and zinc, it tends to have a high fat content. The problem lies in the fact that the fat in meat is primarily in the saturated fat category. Also, the fat in it runs through the red muscle of the meat so that even after all visible fat is removed it is impossible to get rid of it the way you can by removing the skin and visible fat from poultry.

Beef is divided into four grades, prime, choice, good, and select, or very lean, depending on the amount of marbling (fat running through the muscle of the meat) it contains. Select contains the least amount of fat and prime the most. The leanest cuts of beef include flank and round steak.

While veal may be lower in fat content, it is higher in cholesterol than beef. This is because, being baby beef, it is milk-fed. As for lamb, your best low-fat lamb choice is to thread cubes of leg or shoulder onto skewers for lamb kabobs or select extremely lean chops.

When buying meat, always look for the leanest cuts available. Remember the grading on beef and avoid cuts with more fat marbling. Wild game such as elk, venison, and the like, are also good choices. They are leaner because they have run wild rather than being confined in small spaces to prevent them from losing weight.

When possible, it is always better to grind your own meat for things like hamburgers and meat loaf because you can then better control the fat content.

When preparing meat, always carefully remove all visible fat. Use cooking methods that allow the fat to drain off the meat rather than being held in. For example, when you are baking or broiling meat, do so on a rack so that the meat does not sit in the fat. When making stews or soups, try to make them the day before you plan to serve them. Then remove all the visible fat that forms on the top before reheating to serve. This gives you not only a healthier dish but also a more appetizing-looking entree because it will not have the fat globules floating around on the top.

The one thing about cooking meat that is much easier than cooking either fish or shellfish is that cooking time is not so crucial. Even though there are many cuts of meat that are much better served rare rather than well done, there are also many others that can be cooked for long periods and the time only improves both the taste and the texture.

Perhaps the most important tip to remember in preparing and serving meat is to use less of it. Treat all meat as a condiment rather than focusing on it as the main part of the meal.

steak au poivre

This classic preparation of truly tender steak is always a popular item on any menu. The steaks can be coated with the pepper well ahead of time and then cooked just before serving.

4 filets mignons, 4 ounces each and at least 1 inch thick

cracked black pepper

1 teaspoon butter

1/2 cup dry red wine

2 tablespoons brandy

1. Sprinkle both sides of the steaks generously with the black pepper, pressing it into the surface of the steaks with your hands.

2. Melt the butter in a large, heavy skillet and then wipe the surface of the skillet with a paper towel to remove the excess.

3. Heat the skillet to very hot before adding the steaks. Cook the steaks over high heat for about 3 minutes per side. Remove the steaks and add the wine and brandy to the skillet. Bring to a boil, stirring constantly.

4. Spoon the wine mixture over the tops of the steaks before serving.

MAKES 4 SERVINGS

271

• EACH SERVING CONTAINS APPROXIMATELY:

CALORIES: 219 | FAT: 8 g | CHOLESTEROL: 74 mg | SODIUM: 57 mg | CARBOHYDRATES: negligible | PROTEIN: 24 g

teriyaki steak

It is best to make the marinade for this steak at least 1 day before you plan to use it to allow the flavors to marry.

MARINADE:

½ cup reduced-sodium soy sauce

6 ounces frozen pineapple juice concentrate, undiluted

2 garlic cloves, pressed or minced

1 tablespoon peeled and grated fresh gingerroot

1 pound flank steak, all visible fat removed

1. Combine all the marinade ingredients in a bowl and mix well.

2. Place the flank steak in a flat dish and pour the marinade over it. Cover tightly and refrigerate. Allow the steak to marinate for about 2 hours before cooking.

3. Prepare a grill or preheat a broiler. Broil the steak for about 3 minutes per side for rare, 5 minutes for medium, or longer depending on how well done you like your steak. To serve, slice thinly across the grain.

MAKES 4 SERVINGS

272

• EACH SERVING CONTAINS APPROXIMATELY:

CALORIES: **228** | FAT: **12 g** | CHOLESTEROL: **59 mg** | SODIUM: **323 mg** | CARBOHYDRATES: **5 g** | PROTEIN: **23 g**

herb-roasted tenderloin of beef with port wine sauce

This savory, rich-tasting roast is excellent served with just mashed potatoes and fresh vegetables. The sauce provides a fabulous flavor to anything else on the plate. Leftover roast is wonderful chopped, mixed with the sauce, and served over wild rice.

1/2 teaspoon extra-virgin olive oil

1 pound beef tenderloin, all visible fat removed

1 teaspoon coarse-grain mustard

1/2 teaspoon salt

1/2 teaspoon freshly ground black pepper

1 teaspoon dried chervil, crushed

1 teaspoon dried savory, crushed

1 teaspoon dried thyme, crushed

1 teaspoon dried rosemary, crushed

PORT WINE SAUCE:

1 1/2 cups port wine

1 1/2 cups fat-free veal or beef stock

reduced pan juices

1 teaspoon butter

1. Preheat the oven to 450°F.

2. Heat the oil in a medium-size skillet. Add the meat and sear over high heat for 1 to 2 minutes to seal in the juice.

3. Remove the tenderloin from the pan and allow to rest for 5 minutes. Remove any fat from the pan. Combine the mustard with the salt, pepper, and all the herbs. Mix well and coat the beef with the mixture.

4. Place the herb-coated tenderloin in a small roasting pan and roast for 5 minutes, or until medium-rare.

5. Remove from the oven. Place the tenderloin in a separate pan while making the sauce. Deglaze the roasting pan with the port wine and reduce the liquid by half. Add the veal stock and again reduce by half.

6. Pour any meat juices from the resting meat into the pan with the reduced stock. Swirl in the butter. Divide the meat into 4 servings and serve with the sauce.

MAKES 4 SERVINGS

273

about tenderloin
The elongated tenderloin, when separated from the bone and the rest of the short loin, is sold as a tenderloin roast, often called chateaubriand. The tenderloin can also be cut into tournedos or filet mignon steaks.

• EACH SERVING CONTAINS APPROXIMATELY:

CALORIES: 265 | FAT: 10 g | CHOLESTEROL: 75 mg | SODIUM: 416 mg | CARBOHYDRATES: 4 g | PROTEIN: 24 g

canyon ranch burger

The simple but delicious and satisfying hamburger that is served with Coleslaw (see page 99) and Oven Fries (see page 301) has for years ranked among the most popular items on our menus whenever we do a guest poll. We warm the hamburger buns, but if you prefer, you can toast them.

1 pound extra-lean ground round

8 small whole-wheat hamburger buns

1/3 cup thousand island dressing
(see page 151)

tomato and onion slices

lettuce

1. Form the meat into 2-ounce patties and cook as desired.

2. Spread each bun with 2 teaspoons of Thousand Island dressing.

3. Place 1 patty on each bun and garnish with tomato and onion slices and lettuce.

MAKES 8 BURGERS

274

• EACH 2-OUNCE BURGER ON A BUN CONTAINS APPROXIMATELY:

CALORIES: **246** | FAT: **12 g** | CHOLESTEROL: **39 mg** | SODIUM: **238 mg** | CARBOHYDRATES: **19 g** | PROTEIN: **15 g**

dijon-crusted club steak

This is an ideal company dish for busy people because you can prepare the steaks many hours or even a day in advance, cover them tightly, and refrigerate until you are thirty-four minutes from the time you want to serve them. Also, if you leave them in the oven for a little longer than thirty minutes after the oven is turned off, the steaks will still be medium-rare. If you prefer your steaks well done, bake them for 5 minutes instead of 4 minutes before turning the oven off. Because the fat is high in this dish you will need to balance your fat intake for the day.

4 club steaks, 6 ounces each and 1½ inches thick, all visible fat removed

1 large lemon, halved

1 teaspoon garlic salt

1 teaspoon freshly ground black pepper

⅓ cup dijon-style mustard

4 teaspoons unprocessed wheat bran

1 cup finely chopped parsley

1. Preheat the oven to 500°F.
2. Place the steaks in a flat baking pan and rub both sides with lemon. Sprinkle garlic salt and pepper on both sides of each steak.
3. Combine the mustard, bran, and parsley in a bowl and mix well. Top each steak with the mustard mixture and press it down firmly, using the palm of your hand.
4. Place the steaks in the preheated oven for 4 minutes and then turn the oven off. Do not open the oven door for 30 minutes. At the end of the 30 minutes, the steaks will be cooked medium-rare.

MAKES 4 SERVINGS

276

• EACH SERVING CONTAINS APPROXIMATELY:

CALORIES: **302** | FAT: **17 g** | CHOLESTEROL: **73 mg** | SODIUM: **387 mg** | CARBOHYDRATES: **13 g** | PROTEIN: **28 g**

club steak

The short loin is the most tender cut of beef because of its location. It lies in the center of the back, between the sirloin and the rib where the muscles do little to toughen it. The tenderloin and top loin are the two main muscles in the short loin. The top loin with the bone attached is called a club steak. When separated from the bone, the same cut of meat is called a New York or Kansas City strip steak or a Delmonico steak. When portions of both the tenderloin and top loin are left on the bone, the resulting short loin steaks are called porterhouse and T-bone.

eye of round roast

All round steaks and roasts come from the hind leg of the beef where the muscles are toughened by exercise, thus producing less tender cuts of meat. There are 6 major sections into which the round can be divided: the rump, the heel, and the 4 main muscles which include top round, sirloin tip, bottom round, and eye of round. Although eye of round is extremely flavorful, it is the least tender of the muscle groups and requires slow moist heat when cooking.

64

osso bucco

This delicious Italian dish is usually made with veal shanks. At Canyon Ranch we sometimes use lamb shanks instead, which are also very good. It is classically served with a little gremolada, a piquant mixture of minced lemon zest, parsley, and garlic, sprinkled over the top.

4 (6-ounce) veal or lamb shanks (1½ pounds), all visible fat removed

1 small carrot, diced

½ leek, white part only, sliced

1 small potato, diced (3/4 cup)

1 teaspoon whole black peppercorns

⅓ cup dry white wine

2 cups fat-free chicken stock (see page 54)

2 cups fat-free beef stock

VEGETABLE RELISH:

2 tablespoons chopped red onion

2 tablespoons chopped scallion, white part only

¼ cup diced zucchini

1 small red pepper, seeded and diced

1 garlic clove, pressed or minced

¼ cup diced tomato

pinch freshly ground black pepper

2 tablespoons chopped parsley

1. Lightly spray a large, heavy saucepan or a Dutch oven with non-stick cooking spray. Place over medium-high heat until drops of water dance on the surface. Cook the shanks until browned on all sides. Remove the shanks from the pan and set aside.

2. Combine the carrot, leek, potato, black peppercorns, and white wine in the same saucepan and cook over medium heat for 2 minutes. Add the stocks and bring to a boil. Put the shanks back into the saucepan, cover, and cook over medium-low heat until the meat is fork-tender, about 1½ hours.

3. Meanwhile, combine all the vegetable relish ingredients in a skillet and cook over medium-low heat until tender but still firm. Set aside.

1 tablespoon grated lemon zest

1/2 cup finely chopped parsley

2 cloves garlic, finely chopped

shank

The shank is the front leg of beef, veal, lamb, or pork. It is extremely flavorful but also very tough. For this reason it requires a long, slow, moist method of cooking. It is ideal for Crock-Pot dishes.

4. Combine all the gremolada ingredients in a bowl, mix well, and set aside.

5. Lift the shanks out of the saucepan and set aside, covered, to keep warm. Strain the liquid through a strainer or a colander lined with cheesecloth. Return the liquid to the pan and cook over medium-high heat until reduced by half.

6. Serve each shank with 1/4 cup of the vegetable relish and 2 tablespoons of sauce. Sprinkle 1 tablespoon of the gremolada over the top of each serving.

MAKES 4 SERVINGS

• **EACH SERVING CONTAINS APPROXIMATELY:**

CALORIES: **300** | FAT: **10 g** | CHOLESTEROL: **81 mg** | SODIUM: **140 mg** | CARBOHYDRATES: **25 g** | PROTEIN: **25 g**

veal marsala

If you would rather not spend the time to make your own veal glaze, you can buy it already prepared in gourmet markets and some supermarkets. It is called glace de viande and is an extremely concentrated stock used for glazing and as a flavoring agent. Because it is also low in fat it is an important ingredient in spa cuisine as a substitute for oil and butter.

GLAZE:

5 pounds veal bones

1 pound onions, unpeeled and quartered

1/2 pound celery, coarsely chopped

1/2 pound carrots, coarsely chopped

1 pound veal fillets, all fat removed

1 tablespoon fresh lemon juice

1/2 cup dry marsala wine

2 cups thinly sliced mushrooms

marsala
Marsala is a fortified wine from the city of the same name in western Sicily. It has a rich, smoky flavor and can range in taste from sweet to dry.

1. Preheat the oven to 450°F.

2. Put the bones in a roasting pan and place in the preheated oven for 45 minutes, or until well browned. Add the onions, celery, and carrots and roast for another 45 minutes.

3. Transfer all the roasted ingredients to a pot, being sure to scrape all flavorful, roasted bits off the bottom of the pan. Add enough water to cover the ingredients and bring to a boil. Reduce the heat to low and simmer for several hours, or until the liquid is of a thick consistency.

4. Strain the liquid and discard the bones and vegetables.

5. Return the liquid to the pot and cook over medium heat for about 10 minutes, or until reduced to a glaze that is thick enough to coat the back of a spoon. Set aside.

6. Divide the veal into 4 equal portions.

7. Heat a large skillet over medium heat and add enough of the glaze to cover the surface of the pan. Add the veal in 1 layer and lightly brown on both sides. Remove the browned veal and set aside. Cover and keep warm.

8. Add the lemon juice and Marsala and deglaze the pan over high heat. Add the mushrooms and cook just until tender.

9. To serve, spoon a little of the sauce over each veal fillet.

MAKES 4 SERVINGS

• EACH SERVING CONTAINS APPROXIMATELY:

CALORIES: **297** | FAT: **6 g** | CHOLESTEROL: **100 mg** | SODIUM: **156 mg** | CARBOHYDRATES: **22 g** | PROTEIN: **30 g**

veal parmigiano

Parmigiano is a term describing food that is made or cooked with Parmesan cheese. For example, veal Parmigiano is a pounded veal cutlet dipped in egg and then coated with a cheese and bread crumb mixture. The cutlet is then cooked in a hot skillet and covered with a tomato sauce. In this recipe you can substitute chicken breasts for the veal if you prefer. Pound them into paillards just as you do the veal.

4 small veal cutlets (1 pound)

1 medium onion, finely chopped

2 garlic cloves, pressed or minced

2½ cups peeled and diced tomatoes

½ teaspoon freshly ground black pepper

8 ounces low-sodium tomato sauce

1 tablespoon chopped fresh oregano

1 tablespoon chopped fresh basil

2 egg whites, lightly beaten

¼ cup freshly grated parmesan cheese

½ cup whole-wheat bread crumbs

1 teaspoon extra-virgin olive oil

4 ounces low-fat mozzarella cheese, grated (1 cup)

1. Place the veal cutlets on a flat surface and cover with plastic wrap. Using the flat side of a meat mallet pound each cutlet to ¹/8-inch thickness. Set aside.

2. Combine the onion and garlic in a large skillet and cook, covered, over low heat about 10 minutes, until the onion is soft and translucent. Uncover and continue cooking, stirring frequently, until golden brown. Add the tomatoes and pepper and simmer, uncovered, for 15 minutes. Add the tomato sauce, oregano, and basil and simmer over low heat for 30 more minutes.

3. Preheat the oven to 350°F.

4. Put the egg whites in a shallow bowl. Combine the Parmesan cheese and bread crumbs on a plate. Dip each veal cutlet into the egg whites and then into the cheese mixture.

5. Spray a large skillet with non-stick cooking spray and place over medium heat. Add the olive oil and heat until drops of water dance on the surface. Carefully arrange the coated veal in the hot skillet and cook for 2 minutes per side, or until a golden brown on both sides. Do not overcook.

6. Place the browned veal in a 7 x 11-inch baking dish. Spoon the tomato sauce evenly over the top. Sprinkle the mozzarella cheese over the sauce. Bake, uncovered, in the preheated oven for 20 minutes.

7. To serve, arrange 1 veal cutlet on each of 4 dinner plates and top evenly with any remaining sauce.

MAKES 4 SERVINGS

• EACH SERVING CONTAINS APPROXIMATELY:

CALORIES: **310** | FAT: **11 g** | CHOLESTEROL: **91 mg** | SODIUM: **602 mg** | CARBOHYDRATES: **20 g** | PROTEIN: **32 g**

veal piccata

This classic Italian veal dish is already a light choice on most menus. It consists of a seasoned and floured veal cutlet that is quickly cooked in a very hot skillet and served with a sauce made from the pan drippings, lemon juice, and parsley. At Canyon Ranch we include capers for added flavor and cook it in less oil for an even lighter dish. This dish can also be made with chicken breast if you prefer. It is good served with pasta and a fresh green vegetable on the side.

4 small veal cutlets (1 pound)

$1/4$ cup all-purpose flour

1 tablespoon fresh lemon juice

$1/2$ cup fat-free veal stock or chicken stock (see page 54)

$1/4$ cup capers, drained

1 tablespoon extra-virgin olive oil

2 tablespoons finely chopped parsley

284

1. Place the veal cutlets on a flat surface between pieces of plastic wrap. Using the flat side of a meat mallet, pound each cutlet to $1/8$-inch thickness.
2. Place the flour on a large plate and press both sides of each pounded cutlet in the flour. Set aside.
3. Combine the lemon juice, stock, and capers in a small bowl and mix well. Set aside.
4. Spray a large skillet with non-stick cooking spray and place over medium-high heat. Add the olive oil to the skillet and when it is hot enough for drops of water to dance on the surface arrange the cutlets in the hot skillet. Cook for about 2 minutes per side, or until golden brown on both sides. Add the caper mixture, turn the heat to high, and cook, stirring frequently, for 2 minutes, or until the sauce starts to thicken.
5. To serve, place 1 veal cutlet on each of 4 dinner plates and top each serving evenly with any remaining sauce and $1/2$ tablespoon of chopped parsley.

MAKES 4 SERVINGS

• EACH SERVING CONTAINS APPROXIMATELY:

CALORIES: 160 | FAT: 5 g | CHOLESTEROL: 72 mg | SODIUM: 197 mg | CARBOHYDRATES: 7 g | PROTEIN: 19 g

veal tenderloin with tarragon cream

This opulent-tasting veal is an excellent example of how just a small amount of butter can be used to change the perception of richness for the entire dish even when the rest of the sauce is made with totally fat-free ingredients. Served with Garlic Mashed Potatoes (page 304) and a colorful combination of fresh vegetables, it becomes an excellent Canyon Ranch dinner party menu.

TARRAGON CREAM:

1 teaspoon butter

1/2 garlic clove, pressed or minced

1 shallot, minced

1/4 cup dry white wine

2 2/3 cups fat-free veal stock or chicken stock (see page 54)

1/4 cup evaporated skim milk

1 teaspoon arrowroot

1 tablespoon fresh chopped tarragon leaves

pinch dry mustard

pinch freshly ground black pepper

1 teaspoon salt

1 1/2 pounds veal tenderloin, all visible fat removed

1. Melt the butter in a small skillet over medium heat. Add the garlic and shallot and cook until translucent. Add the wine and reduce until almost dry. Add the stock, bring to a simmer over low heat, and reduce by half.

2. Combine the milk with the arrowroot to make a thin paste. Remove the sauce from the heat and add the arrowroot mixture, blending well with a wire whisk.

3. Place the saucepan over medium heat and simmer the sauce for 10 minutes. Remove from the heat and stir in the tarragon, mustard, pepper, and salt.

4. Preheat the broiler. Spray a broiler rack with non-slick cooking spray.

5. Put the veal on the prepared rack and place under the hot broiler for about 5 minutes per side for medium-rare.

6. Cut the cooked tenderloin into 6 pieces, 3 ounces each, and top each serving with 2 tablespoons of the sauce.

285

MAKES 6 SERVINGS

• **EACH SERVING CONTAINS APPROXIMATELY:**

CALORIES: **215** | FAT: **11 g** | CHOLESTEROL: **92 mg** | SODIUM: **532 mg** | CARBOHYDRATES: **3 g** | PROTEIN: **23 g**

mustard-topped rack of lamb with spinach salad

You can save a lot of time making this recipe by using prewashed baby spinach leaves available in cellophane bags in most supermarkets. This is another dish that is perfect for entertaining because everything except the lamb can be prepared ahead of time and assembled just before serving.

COLD MUSTARD SAUCE:

¹/₃ cup fat-free mayonnaise

1 tablespoon dijon mustard

¹/₂ teaspoon whole-grain mustard

¹/₂ teaspoon green peppercorn mustard

1 tablespoon fresh lemon juice

pinch chopped fresh mint

1 tablespoon minced shallots

1 pound rack of lamb (8 chops)

¹/₄ cup canyon ranch dressing
   (see page 138)

¹/₂ pound spinach, washed and tough stems removed

¹/₄ pound mushrooms, sliced (1 cup)

8 thinly sliced red onion rings

1 small tomato, diced

1. Place the cold mustard sauce ingredients in a small bowl and mix well. Cover tightly and refrigerate.

2. Preheat the oven to 400°F.

3. Place the rack on a baking sheet and bake in the preheated oven for 25 minutes for medium-rare. Slice into 8 chops.

4. While the rack is baking, heat the Canyon Ranch dressing in a small pan until hot to the touch but not boiling.

5. Combine the spinach, mushrooms, red onions, and tomato in a bowl. Pour the warm dressing over them and mix until wilted.

6. Divide the warm salad mixture among 4 plates and top each serving with 2 lamb chops and 2 tablespoons of the cold mustard sauce.

MAKES 4 SERVINGS

about a rack of lamb
A rack of lamb comes from the rib section of the animal and the chops are very small. For this reason it is better to cook the entire rack and cut them apart after cooking so that they retain their juices.

• **EACH SERVING CONTAINS APPROXIMATELY:**

CALORIES: **310** | FAT: **14 g** | CHOLESTEROL: **108 mg** | SODIUM: **543 mg** | CARBOHYDRATES: **10 g** | PROTEIN: **39 g**

zenzero grilled lamb chops with cucumber sauce

When I first tasted these subtly seasoned, sensational-tasting chops I was anxious to have the recipes for both the marinade and the sauce. The recipes necessary for this unusual dish were created by Fred Iwasake, the extremely talented chef at Zenzero in Santa Monica, California. Chef Iwasake recommends making the marinade 2 to 3 days before using it in order for the flavors to properly marry. He also prefers to use only the peel of the cucumbers in his sauce for a fuller flavor, so I suggest keeping the peeled cucumbers in a tightly sealed container in your refrigerator to use in a soup or salad the next day.

1-MINUTE MARINADE:

1/3 cup reduced-sodium soy sauce

1/3 cup mirin

1/3 cup sake

3 tablespoons finely chopped garlic

3 tablespoons finely chopped gingerroot

CUCUMBER SAUCE:

peel from 2 large cucumbers

1 1/2 tablespoons rice vinegar

1 tablespoon canola oil

1/4 teaspoon salt

1/4 teaspoon freshly ground black pepper

4 loin lamb chops, all visible fat removed

about mirin

Mirin is a low-alcohol sweet golden wine made from glutinous rice. It adds sweetness and flavor to a variety of traditional dishes.

1. Combine all the marinade ingredients in a bowl and mix well. If possible, allow to stand for at least 2 days before using.

2. Combine all the sauce ingredients in a blender and puree. Pour through a strainer, pressing the liquid through with the back of a spoon. (You will have about 3/4 cup of the strained sauce.)

3. Before grilling or broiling the lamb chops, dip each one in the marinade, allowing it to remain for 1 minute. Cook the lamb until a bright pink in color, about 4 minutes per side. Serve each lamb chop with 3 tablespoons of the cucumber sauce.

MAKES 4 SERVINGS

• **EACH 1-CHOP SERVING CONTAINS APPROXIMATELY:**

CALORIES: **204** | FAT: **16 g** | CHOLESTEROL: **41 mg** | SODIUM: **168 mg** | CARBOHYDRATES: **4 g** | PROTEIN: **10 g**

peachy spiced lamb chops

This recipe is a wonderful example of how dried fruit can give a fat-free sauce a rich and creamy texture. The combination of the dried peaches, herbs, and spices also adds a complex blend of flavors that go well with the lamb.

4 (6-ounce) loin lamb chops, 1½ inches thick, all visible fat removed

½ teaspoon garlic salt

½ teaspoon freshly ground black pepper

SAUCE:

6 ounces dried peach halves (1 cup)

2 cups fat-free chicken stock (see page 54)

½ teaspoon dried oregano, crushed

¼ teaspoon ground allspice

¼ teaspoon ground coriander

¼ teaspoon ground cumin

¼ teaspoon paprika

¼ teaspoon salt

½ teaspoon balsamic vinegar

1. Sprinkle both sides of the lamb chops evenly with the garlic salt and pepper, cover tightly, and set aside.

2. Combine the dried peaches and chicken stock in a saucepan and bring to a boil over high heat. Reduce the heat to medium and boil, uncovered, for 5 minutes. Allow to cool slightly and then spoon the cooked peaches and all the liquid in the pan into a blender or a food processor. Add all the remaining ingredients and puree. If you want a thinner consistency, add a little water. Pour the mixture back into the same pan to reheat.

3. Prepare the grill or preheat the broiler. Broil the lamb chops 4 minutes per side for medium-rare.

4. To serve, place one lamb chop on each of 4 dinner plates and spoon about ½ cup of sauce over the top of each chop.

MAKES 4 SERVINGS

289

loin lamb chops
Loin lamb chops come from the leg and can be cut much thicker than the rib chops in a rack. They are more flavorful but not quite as tender as the rib chops. Boneless, skewered loin lamb chops, which are cut off the very top of the leg, can be substituted for the chops with bones.

• EACH SERVING CONTAINS APPROXIMATELY:

CALORIES: 374 | FAT: 19 g | CHOLESTEROL: 27 mg | SODIUM: 363 mg | CARBOHYDRATES: 27 g | PROTEIN: 23 g

pastitsio

Pastitsio is an extremely popular Greek dish that is usually made with ground lamb, as it is in this recipe. However, for a vegetarian offering this recipe can also be made without any meat at all.

LAMB MIXTURE:

1 large onion, chopped (2 cups)

3/4 pound lean ground lamb

16 ounces whole canned tomatoes, drained and mashed

8 ounces tomato sauce

1/2 teaspoon salt

1/8 teaspoon freshly ground black pepper

1/2 teaspoon oregano, crushed

1/4 teaspoon ground cinnamon

1 slice whole-wheat bread, toasted and crumbled (3/4 cup)

SAUCE:

1 tablespoon extra-virgin olive oil

1/3 cup whole-wheat flour

2 1/2 cups non-fat milk, simmering

1/2 teaspoon salt

1/4 teaspoon ground cinnamon

1/8 teaspoon white pepper

3 egg whites, lightly beaten

1. To make the lamb mixture, place the onion in a large saucepan and cook, covered, over low heat for 10 minutes, or until soft. Add a little water if necessary to prevent scorching. Add the lamb and increase the heat to medium. Cook until the lamb is no longer pink, about 5 minutes, stirring frequently to keep crumbly. Add the tomatoes, tomato sauce, salt, pepper, oregano, and cinnamon and mix well. Cover and simmer for 10 minutes, stirring occasionally. Add the bread crumbs and mix well.

2. Preheat the oven to 350°F.

3. To make the sauce, heat the oil in a skillet over medium heat. Add the flour and cook for 3 minutes, stirring constantly. Add the hot milk, stirring constantly until smooth. Add the salt, cinnamon, and white pepper and cook, stirring frequently, until thickened, about 15 minutes. Remove from the heat and slowly add the egg whites, stirring constantly. Combine 1 cup of the sauce with the ricotta cheese. Mix well and set aside.

4. Spray a 3-quart baking dish with non-stick cooking spray. Spread half of the cooked pasta in the dish and top with the

1/2 cup part-skim ricotta cheese

16 ounces tubular pasta, cooked al
   dente according to package
   directions and drained, divided use

1 cup freshly grated romano cheese
   (4 ounces), divided use

sauce without the added ricotta cheese. Spread all the lamb mixture evenly over the top, then sprinkle half of the grated Romano cheese over it. Cover with the remaining pasta and bake in the preheated oven for 30 minutes.

5. Remove from the oven and increase the temperature to 400°F. Spread the reserved sauce mixed with the ricotta cheese over the top and sprinkle evenly with the remaining Romano cheese. Bake for another 20 to 30 minutes, or until lightly browned. Cool for 10 minutes before serving.

MAKES 12 SERVINGS

• EACH 1-CUP SERVING CONTAINS APPROXIMATELY:

CALORIES: 339 | FAT: 12 g | CHOLESTEROL: 34 mg | SODIUM: 544 mg | CARBOHYDRATES: 39 g | PROTEIN: 18 g

side dishes

This chapter contains primarily the basic recipes for side dishes we serve at Canyon Ranch, such as baked and oven-fried potatoes and grilled, steamed, and roasted vegetables. We don't place a great deal of emphasis on more elaborate side dishes because our suggested menus always include either a soup or a salad and an entree served with a starch such as Creamy Polenta or Whole-Wheat Spaetzle and fresh vegetables.

All of the side dishes that follow in this section go well with fish, poultry, or meat. You can also combine two or three of them for a complete vegetarian meal. Plant foods are important for their fiber, complex carbohydrates, vitamins, and minerals such as beta carotene and magnesium. Other disease-fighting compounds, such as substances called indoles, are found in the cruciferous vegetables, which include broccoli, cauliflower, cabbage, brussels sprouts, kale, and kohlrabi. Legumes, which include all dried beans and peas, peanuts, and all the soybean by-products, such as tofu and tempeh, contribute protein as well.

The dominant message in preventive nutrition used to focus on foods to avoid. Fortunately, during the past decade, as we have learned about eating less fat, the message has become more positive and has changed into what we should eat. And vegetables lead the list!

braised red cabbage

This colorful side dish is good served hot or cold. You can substitute green cabbage in this recipe, but the red makes a more attractive presentation. If you're in a hurry, you can use coleslaw mix for the cabbage leaves.

1/2 teaspoon olive oil

1/2 cup thinly sliced onion

2 1/2 cups packed red cabbage leaves, shredded

1 bay leaf

pinch ground cloves

1/4 teaspoon freshly ground black pepper

pinch salt

1/4 teaspoon caraway seeds
(see page 303)

2 tablespoons dry red wine

1 tablespoon red wine vinegar

1/2 cup vegetable stock
(see page 56)

1 small apple, peeled and cut into matchstick-size pieces (1/2 cup)

1 tablespoon red currant jelly

1 1/2 tablespoons minced parsley for garnish

1. Preheat the oven to 350°F.

2. Heat the olive oil in a medium-size, ovenproof skillet over medium heat. Add the onion and cook, stirring frequently, until golden brown.

3. Add the red cabbage, cover, and cook for about 2 minutes. Add the bay leaf, cloves, pepper, salt, caraway seeds, red wine, red wine vinegar, and vegetable stock. Mix well and cover the skillet.

4. Transfer the covered skillet to the preheated oven and bake for 25 minutes, or until the cabbage is completely wilted.

5. Add the sliced apple and red currant jelly and mix well. Return to the oven and bake for an additional 10 minutes.

6. To serve, place 1/2 cup of the cabbage mixture on each of 4 plates and garnish with chopped parsley.

MAKES 4 SERVINGS

294

the cabbage family

The cabbage family includes all the cruciferous vegetables, which are believed to prevent certain types of cancer. These include broccoli, brussels sprouts, cabbage, cauliflower, kale, and kohlrabi. The name cruciferous comes from the cross-shaped blossoms . Cabbages come in many shapes from almost flat to round and the leaves range from curly to smooth. The waxy-textured smooth leaves are tightly wrapped and range in color from almost white to green and red. When buying cabbage, look for a head that is heavy for its size with crisp, fresh-looking outer leaves. Cabbage is a good source of vitamin C and contains some vitamin A.

• EACH 1/2-CUP SERVING CONTAINS APPROXIMATELY:

CALORIES: **55** | FAT: **negligible** | CHOLESTEROL: **0** | SODIUM: **71 mg** | CARBOHYDRATES: **10 g** | PROTEIN: **1 g**

celery root and potato puree

The unusual flavor created by combining celery root with potatoes and the creamy satin-smooth texture of the puree make this a truly unusual side dish. The tasty mixture is a delightfully different alternative to plain mashed potatoes on a variety of menus.

2 cups peeled and diced celery root

3 cups peeled and diced potato

1/3 cup low-fat (2 percent) milk

1 2/3 cups vegetable stock
(see page 56)

1/8 teaspoon freshly ground nutmeg

1/8 teaspoon freshly ground
white pepper

1. Combine the celery root and potato in a large saucepan and cover with water. Bring to a boil over medium-high heat. Reduce the heat to low and cook for about 15 minutes, or until tender.

2. Drain thoroughly and spoon into a blender. Add all the remaining ingredients and puree. Return to the saucepan and reheat to the desired temperature before serving.

MAKES 6 SERVINGS

• EACH 3/4-CUP SERVING CONTAINS APPROXIMATELY:

CALORIES: 84 | FAT: negligible | CHOLESTEROL: 1 mg | SODIUM: 63 mg | CARBOHYDRATES: 18 g | PROTEIN: 3 g

gingered spiced carrots

These spicy carrots are a wonderful side dish for grilled poultry or meat. They are also delicious served cold as an appetizer or a salad. In fact, I often make this dish specifically to serve cold. If tightly covered, it keeps well in the refrigerator for at least 1 week, and the flavor just gets better each day.

1 tablespoon olive oil

1 medium onion, finely diced (1¹/₂ cups)

2 tablespoons finely chopped fresh gingerroot

1 teaspoon ground cinnamon

2 teaspoons ground cumin

3 tablespoons light brown sugar

2 pounds carrots, sliced (6 cups)

2 cups vegetable stock (see page 56)

1 teaspoon salt (omit if using salted stock)

2 tablespoons fresh dill

1. Heat the oil in a large skillet over medium heat. Add the onion and cook until it turns a golden color.

2. Add the remaining ingredients, except for the salt and dill. Simmer until the carrots are tender but not mushy, about 15 minutes.

3. Remove from the heat and allow to cool for 5 minutes. Stir in the salt and dill.

MAKES 6 CUPS

296

naan bread

This delicious Indian bread is perfect served with Indian menus and curried dishes of all types. It can also be cut into wedges to serve with dips or to make sandwiches. Naan is an Indian flat bread, made with white flour and traditionally baked at a very high heat by being thrown against the wall of a tandoor oven. This baking method not only cooks the bread in less than a minute, it also gives it a slightly smoky flavor.

1 teaspoon sugar

1 teaspoon active dry yeast

1/3 cup water

1/3 cup plus 4 teaspoons non-fat plain yogurt, divided use

1 teaspoon salt

1 1/2 cups bread flour

4 teaspoons sesame seeds

1. Combine the sugar, yeast, and water in a small bowl and set aside until foamy.

2. Combine 1/3 cup of the yogurt, salt, and the foaming yeast mixture in an electric mixer bowl fitted with a dough hook. While the mixer is running at medium speed, add the flour and knead until smooth and elastic, about 10 minutes. If not using an electric mixer, combine the yogurt, salt, and yeast mixture in a bowl and mix well. Stir in as much flour as possible and then place on a flat surface and knead in the remaining flour. Continue to knead until smooth and elastic, about 10 minutes.

3. Transfer the dough to another bowl, cover, and allow to rise in a warm place for 45 minutes.

4. Preheat the oven to 500°F.

5. Lightly spray 2 baking sheets with non-stick cooking spray.

6. Punch the dough down and divide into 8 balls. Knead each piece of dough into a round-shaped roll and place 4 dough balls on each prepared baking sheet. Cover and allow to rise until doubled in size, about 15 minutes.

7. Stretch each roll into a 4-inch round and allow to rise an additional 5 minutes. Spread 1/2 teaspoon of the remaining non-fat yogurt and 1/2 teaspoon of sesame seeds on top of each round. Bake in the preheated oven for 12 minutes, or until golden brown.

MAKES 8 SERVINGS

• EACH SERVING CONTAINS APPROXIMATELY:

CALORIES: **112** | FAT: **1 g** | CHOLESTEROL: **negligible** | SODIUM: **277 mg** | CARBOHYDRATES: **20 g** | PROTEIN: **4 g**

lentil dhal

For an interesting and unusual Indian vegetarian dinner, serve this tasty dhal with Curried Basmati Rice (page 314), Cucumber Raita (page 40), and Naan Bread, (page 298) Dhal, or dhall, is a spicy dish that can be made with lentils or other pulses, onions, and sometimes tomatoes or other vegetables, and a variety of different seasonings. In India the word *dal* refers to any of about 60 varieties of dried pulses, including lentils, peas, and mung beans.

¼ cup diced onion

1 teaspoon coriander seeds

2 cloves garlic, pressed or minced

1 teaspoon minced fresh gingerroot

¾ cup red lentils

1¼ cups vegetable stock
(see page 56)

1 tablespoon chopped cilantro

1. Lightly spray a medium saucepan with non-stick cooking spray. Cook the onion and coriander seeds over medium heat, stirring to prevent burning, until golden.
2. Add the garlic and ginger and cook for an additional 2 minutes. Add the lentils and vegetable stock and simmer for about 20 minutes, or until tender. Stir in the cilantro just before serving.

MAKES 4 SERVINGS

300

• EACH ½-CUP SERVING CONTAINS APPROXIMATELY:

CALORIES: **129** | FAT: **negligible** | CHOLESTEROL: **0** | SODIUM: **42 mg** | CARBOHYDRATES: **22 g** | PROTEIN: **11 g**

oven fries

These oven fries are a big hit at Canyon Ranch. Many of our guests are truly surprised to find burgers and fries on our menus, and the combination is always one of our most popular meals. I think they are actually better-tasting than classic french fries that are deep-fried in oil because you can really taste the potato. Also, they are easy to make, and cleanup is a snap with no spattered oil to worry about. You can use this same method to make sweet potato fries, but you have to watch them more carefully because they burn easily.

2 russet potatoes, scrubbed very clean

1. Preheat the oven to 375°F.
2. Cut the clean, unpeeled potatoes into strips the size of large french fries, about 1 inch in diameter.
3. Spray a large baking sheet with non-stick cooking spray. Arrange the potato strips on the baking sheet, being careful not to overlap them. Spray the potatoes with the non-stick cooking spray.
4. Bake in the preheated oven for about 1 hour and 20 minutes. Turn them over after the first 30 minutes. Continue turning them over every 15 minutes until browned and crisp.

MAKES 4 SERVINGS

301

• EACH 1-CUP SERVING (ABOUT 5 FRIES) CONTAINS APPROXIMATELY:

CALORIES: 44 | FAT: negligible | CHOLESTEROL: 0 | SODIUM: 3 mg | CARBOHYDRATES: 10 g | PROTEIN: 1 g

mashed potato and shallot casserole

This casserole can be made ahead and then baked just before serving. Leftovers can be formed into patties for delicious potato pancakes.

1 tablespoon corn oil margarine

4 medium shallots (3 ounces), thinly sliced (2/3 cup)

1 teaspoon sugar

2 pounds russet potatoes, peeled and cut into 2-inch cubes (6 cups)

4 ounces non-fat cream cheese

1/2 cup non-fat sour cream

1/2 teaspoon salt

1/4 teaspoon freshly ground black pepper

paprika

1. Preheat the oven to 400°F.

2. Spray a 2-quart casserole with non-stick cooking spray and set aside.

3. Melt the margarine in a skillet over medium heat. Add the shallots, stir to coat with the margarine, and then sprinkle with sugar. Cook until the shallots are golden, stirring occasionally, about 10 minutes. Set aside.

4. Put the potatoes in a large saucepan, cover with water, and bring to a boil. Reduce the heat to low and simmer until tender, about 20 to 25 minutes.

5. While the potatoes are cooking, beat together the cream cheese, sour cream, salt, and pepper. Stir in the cooked shallots.

6. Drain the potatoes and mash with a potato masher or an electric mixer. Add the cream cheese mixture and beat until fluffy and smooth.

7. Spread the potato mixture evenly in the prepared casserole and sprinkle lightly with paprika. Cover and bake in the preheated oven for 25 minutes. Remove the cover and continue to bake for 10 more minutes.

MAKES 4 CUPS, OR 8 SERVINGS

• EACH 1/2-CUP SERVING CONTAINS APPROXIMATELY:

CALORIES: **130** | FAT: **1 g** | CHOLESTEROL: **0** | SODIUM: **195 mg** | CARBOHYDRATES: **26 g** | PROTEIN: **40 g**

caraway mashed potatoes

Cooking the potatoes in stock rather than water and then allowing the potatoes to absorb all of the stock greatly enhances their flavor. The combination of russet potatoes, which have a low moisture and high starch content, and red potatoes, which contain less starch and more moisture, is perfect for making creamy mashed potatoes with very little fat. Also, leaving the red potatoes unpeeled provides an interesting texture as well as a touch of color, and the caraway seeds add a wonderful and unusual flavor. Leftovers are wonderful served cold as potato salad or reheated along with poultry or meat for a hot entree. For a vegetarian dish substitute vegetable stock for the chicken stock.

1 3/4 cups fat-free chicken stock
(see page 54)

1 pound russet potatoes, peeled and diced (3 cups)

1 pound red boiling potatoes, diced (3 cups)

1 tablespoon butter

3/4 cup hot non-fat milk

1/2 teaspoon seasoned salt

1/2 teaspoon caraway seeds

1/4 cup chopped chives

caraway seeds
Caraway seeds come from an herb in the parsley family. They have a unique, slightly aniselike flavor and are often used in rye breads for added taste and texture. They are popular in Alsatian, Austrian, German, and Hungarian cuisines and are often added to vegetables, stews, meats, cheeses, breads, and cakes. Caraway seeds are also used to make the liqueur called kümmel.

1. Combine the chicken stock and diced potatoes in a large saucepan and bring to a boil. Reduce the heat to low and cook, uncovered, for 10 minutes. Turn the heat back to high and boil until almost dry and the potatoes can be pierced easily with a fork, about 10 more minutes.

2. Place the cooked potatoes in a large bowl. Add the butter, milk, seasoned salt, and caraway seeds and mash well.

3. Stir in the chopped chives and serve immediately.

MAKES 4 CUPS, OR 8 SERVINGS

• EACH 1/2-CUP SERVING CONTAINS APPROXIMATELY:

CALORIES: **115** | FAT: **1 g** | CHOLESTEROL: **4 mg** | SODIUM: **303 mg** | CARBOHYDRATES: **22 g** | PROTEIN: **4 g**

garlic mashed potatoes

In this recipe the amount of garlic is listed as 2 cloves or to taste because when it comes to garlic, personal preference varies dramatically. Leftover mashed potatoes can be formed into patties and made into garlic potato pancakes.

3 medium russet potatoes (2¼ pounds)

1 cup non-fat milk

2 garlic cloves, pressed or minced, or to taste

1 tablespoon chopped chives

1 teaspoon salt

1 teaspoon freshly ground black pepper

1 tablespoon extra-virgin olive oil

1. Peel the potatoes and cut them into large cubes. Place them in a medium pot of boiling water to cover and partially cook, about 10 minutes.

2. In a medium-size saucepan over medium-low heat, bring the milk to a simmer.

3. When the potatoes are partially cooked, drain well and transfer to the preheated milk. Continue cooking until the potatoes are soft, about 15 minutes. If the potatoes become dry, add a little more milk.

4. Combine the potatoes with the remaining ingredients. Mash with a hand masher or an electric mixer until smooth.

MAKES 4 CUPS, OR 8 SERVINGS AS A SIDE DISH

• EACH ¹/₂-CUP SERVING CONTAINS APPROXIMATELY:

CALORIES: **139** | FAT: **2 g** | CHOLESTEROL: **negligible** | SODIUM: **291 mg** | CARBOHYDRATES: **28 g** | PROTEIN: **4 g**

scalloped potatoes

Scalloped potatoes are a wonderful side dish with almost any entree because of their mild flavor. You can also add cheese, fish, poultry, or meat and additional seasoning to this recipe and serve it as an entree.

2 medium white rose potatoes, thinly sliced (3 cups)

3/4 cup thinly sliced onion

1 cup low-fat milk

1 tablespoon flour

1/2 teaspoon salt

1/2 teaspoon freshly ground black pepper

1 1/2 teaspoons corn oil margarine

white rose or california long white potatoes
The potatoes known as white rose, or California long whites, named after the state in which they were developed, are similar to the russet in shape. However, they have thin, pale gray-brown skins with almost imperceptible eyes and can be baked, boiled, or fried.

1. Preheat the oven to 425°F.

2. Spray a 9-Inch-square baking dish with non-stick cooking spray.

3. Place half of the potatoes in the dish and cover with the sliced onion. Top with the remaining sliced potatoes.

4. Combine the milk, flour, salt, pepper, and margarine in a blender and blend until well mixed. Pour evenly over the potatoes.

5. Bake, covered, in the preheated oven for 45 minutes. Uncover and continue to bake for 15 more minutes, or until the potatoes reach the desired crispness on the top.

MAKES 6 SERVINGS

305

• EACH 1/2-CUP SERVING CONTAINS APPROXIMATELY:

CALORIES: 67 | FAT: 2 g | CHOLESTEROL: 3 mg | SODIUM: 288 mg | CARBOHYDRATES: 11 g | PROTEIN: 3 g

crisp potato pancakes

By pureeing part of the cooked potatoes to help hold the pancakes together you don't need to add as much flour and thereby have a crispier pancake. If you have an allergy to wheat, you can substitute potato starch for the flour called for in this recipe.

2 cups water

2 pounds russet potatoes, peeled and shredded

3 tablespoons chopped onions

2 tablespoons chopped parsley

1 scallion, chopped

3 tablespoons all-purpose flour

pinch salt

pinch freshly ground black pepper

¼ cup light sour cream, optional

1. Put the 2 cups of water in a saucepan and bring to a boil. Arrange the shredded potatoes in a steamer basket and place over the boiling water. Cover the pan and steam for about 6 minutes, or until the potatoes are al dente. Remove three-fourths of the potatoes from the basket and set aside. Continue to steam the remaining potatoes until they are soft enough to puree easily. Transfer the soft potatoes to a blender and puree.

2. Combine the steamed shredded potatoes, pureed potatoes, and all the remaining ingredients, except the sour cream, in a bowl and mix well.

3. Spray a skillet with non-stick cooking spray and place it over medium-high heat, or heat an electric skillet to 400°F. Divide the potato mixture into 4 equal portions and spoon onto the hot skillet. Cook until brown and crispy and then turn over and brown the other side.

4. To serve, top each pancake with 1 tablespoon of sour cream, if desired.

MAKES 4 SERVINGS

• EACH PANCAKE CONTAINS APPROXIMATELY:

CALORIES: **214** | FAT: **negligible** | CHOLESTEROL: **1 mg** | SODIUM: **88 mg** | CARBOHYDRATES: **48 mg** | PROTEIN: **6 g**

oven-fried squash

For variety you can add any of your favorite herbs or spices to the cornmeal coating. For a thicker coating you can dip the squash slices in lightly beaten egg white before rolling them in the cornmeal.

½ cup cornmeal

½ teaspoon salt

½ teaspoon freshly ground black pepper

6 medium zucchini or yellow squash, thinly sliced lengthwise into strips

1. Preheat the oven to 375°F.

2. Spray a large baking sheet with non-stick cooking spray.

3. Combine the cornmeal, salt, and pepper in a shallow bowl and mix well. Roll each squash slice in the cornmeal mixture and place it on the prepared baking sheet. Spray the squash slices with the non-stick cooking spray.

4. Bake in the preheated oven for 30 minutes. Carefully turn the slices over and bake them for 15 more minutes, or until browned.

MAKES 4 SERVINGS

• EACH 3/4-CUP SERVING CONTAINS APPROXIMATELY:

CALORIES: 59 | FAT: **negligible** | CHOLESTEROL: 0 | SODIUM: **139 mg** | CARBOHYDRATES: **13 g** | PROTEIN: **3 g**

roasted vegetables

The timing for this method of cooking vegetables will vary greatly from one vegetable to another. For example, asparagus will roast in about 7 minutes, sliced cauliflower and broccoli florets in about 8 minutes, and mushrooms, due to their high moisture content, will usually take about 12 minutes. You can also vary the flavor range by using seasoned oils, adding a sprinkle of salt, freshly ground black pepper, or herbs. I particularly like cauliflower prepared in this manner when the florets are sliced, rather than separated into small pieces, because it looks like browned lace.

1 tablespoon extra-virgin olive oil

1 pound fresh vegetables, such as whole asparagus spears, small or sliced cauliflower or broccoli florets, halved mushrooms, sliced squash, or sliced eggplant

1. Preheat the oven to 500°F.

2. Brush the olive oil evenly over the bottom of a baking sheet.

3. Add the vegetables to the baking sheet, rolling or turning them to coat them with the oil. Place in the oven and roast for about 7 to 8 minutes, or until they are well browned and can be pierced easily with a fork.

MAKES 4 SERVINGS

• EACH 1/2-CUP SERVING CONTAINS APPROXIMATELY:

CALORIES: 70 | FAT: 4 g | CHOLESTEROL: 0 | SODIUM: 3 mg | CARBOHYDRATES: 8 g | PROTEIN: 4 g

grilled vegetables

Grilled vegetables are a delightful accompaniment to almost any meal. They can be served over pasta, rice, or beans as an entree, as a hot side dish with fish, poultry, or meat, or cold as an appetizer or salad course. And you can change the flavor range of grilled vegetables dramatically just by using different types of vinegar and oil or by adding fresh herbs to the marinade.

MARINADE:

¼ cup balsamic vinegar

1 teaspoon ground thyme

1 tablespoon dijon mustard

2 teaspoons extra-virgin olive oil

pinch freshly ground black pepper

1 cup vegetable stock (see page 56)

VEGETABLES:

1 head endive, quartered

1 medium zucchini, diagonally cut into ¼-inch-thick slices

2 large red bell peppers, seeded and quartered

1 small head radicchio, quartered

1 small red onion, sliced into ⅛-inch rounds

1. Prepare hot coals for grilling or preheat the broiler.

2. Combine the marinade ingredients in a large bowl and mix well. Place the vegetables in the marinade for 10 to 15 minutes.

3. Grill the marinated vegetables for 1 to 2 minutes per side, turning once. Do not allow them to turn black.

MAKES 4 SERVINGS

• EACH ¹/₂-CUP SERVING CONTAINS APPROXIMATELY:

CALORIES: **80** | FAT: **2 g** | CHOLESTEROL: **0** | SODIUM: **164 mg** | CARBOHYDRATES: **16 g** | PROTEIN: **3 g**

herbed vegetable medley

You can substitute any other aromatic fresh herb such as oregano, tarragon, thyme, rosemary, or marjoram for the fresh basil called for in this recipe.

2 medium onions, diced (3 cups)

2 garlic cloves, finely chopped

1/2 teaspoon salt

3 tablespoons chopped fresh basil leaves

1 cup chopped parsley

6 cups diced and steamed vegetables (a colorful assortment)

1. Combine the onions and garlic in a pan and cook, covered, over low heat until soft, about 10 minutes, adding a little water if necessary to prevent scorching. Add the salt, basil, and parsley, mix well, and cook for 5 more minutes.

2. Add the vegetables, mix well, and cook just until thoroughly heated.

MAKES 8 SERVINGS

• EACH 3/4-CUP SERVING CONTAINS APPROXIMATELY:

CALORIES: **71** | FAT: **negligible** | CHOLESTEROL: **0** | SODIUM: **339 mg** | CARBOHYDRATES: **15 g** | PROTEIN: **4 g**

herbed zucchini and tomatoes

Vary this recipe by substituting another green vegetable, such as brussels sprouts or asparagus, for the zucchini.

1/2 pound zucchini, sliced into 1-inch rounds (2 cups)

1 tablespoon extra-virgin olive oil

1/8 teaspoon salt

1 tablespoon finely chopped fresh oregano, or 1/2 teaspoon dried, crushed

1/4 cup finely chopped parsley

1/4 cup finely chopped scallions

3/4 pound cherry tomatoes, stems removed (2 cups)

1. Steam the zucchini until crisp-tender, about 3 minutes.

2. Heat the olive oil in a large skillet over medium heat until fragrant. Add the salt, oregano, parsley, and scallions and cook until wilted.

3. Add the zucchini and tomatoes and cook, tossing gently, until heated through, about 2 to 3 minutes.

MAKES 4 SERVINGS

• EACH 1-CUP SERVING CONTAINS APPROXIMATELY:

CALORIES: 66 | FAT: 4 g | CHOLESTEROL: 0 | SODIUM: 86 mg | CARBOHYDRATES: 8 g | PROTEIN: 2 g

curried basmati rice

This rice is wonderful served with Lentil Dhal, which appears earlier in this chapter (page 300). For a complete Indian vegetarian meal, serve this fragrant rice with the Naan Bread (see page 298) and Cucumber Raita (see page 40) on the side.

3/4 cup basmati rice

1/2 cup sliced mushrooms

1/2 cup diced eggplant

1/2 cup diced zucchini

3/4 teaspoon curry powder

1 1/2 cups vegetable stock
(see page 56)

1. Rinse the rice and drain thoroughly.

2. Lightly spray a saucepan with non-stick cooking spray and place it over medium heat. Add the mushrooms, eggplant, and zucchini and cook, stirring frequently, for 5 minutes.

3. Add the rice and curry powder, and stir to coat the grains. Add the vegetable stock and bring to a boil. Reduce the heat to low, cover, and cook for 15 minutes, or until the water is absorbed. Remove from the heat and fluff the rice with a fork.

MAKES 3 CUPS, OR 6 SERVINGS

• EACH 1/2-CUP SERVING CONTAINS APPROXIMATELY:

CALORIES: 45 | FAT: **negligible** | CHOLESTEROL: 0 | SODIUM: 0 | CARBOHYDRATES: **10 g** | PROTEIN: **1 g**

creamy polenta

You can cook the cornmeal in stock or in a combination of stock and milk and add your favorite herbs or spices for variety. For a vegan side dish use vegetable stock, water, or juice. Polenta is delicious topped with cheese or mixed with sun-dried tomatoes. Leftover polenta can be formed into patties and browned on a griddle for hot corn cakes. They are wonderful for breakfast with maple or fruit syrup!

4 cups low-fat (1 percent) milk

1 cup cornmeal

pinch salt

pinch freshly ground black pepper

1/2 cup freshly grated parmesan cheese, optional

about polenta

Polenta is mush made from cornmeal and is a staple starch in northern Italy where it is often served as a first course. It can be eaten hot in its original cereal consistency or cooled, cut into squares, and browned in a skillet or on a grill.

1. Pour the milk into a saucepan and bring to a boil over medium heat. Slowly add the cornmeal, salt, and pepper, stirring constantly to prevent lumps. Reduce the heat to low and continue to cook for about 6 more minutes, stirring occasionally, or until the polenta is the consistency of Cream of Wheat.

2. To serve, allow 1/2 cup per serving and top with 1 tablespoon of Parmesan cheese, if desired.

MAKES 8 SERVINGS

315

• EACH 1/2-CUP SERVING CONTAINS APPROXIMATELY:

CALORIES: 147 | FAT: 4 g | CHOLESTEROL: 13 mg | SODIUM: 171 mg | CARBOHYDRATES: 20 g | PROTEIN: 8 g

wild rice

For variety try cooking wild rice in half orange juice and half stock or water. For more texture, toss a few toasted nuts or chopped crunchy vegetables into the cooked rice. Leftover rice can be dressed and served as a salad or added to soups.

3 cups fat-free chicken stock
(see page 54)

1 cup wild rice (5 1/2 ounces)

wild rice

Wild rice is not really a rice at all. It is a long-grain marsh grass native to the northern Great Lakes region of this country where it was very popular with the Native Americans. They called it manomin, meaning "good berry." It is now grown commercially in California and in several midwestern states. Wild rice is higher in protein than white rice and contains the amino acid lysine, not found in most other grains. It is first fermented at a warm temperature, then parched to caramelize and slightly brown the green seeds before threshing. It has a wonderful nutty flavor and a slightly chewy texture. Before cooking wild rice, it is important to clean it thoroughly by covering it with cold water. The debris will float to the top where it can easily be removed. Overcooking will destroy its chewy texture and make it mushy.

1. Pour the stock into a saucepan that has a tight-fitting lid and bring to a boil. Stir in the wild rice and reduce the heat to low. Cover and simmer for about 45 to 50 minutes, or until the rice kernels burst and are tender.

2. Remove from the heat and fluff with a fork.

MAKES 4 CUPS, OR 8 SERVINGS

316

• EACH 1/2-CUP SERVING CONTAINS APPROXIMATELY:

CALORIES: 78 | FAT: **negligible** | CHOLESTEROL: 0 | SODIUM: **121 mg** | CARBOHYDRATES: **15 g** | PROTEIN: 4 g

whole-wheat spaetzle

This light version of a classic German dish can be served as a side dish or can be added to soups or stews. It can also be topped with sauce just like a pasta. Spaetzle is a German side dish of tiny noodles or dumplings made with flour, salt, eggs, and water or milk. Nutmeg is often added for seasoning. The dough can be firm enough to be rolled out and cut into matchstick-size pieces, or soft enough to be forced through the large holes of a colander. The dough pieces are boiled before being tossed with butter or oil. In Germany this popular dish is often topped with gravy.

1/4 cup non-fat milk

2 egg whites

pinch salt

pinch nutmeg

1/2 cup whole-wheat flour

2 tablespoons all-purpose flour

2 quarts water

1/2 teaspoon extra-virgin olive oil

1 tablespoon chopped parsley

1 1/2 teaspoons chopped chives

pinch freshly ground black pepper

1. Pour the milk in a bowl. Add the egg whites, salt, and nutmeg and mix well.

2. Add in the flours and mix until smooth.

3. Bring the 2 quarts of water to boil in a saucepan. Using a rubber spatula, push the spaetzle mix through a colander with large holes into the boiling water. Cook the spaetzle until they rise to the surface. Remove with a slotted spoon.

4. In a large non-stick sauté pan over medium heat, cook the spaetzle in the olive oil until golden brown. Toss with the parsley, chives, and pepper. Serve immediately.

MAKES 4 SERVINGS

317

• EACH 1/4-CUP SERVING CONTAINS APPROXIMATELY:

CALORIES: 80 | FAT: negligible | CHOLESTEROL: negligible | SODIUM: 66 mg | CARBOHYDRATES: 15 g | PROTEIN: 4 g

sauces and spreads

All you really need to turn a piece of grilled fish, poultry, meat, or a plate of pasta into a memorable gourmet dish is a great-tasting sauce, and the following recipes are designed for just that purpose. The beauty of something as multi-purpose as the Low-Fat White Sauce is that it can easily be transformed into any flavor range desired, such as curry, mustard, paprika, or tomato. Our Marinara Sauce freezes so well that you can always have it on hand for spur-of-the-moment Canyon Ranch meals. It is not only good on pasta but can be used as a pizza topping or as a sauce on fish, poultry, or meat.

Even though sauces are of vital importance in Canyon Ranch menu planning this is a very short chapter because there are already sensational sauces incorporated into many of our recipes. Good examples are the Citrus Sauce served with the

Israeli Cabbage Rolls and the Roasted Red Pepper Sauce served over the Hummus in the Appetizers chapter; the Pesto served with the White Bean Soup; the vinaigrettes and the Blue Cheese Dressing in the Salads and Salad Dressings chapter; the Broiled Eggplant and Artichoke Sauce on the Linguini in the Vegetarian chapter; the Sorrel Sauce on the salmon in the Fish and Shellfish chapter; the Barbecue Sauce and Three Mustard Sauce in the Poultry chapter; the Port Wine Sauce on the Herb-Roasted Tenderloin of Beef and the Cucumber Sauce on the Zenzero Grilled Lamb Chops in the Meat chapter. Also there are the sauces that are most frequently served with certain dishes. These either follow the recipe, such as Light Rouille after Bouillabaisse, or are most appropriate in a particular chapter, such as Poultry Gravy found in the Poultry chapter.

cranberry concassé

This sensational condiment always creates a huge sensation at holiday time, but I like it so much that I serve it all year round. Recently I served it with turkey curry instead of the more traditional chutney, and all my guests asked for the recipe. Concassé, a French term, defines a mixture that is coarsely ground or chopped. In this recipe, however, the cranberries naturally break apart to create a similar texture.

3/4 cup water

1 1/2 cups sugar

3 whole cloves

3 whole allspice

2 cinnamon sticks

12 ounces fresh cranberries

1 tablespoon grated fresh orange zest

1. Combine the water, sugar, cloves, allspice, and cinnamon sticks in a large saucepan and bring to a boil over medium heat. Cook, stirring constantly, until the syrup is clear, about 3 minutes. Add the cranberries and cook for about 5 more minutes, or until the cranberries begin to pop.

2. Remove from the heat and stir in the grated orange zest.

3. Cool to room temperature and then refrigerate, tightly covered, for at least 3 days before serving.

MAKES 2 1/2 CUPS

320

• EACH 2-TABLESPOON SERVING CONTAINS APPROXIMATELY:

CALORIES: 66 | FAT: 0 | CHOLESTEROL: 0 | SODIUM: negligible | CARBOHYDRATES: 18 g | PROTEIN: negligible

mango or papaya salsa

This tasty tropical fruit salsa is a refreshing change from the more usual tomato varieties. It is particularly good served with fish and poultry dishes and can be used as a dressing on fruit salads.

2 cups peeled and diced mango or papaya

1 shallot, minced

1 garlic clove, pressed or minced

2 tablespoons chopped cilantro leaves

1/4 cup canned diced green chiles

1 tablespoon rice vinegar

2 teaspoons fresh lime juice

Combine all the ingredients and mix well. Cover tightly and refrigerate until ready to use.

MAKES ABOUT 2 CUPS

321

• EACH 1/4-CUP SERVING CONTAINS APPROXIMATELY:

CALORIES: 41 | FAT: negligible | CHOLESTEROL: 0 | SODIUM: 7 mg | CARBOHYDRATES: 10 g | PROTEIN: negligible

gingered carrot sauce or dressing

This colorful concoction meets every recipe criteria our guests request. It's great-tasting, versatile, and healthful. Plus, its vibrant color makes even the most mundane-looking dish more attractive. Serve it as a sauce on grilled fish, poultry, meat, and vegetables, or as a light dressing on salads of all types. You can change the whole personality of this sauce just by substituting another oil. For more of a pure ginger-carrot flavor use canola oil. For an entirely different taste range, use walnut or extra-virgin olive oil. Or omit the oil entirely and serve this, hot or cold, as a tasty and unusual soup that can be made in minutes. Lastly, this adds enormously to the nutritional profile of anything it's served on because it is extremely high in vitamin A and an excellent source of fiber.

8 ounces new potatoes

1 cup fresh carrot juice

1 tablespoon finely chopped fresh gingerroot

¼ teaspoon salt

1 teaspoon dark sesame oil

322

1. Put the potatoes in a saucepan and cover with water. Cook over high heat until the water comes to a boil. Reduce the heat to low and simmer until the potatoes can be pierced easily with a fork, about 14 minutes. Drain and let cool.
2. Pour the carrot juice into a blender. Add the potatoes, ginger, and salt and puree. Slowly add the oil while the blender is running. Serve warm as a sauce or refrigerate and use as a salad dressing.

MAKES 2 CUPS

• EACH ¼-CUP SERVING CONTAINS APPROXIMATELY:

CALORIES: 40 | FAT: negligible | CHOLESTEROL: 0 | SODIUM: 77 mg | CARBOHYDRATES: 8 g | PROTEIN: negligible

tomato salsa

This fresh tomato salsa, often called pico de gallo, is a staple in Mexican cuisine. It is served with almost everything, and bowls of it are usually found on the table, along with chips, in all Mexican restaurants. If you prefer a hotter salsa, add more jalapeño; if you don't like hot sauces, omit it. At Canyon Ranch we always have salsa on our salad bar. Also, it is often served with baked corn chips as an appetizer on Southwestern menus.

6 medium tomatoes (2 pounds), diced (4 cups)

1 medium onion, diced (1½ cups)

¼ cup finely chopped cilantro leaves

1 jalapeño pepper, seeded and finely chopped, or to taste

1 garlic clove, pressed or minced

1½ teaspoons dried oregano, crushed

½ teaspoon ground cumin

¼ teaspoon salt

¼ teaspoon freshly ground black pepper

1 tablespoon fresh lemon juice

1 tablespoon fresh lime juice

1. Combine all the ingredients in a large bowl and mix well.
2. Cover tightly and refrigerate for at least 2 hours before serving.

MAKES 6 CUPS

• EACH ¼-CUP SERVING CONTAINS APPROXIMATELY:

CALORIES: 22 | FAT: negligible | CHOLESTEROL: 0 | SODIUM: 98 mg | CARBOHYDRATES: 5 g | PROTEIN: negligible

low-fat white sauce

This sensational low-fat white sauce can be used to replace the white sauce called for in any recipe. It takes longer to thicken than white sauce made with higher-fat milk, but it's worth the wait for the enormous reduction in both calories and fat.

2 teaspoons corn oil margarine or butter

1 tablespoon all-purpose flour

12 ounces canned evaporated skim milk, heated to simmering

1/4 teaspoon salt

1. Melt the margarine or butter in a saucepan over low heat. Add the flour and cook, stirring constantly, for 2 full minutes, being careful not to brown the flour.

2. Remove from the heat and add the simmering milk, stirring constantly with a wire whisk.

3. Add the salt and return the sauce to low heat. Cook slowly, stirring occasionally, for about 20 to 30 minutes, or until thickened.

MAKES 1 1/4 CUPS

325

• EACH 1/4-CUP SERVING CONTAINS APPROXIMATELY:

CALORIES: 72 | FAT: 2 g | CHOLESTEROL: 7 mg | SODIUM: 200 mg | CARBOHYDRATES: 9 g | PROTEIN: 5 g

marinara sauce

This sauce is even better if made a day or two before you plan to use it. Also, because it freezes well, you may want to double or triple the recipe and store it, tightly covered, in the freezer. It will keep for several months and is wonderful to have on hand for unexpected guests.

1 cup chopped onion

1 tablespoon minced garlic

1 teaspoon finely chopped fresh oregano

3/4 teaspoon finely chopped fresh basil

1 bay leaf

1/2 teaspoon freshly ground black pepper

1/2 cup vegetable stock (see page 56)

2 cups sliced fresh mushrooms

3 cups canned tomato sauce

2 cups canned tomato puree

1. Combine the onion, garlic, oregano, basil, bay leaf, pepper, and stock in a large saucepan and cook until the onion is soft and translucent. Add the mushrooms and cook for 5 more minutes.

2. Stir in the tomato sauce and puree. Cover and simmer over low heat for at least 1 hour. Remove the bay leaf before serving over pasta.

MAKES 3 CUPS

• EACH 1/2-CUP SERVING CONTAINS APPROXIMATELY:

CALORIES: **50** | FAT: **negligible** | CHOLESTEROL: **11 mg** | SODIUM: **395 mg** | CARBOHYDRATES: **11 g** | PROTEIN: **2 g**

pesto sauce

Pesto is an uncooked Italian sauce that originated in the city of Genoa. It is classically made with fresh basil, garlic, pine nuts, Parmesan cheese, and olive oil. This dairy-free variation substitutes miso for the cheese and was created for our vegan menus by John Luzader, the executive chef at the Canyon Ranch in Tucson. We usually serve this sauce over pasta, but it is also a delicious topping for rice and vegetables and an unusual dip.

1 garlic clove, pressed or minced

1 tablespoon pine nuts, roasted

1/2 cup chopped fresh basil leaves

1/2 cup chopped fresh spinach leaves

2 cups chopped parsley leaves

2 1/2 tablespoons brown rice miso

1/2 tablespoon extra-virgin olive oil

1 tablespoon vegetable stock
(see page 56)

1. Spray a small skillet with non-stick cooking spray. Add the garlic and cook over low heat until just golden. Do not overcook.

2. Combine the garlic, pine nuts, basil, spinach, parsley, and miso in a blender and blend until smooth.

3. With the machine running, slowly add the olive oil and vegetable stock.

MAKES ABOUT 1 1/2 CUPS

• EACH 1/4-CUP SERVING CONTAINS APPROXIMATELY:

CALORIES: 460 | FAT: 4 g | CHOLESTEROL: 0 | SODIUM: 278 mg | CARBOHYDRATES: 91 g | PROTEIN: 16 g

puttanesca sauce

The name puttanesca is a derivation of *puttana,* which in Italian means "ladies of the evening." According to legend, the name comes from the fact that the intense fragrance of this sauce was like a siren's call to the men seeking their favors. Classically, this spicy sauce, usually served over pasta, includes anchovies. This recipe does not so that we can include it on our vegetarian menus. Using already pitted kalamata olives will save you time when making this sauce.

¼ cup finely chopped garlic

¾ cup diced onion

½ cup dry red wine

4 medium tomatoes (1⅓ pounds), peeled and diced (2½ cups)

10 kalamata olives, pitted and thinly sliced

1 teaspoon grated or finely chopped orange zest

¼ teaspoon dried thyme, crushed

2 tablespoons tomato paste

6 tablespoons freshly grated parmesan cheese

1. Lightly spray a medium skillet with non-stick cooking spray. Add the garlic and onion and cook over medium heat until the onion is soft and translucent.
2. Add the red wine and deglaze the skillet by cooking until the skillet is almost dry. Add the tomatoes, olives, orange zest, thyme, and tomato paste. Cook for 25 minutes, or until slightly thickened and the consistency of tomato sauce. Stir in the Parmesan cheese.

MAKES 3 CUPS

328

• EACH ½-CUP SERVING CONTAINS APPROXIMATELY:

CALORIES: 75 | FAT: 3 g | CHOLESTEROL: 4 mg | SODIUM: 175 mg | CARBOHYDRATES: 8 g | PROTEIN: 3 g

spicy peanut sauce

We serve this piquant sauce on cold Asian-style soba noodles in our low-calorie rendition of Szechuan Noodles with Spicy Peanut Sauce on page 125. It also makes a wonderful dip for Indonesian satés, and you can find one in the Poultry chapter, on page 236. If you prefer a milder sauce, use less red pepper flakes. If stored tightly covered in the refrigerator, this sauce will keep well for at least a week.

1½ teaspoons cornstarch

⅔ cup water

⅓ cup rice vinegar

⅓ cup unhomogenized smooth peanut butter (see below)

2 tablespoons reduced-sodium soy sauce

¼ teaspoon dark sesame oil

4 garlic cloves, minced

2 teaspoons sugar

1 teaspoon crushed red pepper flakes, or to taste

1. Combine the cornstarch and water in a saucepan and stir until the cornstarch is completely dissolved. Bring to a boil, reduce the heat, and stir constantly until thickened. Remove the pan from the heat and set aside to cool to room temperature.

2. Combine all the remaining ingredients in a blender and puree. Add the puree to the cooled cornstarch mixture and mix well with a whisk.

MAKES 1½ CUPS

unhomogenized peanut butter
You can make your own unhomogenized peanut butter by grinding roasted skinned peanuts in a food processor to the desired consistency, either chunky or satin smooth. In fact, it is the best way to always have truly fresh-tasting peanut butter for any use. One cup of peanuts will yield about ½ cup of peanut butter. Stored, tightly covered, in the refrigerator, it will last for several weeks — provided you don't have any real peanut-butter lovers in the house!

329

• EACH 2-TABLESPOON SERVING CONTAINS APPROXIMATELY:

CALORIES: 50 | FAT: 3 g | CHOLESTEROL: 0 | SODIUM: 102 mg | CARBOHYDRATES: 3 g | PROTEIN: 2 g

sweet yellow pepper sauce

At Canyon Ranch we serve this fruit and vegetable mélange over a colored pasta such as spinach or basil. It is also an excellent sauce on vegetables, fish, and poultry. It can even be served as a soup! If yellow bell peppers are not available, use red bell peppers.

1¹/₂ teaspoons olive oil

4 yellow bell peppers, seeded and chopped

²/₃ cup thinly sliced carrots

1 cup canned tomatoes, drained and diced

¹/₃ cup tomato puree

1 teaspoon minced garlic

¹/₈ teaspoon freshly ground black pepper

¹/₂ cup peeled and chopped fresh pears

¹/₂ teaspoon finely chopped fresh basil

1. Heat the olive oil in a large skillet over medium heat. Add the peppers and carrots and cook, stirring, until soft.
2. Add all the remaining ingredients and simmer for 30 minutes, or until the vegetables are soft.
3. Pour the mixture into a blender and puree.

MAKES 4 CUPS

330

• EACH ¹/₂-CUP SERVING CONTAINS APPROXIMATELY:

CALORIES: 40 | FAT: 1 g | CHOLESTEROL: 0 | SODIUM: 56 mg | CARBOHYDRATES: 6 g | PROTEIN: 56 g

tomato olive sauce

This zesty sauce serves as an accompaniment to Grilled Vegetable Strudel on page 176. It is also an excellent topping on other vegetable dishes, pasta, rice, grilled fish, poultry, or meat. Unlike so many other sauces, it has little fat and much flavor. It will keep for at least 1 week if stored, tightly covered, in the refrigerator.

1 medium red onion, cut into ⅛-inch-thick rounds

4 plum tomatoes, seeded and quartered

1 teaspoon extra-virgin olive oil

1 garlic clove, pressed or minced

¼ cup vegetable stock (see page 56)

1 tablespoon pitted and chopped kalamata olives

1 teaspoon balsamic vinegar

pinch salt

pinch freshly ground black pepper

1 tablespoon chopped fresh basil leaves

1. Prepare the grill or preheat the broiler. Grill or broil the onion slices for about 8 minutes, turning as needed for even browning. Add the tomatoes and continue to grill or broil for about 3 more minutes, or until tender.

2. Put the grilled vegetables in a blender and puree. Strain the puree into a small saucepan and bring to a simmer. Cook over low heat for 10 to 15 minutes, or until thickened.

3. Heat the olive oil in a medium skillet and cook the garlic until soft. Add the puree and all the remaining ingredients and cook until heated through.

MAKES 1½ CUPS

331

• EACH ¼-CUP SERVING CONTAINS APPROXIMATELY:

CALORIES: 10 | FAT: negligible | CHOLESTEROL: 0 | SODIUM: 80 mg | CARBOHYDRATES: 2 g | PROTEIN: negligible

roasted garlic spread

This fat-free, smooth-textured, and aromatic spread is a great substitute for butter and other high-fat toppings frequently used on bread and baked potatoes, and it is a tasty addition to many other dishes.

2 large heads garlic

2 teaspoons extra-virgin olive oil

garlic

Garlic, a member of the lily family, is a cousin to onions, leeks, chives, and shallots. The bulb, which grows beneath the ground, is made up of cloves ranging from 1/2 to 1 1/2 inches in size. The Paul Bunyanesque white-skinned elephant garlic has bulbs the size of a large orange and huge cloves, averaging about 1 ounce each. The most popular garlic is the white-skinned, strongly flavored American garlic. The lavender-skinned Mexican garlic has a milder flavor, and elephant garlic is the mildest of all. Garlic has been used for a variety of medicinal purposes for centuries, and it was fed to the Egyptian slaves building the giant pyramids to provide and prolong greater physical strength. The only negative comment that can be made about garlic is that its essential oils permeate the lung tissue, causing it to remain with the body for hours after it's eaten, affecting both breath and skin odor.

1. Preheat the oven to 350°F.

2. Slice the tops off both heads of garlic and place the heads, cut side up, in a small baking pan. Drizzle 1 teaspoon of the olive oil over the top of each head.

3. Cover the pan with aluminum foil and bake in the preheated oven for 30 minutes. Remove the foil and bake, uncovered, for 15 to 30 minutes more, or until the garlic is a soft, spreadable consistency when squeezed from the cloves.

MAKES ABOUT 6 TABLESPOONS

332

• EACH 1-TABLESPOON SERVING CONTAINS APPROXIMATELY:

CALORIES: 36 | FAT: 1 g | CHOLESTEROL: 0 | SODIUM: 3 mg | CARBOHYDRATES: 5 g | PROTEIN: negligible

quick breads
and breakfast treats

At Canyon Ranch our emphasis is on whole-grain rather than refined flours in all of our baked goods. This is because they contain the valuable vitamins, minerals, and fiber that are all removed in the refining process. In the nineteenth century the roller mill was invented, and the British were able to produce a pure white flour by removing the germ and the outside bran coating of the wheat kernel, leaving only the endosperm, or soft white center portion of the kernel. This new white bread was very expensive to produce and was in such limited supply that only royalty and the upper classes could afford it. Therefore, it was the peasants who were eating the dark, rough, whole-grain breads and they were all much healthier than the upper classes who were eating the refined bread. To this day this rough bread is called peasant bread.

Wheat, although certainly the most popular and often-used grain, is certainly not the whole grain story. There are many other healthy and tasty grains available that are excellent for both cereals and breads, such as cornmeal, rolled oats, and kashi, which combines 7 grains with sesame seeds.

Most of the bread recipes in this chapter are for quick breads rather than yeast breads. The name, quick breads, comes from the fact that they are so much quicker to make than yeast breads. Quick breads don't require any kneading or any time to rise because they contain baking powder or baking soda instead of yeast. You can now have easy-to-make quick breads whenever you want to just by using the recipes in this chapter.

It's important to start the day with enough calories and carbohydrates to give you the energy for all your morning activities. At Canyon Ranch we recommend that breakfast be centered around a high complex carbohydrate such as whole-grain bread, muffins, waffles, pancakes, or cereal accompanied by fruit. A glass of non-fat or low-fat milk or a carton of non-fat yogurt can provide a healthy portion of the calcium and protein you need daily.

One of our most popular breakfast menus includes Gingerbread Pancakes served with Fresh Apple Butter and Fitness Cheese and another is Banana Waffles with Maple Walnut Syrup and grilled banana.

I have included many of our other breakfast favorites — quick breads, muffins, pancakes, and waffles, and a handful of wonderful spreads. Also, in the Beverages chapter you will find healthy drinks that offer satisfying ways to start the day, such as a Banana Yogurt Smoothie (see page 411) and an Orange Shake (see page 409).

banana bread

Whenever you find that you have too many bananas getting ripe at the same time, it is a good idea to make a loaf or two of this delicious bread. It freezes well, and for added convenience, slice it first and freeze each slice in a separate plastic bag. When you're in a hurry in the morning, just pop a slice of frozen banana bread in the microwave for about 30 seconds. The easiest way to cut any standard-size loaf into 16 equal slices is to first cut the bread in half, then cut each half in half again into 4 pieces, which you will cut in half again into 8 pieces and again in half to 16 slices.

3 ripe bananas, mashed (about 2 cups)

1¹/₂ teaspoons vanilla extract

1 large egg, lightly beaten

¹/₄ cup fructose

1¹/₄ cups whole-wheat flour

2 teaspoons baking powder

2 tablespoons melted corn oil margarine

bananas

Bananas are one of the few fruits that develop better flavor when allowed to ripen after picking. This is a fabulous attribute since they grow only in tropical climates and must be picked and shipped green. Bananas are low in fat and rich in both potassium and vitamin C. Ripen bananas by storing, uncovered, at room temperature (about 70°F.). Ripe bananas will keep for several days in the refrigerator; the peel will turn brown but the flesh will remain unchanged. Overripe bananas can be peeled, sliced, and stored in Ziploc bags in the freezer.

1. Preheat the oven to 350°F.

2. Lightly spray a 5 x 9-inch loaf pan with non-stick cooking spray.

3. Combine the bananas, vanilla, egg, and fructose in a large bowl and mix well. In another bowl combine the flour and baking powder and mix well.

4. Add the flour mixture to the banana mixture and mix lightly. Add the melted margarine and mix just until moistened.

5. Pour the batter into the prepared pan and bake in the preheated oven for 45 minutes to 1 hour, or until a knife inserted in the center comes out clean.

6. Remove the bread from the pan and cool on a wire rack for at least 30 minutes before slicing.

MAKES 16 SERVINGS

337

• **EACH SERVING CONTAINS APPROXIMATELY:**

CALORIES: 85 | FAT: 2 g | CHOLESTEROL: 13 mg | SODIUM: 89 mg | CARBOHYDRATES: 15 g | PROTEIN: 2 g

canyon ranch bread

We have been serving this coarse-textured, low-fat bread since the day we opened in Tucson. It is so popular with our guests that many of them order loaves of it to take home with them when they leave. It is especially good toasted and spread with a little of our Fitness Cheese or Fresh Apple Butter, both of which appear further along in this chapter. I like to store individual slices in sealed bags in the freezer. Just pop a frozen slice in the toaster for an instant breakfast treat.

1½ cups whole-wheat flour

1 cup unprocessed wheat bran

1 tablespoon baking powder

¼ teaspoon baking soda

3 tablespoons fructose

1 teaspoon ground cinnamon

⅓ cup raisins

1½ cups buttermilk

1 egg

1 tablespoon vanilla extract

1. Preheat the oven to 350°F.

2. Spray a standard-size (9 x 5-inch) loaf pan with non-stick cooking spray.

3. Combine the flour, bran, baking powder, baking soda, fructose, and cinnamon in a large bowl and mix well. Add the raisins and mix again.

4. Combine the buttermilk, egg, and vanilla in another bowl and mix.

5. Pour the liquid ingredients into the dry ingredients and mix until moist.

6. Spoon the mixture into the prepared loaf pan and bake in the preheated oven for 45 to 50 minutes, or until a knife inserted in the center comes out clean. Place the bread, while still in the pan, on its side on a wire rack to cool.

7. Store, tightly covered, in the refrigerator.

MAKES 18 SLICES

about unprocessed bran
THE WHEAT BERRY
The wheat kernel, commonly called a wheat berry, is made up of 3 distinct layers: bran, germ, and endosperm. Bran is the outer layer; it has little nutritional value but is a great source of fiber. The germ, essentially the embryo of the berry, is a concentrated source of vitamins, minerals, and protein. The endosperm, which makes up the major part of the kernel, is full of starch, protein, niacin, and iron. This good source of fiber can be found in most supermarkets in the cereal section, as can wheat germ. They are both available in all health food stores.

338

• EACH SLICE CONTAINS APPROXIMATELY:

CALORIES: **80** | FAT: **negligible** | CHOLESTEROL: **16 mg** | SODIUM: **110 mg** | CARBOHYDRATES: **13 g** | PROTEIN: **2 g**

hazelnut bread

The toasted hazelnuts give this quick bread a marvelous taste and texture. It is a great breakfast bread, but it's also wonderful toasted and served with other meals. Applesauce is used in this recipe to replace most of the fat usually found in breads of this type. The chopped pear adds moisture as well as taste to the bread.

2 cups unbleached all-purpose flour

3/4 cup hazelnuts, toasted and skinned (see box)

3/4 cup brown sugar

1 teaspoon baking powder

1/2 teaspoon baking soda

1/2 teaspoon salt

2 egg whites

1 tablespoon canola oil

6 tablespoons unsweetened applesauce

1 whole pear, peeled and coarsely chopped

1/4 cup water

hazelnuts

Hazelnuts grow in clusters on hazel trees around the world. Most of them used to come from Europe; however, many are now grown in Oregon and Washington. They have a fuzzy outer husk that opens as the nut ripens, revealing a hard, smooth shell. The bitter brown skin is best removed by first heating in a 350°F. oven for 15 minutes to loosen the skin and then rolling the nuts vigorously in a dish towel to remove the loosened skins.

1. Preheat the oven to 350°F.

2. Spray a standard-size (9 x 5-inch) loaf pan with non-stick cooking spray.

3. Combine the flour, hazelnuts, brown sugar, baking powder, baking soda, and salt in a food processor and process for about 1 minute, or until the nuts are finely chopped.

4. Add all the remaining ingredients to the food processor and process until blended. Pour the batter into the prepared loaf pan.

5. Bake in the preheated oven for about 50 to 60 minutes, or until a knife inserted in the center comes out clean.

6. Allow to cool for 20 to 30 minutes on a wire rack before removing the bread from the pan. Allow to cool for 30 more minutes before cutting into 16 slices.

MAKES 16 SERVINGS

339

• EACH SERVING CONTAINS APPROXIMATELY:

CALORIES: **145** | FAT: **3 g** | CHOLESTEROL: **0** | SODIUM: **300 mg** | CARBOHYDRATES: **28 g** | PROTEIN: **3 g**

jalapeño corn bread

This tasty Southwestern corn bread has a real bite. It is perfect with grilled dishes and makes an outstanding savory bread pudding or dressing for poultry.

4¹/₂ tablespoons sugar

pinch salt

2 tablespoons non-fat dry milk

¹/₂ tablespoon corn syrup

3 tablespoons corn oil margarine

1 egg

6 tablespoons water

¹/₂ cup yellow cornmeal

1¹/₄ cups unbleached all-purpose flour

2 tablespoons baking powder

1 tablespoon minced jalapeño peppers, rinsed if canned

jalapeño peppers
Jalapeño chile peppers are named after Jalapa, the capital of the state of Veracruz in Mexico. When fresh, they are small, about 2 inches long and 3/4 inch in diameter, smooth-skinned, a dark green color, and range from hot to very hot. The seeds and veins are the hottest part of the chile and can easily be removed if you want a milder flavor. It is best to wear gloves when handling hot peppers of any type because they can irritate your skin, and if you rub your eyes while handling them, they will burn for hours.

1. Preheat the oven to 325°F.

2. Lightly spray a 9-inch-square baking pan with non-stick cooking spray.

3. Combine the sugar, salt, dry milk, corn syrup, and margarine in a bowl. Using an electric mixer, beat until well blended.

4. Add the egg and water and mix until smooth.

5. In a separate bowl combine all the remaining ingredients, mix well, and add to the batter. Mix until smooth.

6. Spoon the batter into the prepared baking pan. Bake in the preheated oven for 35 minutes, or until golden brown and a knife inserted in the center comes out clean.

7. Remove from the oven and cool on a wire rack. To serve, cut into 24 pieces, each about 2¹/₄ x 1¹/₂ inches in size.

MAKES 24 SERVINGS

340

• EACH SERVING CONTAINS APPROXIMATELY:

CALORIES: 55 | FAT: 1 g | CHOLESTEROL: 5 mg | SODIUM: 115 mg | CARBOHYDRATES: 9 g | PROTEIN: 1 g

zucchini bread

This low-fat, whole-wheat zucchini bread is both lower in calories and higher in fiber than most similar quick breads. The addition of pineapple adds a subtle flavor as well as moisture. I recommend doubling this recipe because the bread is so versatile, easy to make, and freezes extremely well. If tightly sealed, it will keep for several months in the freezer.

1½ cups whole-wheat flour

½ cup fructose

1 teaspoon baking powder

½ teaspoon baking soda

¼ teaspoon cinnamon

¼ teaspoon nutmeg

¼ teaspoon ground cloves

1 egg

1 egg white

3 tablespoons corn oil

1¼ cups grated and well-packed zucchini

1 teaspoon vanilla extract

½ cup well-drained canned crushed pineapple

pure crystalline fructose
Fructose is a natural fruit sugar that is one-third sweeter than sucrose, or ordinary table sugar. It comes in both granulated and syrup forms. However, pure crystalline fructose, which is 100 percent fructose, is what we use at Canyon Ranch. It is absorbed more slowly by the body than sucrose and therefore does not cause the equivalent sharp rise and fall in blood sugar which tends to cause spurts of energy followed by fatigue in some people.

1. Preheat the oven to 350°F.

2. Spray a standard-size (9 x 5-inch) loaf pan with non-stick cooking spray.

3. Combine the flour, fructose, baking powder, baking soda, cinnamon, nutmeg, and cloves in a large bowl and mix well.

4. In another bowl combine all the remaining ingredients and mix well.

5. Add the wet ingredients to the dry ingredients and mix just until combined. Pour into the prepared loaf pan and bake in the preheated oven for 50 to 60 minutes, or until a knife inserted in the center comes out clean.

6. Remove from the oven and cool on a wire rack for at least 30 minutes before slicing.

MAKES 16 SLICES

341

• EACH SLICE CONTAINS APPROXIMATELY:

CALORIES: **89** | FAT: **3 g** | CHOLESTEROL: **13 mg** | SODIUM: **71 mg** | CARBOHYDRATES: **14 g** | PROTEIN: **2 g**

bran muffins

Bran muffins are popular for breakfast at Canyon Ranch, especially when spread with our Fitness Cheese (see page 361). They freeze well, so you may want to double the recipe when you make them to have some on hand in your freezer for unexpected breakfast guests.

1 cup whole-wheat flour

1 teaspoon baking soda

¼ teaspoon salt

1½ cups unprocessed wheat bran

3 tablespoons melted margarine

¼ cup blackstrap molasses

1 large egg, lightly beaten

1½ cups buttermilk

½ cup raisins

342

1. Preheat the oven to 375°F.

2. Lightly spray muffin pans with non-stick cooking spray or line them with paper liners.

3. Combine all the dry ingredients in a bowl and mix well. In another bowl combine all the other ingredients, except the raisins, and mix well.

4. Add the liquid ingredients to the dry ingredients and stir just until the dry ingredients are moistened. Do not overmix.

5. Stir in the raisins and fill the prepared muffin pans three-fourths full with the batter.

6. Bake in the preheated oven for 15 to 20 minutes, or until a knife inserted in the center of a muffin comes out clean. Let the muffins cool slightly before removing them from the tin.

MAKES 12 MUFFINS

• EACH MUFFIN CONTAINS APPROXIMATELY:

CALORIES: **140** | FAT: **4 g** | CHOLESTEROL: **9 mg** | SODIUM: **240 mg** | CARBOHYDRATES: **17 g** | PROTEIN: **3 g**

basic fruit muffins

Any diced fruit can be used in this recipe. This includes fresh, canned, and frozen fruit. When using canned fruit, drain it thoroughly before adding it to the other ingredients. Frozen fruit does not have to be thawed. In fact, when it's added frozen, it thaws and plumps up during the cooking process and makes more attractive muffins.

3/4 cup whole-wheat flour

3/4 cup unbleached all-purpose flour

1/4 cup fructose

2 teaspoons baking powder

1/4 teaspoon salt

1 large egg

2/3 cup non-fat milk

2 tablespoons melted corn oil margarine

3/4 cup diced fruit

1/2 teaspoon grated lemon zest

unbleached flour
Like all refined white flour, unbleached all-purpose flour is the ground endosperm of the wheat kernel and contains none of the bran or the germ. The baking qualities of this white flour tend to improve as it ages or matures. Bleaching can bring about similar changes without aging. The trade-off with bleaching is that it destroys nutrients, such as vitamin E, in the process.

1. Preheat the oven to 350°F.

2. Spray 12 muffin cups with non-stick cooking spray or line them with paper liners.

3. Thoroughly mix the flours, fructose, baking powder, and salt in a medium bowl.

4. In another bowl lightly beat the egg, then whisk in the milk and margarine. Pour over the dry ingredients. Add the fruit and grated lemon zest and stir just until mixed.

5. Fill each muffin cup three-fourths full. Bake in the preheated oven for 15 to 20 minutes, or until lightly browned on the top. Let the muffins cool slightly before removing them from the tin.

MAKES 12 MUFFINS

343

• EACH MUFFIN CONTAINS APPROXIMATELY:

CALORIES: **130** | FAT: **3 g** | CHOLESTEROL: **22 mg** | SODIUM: **234 mg** | CARBOHYDRATES: **23 g** | PROTEIN: **3 g**

lime coffee cake

This is a wonderful breakfast coffee cake which can also be served with salads as a luncheon bread.

1 3/4 cups all-purpose flour

2 1/4 teaspoons baking powder

1/2 teaspoon salt

3 tablespoons butter

3 tablespoons canola oil

1 cup sugar

4 egg whites

2/3 cup buttermilk

1 tablespoon fresh lime juice

1 1/2 teaspoons grated lime zest

1 teaspoon vanilla extract

1. Preheat the oven to 350°F.

2. Lightly spray a standard-size (9 x 5-inch) loaf pan with non-stick cooking spray.

3. Combine the flour, baking powder, and salt in a medium bowl and set aside.

4. In another bowl combine the butter, oil, and sugar and mix until smooth. Add the egg whites and beat with an electric mixer until the batter is smooth.

5. Alternately add the flour and buttermilk to the egg mixture, ending with flour. Add the lime juice, grated lime zest, and vanilla and mix until smooth. Pour into the prepared loaf pan.

6. Bake in the preheated oven for 35 to 45 minutes, or until the top is golden brown. Remove from the oven and cool in the pan on a rack for at least 10 minutes before slicing.

MAKES 16 SLICES

344

• EACH SLICE CONTAINS APPROXIMATELY:

CALORIES: **145** | FAT: **4 g** | CHOLESTEROL: **4 mg** | SODIUM: **194 mg** | CARBOHYDRATES: **24 g** | PROTEIN: **2 g**

light popovers

When making these popovers for breakfast I often add a teaspoon of ground cinnamon to the ingredients and serve them with honey or maple syrup. They are also good split and topped with any leftover as a hot entree or served cold stuffed with a salad. Use your imagination and create your own popover specialties. These popovers can be made ahead of time and frozen very successfully. First cool them to room temperature. Then wrap each popover tightly in plastic wrap or aluminum foil before freezing. To serve, unwrap them, place them on a baking sheet, and bake in a preheated 350°F. oven for about 15 minutes.

5 egg whites

1 cup low-fat (2 percent) milk, at room temperature

1 cup all-purpose flour

2 tablespoons corn oil margarine or butter, melted

346

1. Preheat the oven to 450°F.

2. Grease a popover pan or 6 large custard cups, 3 1/2 inches in diameter, with corn oil margarine or butter, being careful to cover the entire inner surface. Lightly dust with all-purpose flour and place on a baking sheet.

3. Combine all the ingredients in a blender and blend at medium speed for 15 seconds. Do not overmix.

4. Divide the batter evenly in the prepared pan or among the custard cups and bake in the preheated oven for 20 minutes. Reduce the heat to 350°F. and bake for 25 more minutes. Pierce the side of each popover with a sharp knife and bake for 5 more minutes.

MAKES 6 SERVINGS

• EACH SERVING CONTAINS APPROXIMATELY:

CALORIES: **139** | FAT: **4 g** | CHOLESTEROL: **2 mg** | SODIUM: **109 mg** | CARBOHYDRATES: **18 g** | PROTEIN: **5 g**

french toast

Everyone loves French toast, and the addition of the fruit butter in this recipe makes it even more appealing. There is no added fat in this recipe and using 2 whole eggs and 2 egg whites instead of 3 whole eggs also lowers both the fat and the cholesterol. Using whole-wheat sourdough bread increases the nutrients and the fiber.

¼ cup non-fat milk

½ cup buttermilk

2 eggs

2 egg whites

pinch cinnamon

pinch nutmeg

8 slices whole-wheat sourdough bread
(1 ounce each)

1 cup pineapple peach butter
(see page 360)

8 whole strawberries, cut into fans,
for garnish, optional

348

1. Combine the milk, buttermilk, eggs, egg whites, and spices in a bowl and mix well.

2. Arrange the bread slices in a single layer on a baking sheet or in a shallow dish and pierce liberally with the tines of a fork.

3. Pour the liquid over the bread and allow to stand until absorbed.

4. Cook each slice on a hot grill sprayed with non-stick cooking spray or under a broiler until golden brown on both sides.

5. Divide each slice in half diagonally and place on a warm plate.

6. Spoon 2 tablespoons of pineapple peach butter over the top of each slice and garnish with a fanned strawberry if desired.

MAKES 8 SERVINGS

• EACH 1-SLICE SERVING WITH 2 TABLESPOONS OF PINEAPPLE PEACH BUTTER CONTAINS APPROXIMATELY:

CALORIES: 335 | FAT: 3 g | CHOLESTEROL: 54 mg | SODIUM: 191 mg | CARBOHYDRATES: 73 g | PROTEIN: 8 g

apple pancakes

These pancakes are wonderful served with Fresh Apple Butter (see page 359) and Fitness Cheese (see page 361). In fact, this dish can also be served as a healthy alternative for dessert. Golden Delicious apples are called for in this recipe because they are so sweet. If not available, however, other apple varieties can be substituted.

2¹/2 cups all-purpose flour

1 cup whole-wheat pastry flour

¹/4 cup fructose

1 tablespoon baking powder

2 teaspoons baking soda

pinch cinnamon

2 eggs

2 egg whites

2 cups buttermilk

2 tablespoons margarine, melted

3 medium golden delicious apples, cored and diced

1. Combine the flours, fructose, baking powder, baking soda, and cinnamon in a bowl and mix well.

2. In a separate bowl combine the eggs and egg whites and beat lightly. Add the buttermilk and mix well.

3. Add the wet ingredients to the flour mixture and stir until well moistened. Add the melted margarine and apples and mix until just combined.

4. Spray a hot skillet or griddle with non-stick cooking spray. Pour the batter, 3 tablespoons at a time, onto the griddle. Cook until the top of each pancake is covered with tiny bubbles and the bottom is browned. Turn and brown the other side.

349

MAKES 30 PANCAKES

• EACH 3-PANCAKE SERVING CONTAINS APPROXIMATELY:

CALORIES: 230 | FAT: 4 g | CHOLESTEROL: 26 mg | SODIUM: 470 mg | CARBOHYDRATES: 43 g | PROTEIN: 7 g

gingerbread pancakes

I developed these sugar-free gingerbread pancakes for our breakfast menu many years ago, and every time we take them off the menu returning guests always ask for them. They are easy to make and can be frozen and reheated for an instant breakfast or snack at home. We serve them with our Fresh Apple Butter and Fitness Cheese.

1 cup whole-wheat flour

3/4 teaspoon baking soda

1/2 teaspoon ground ginger

1/2 teaspoon ground cinnamon

1/4 teaspoon ground cloves

1/4 teaspoon salt

2 teaspoons instant decaffeinated coffee powder

1/4 cup hot water

1 egg, beaten

6 ounces frozen unsweetened apple juice concentrate, undiluted

2 tablespoons corn oil margarine, melted

fitness cheese (see page 361), optional

fresh apple butter (see page 359), optional, or pineapple peach butter (see page 360), optional

350

1. Combine the flour, baking soda, ginger, cinnamon, cloves, and salt in a large mixing bowl. In another smaller bowl, dissolve the instant coffee in the hot water. Add the egg, apple juice concentrate, and melted margarine and mix well. Add the liquid ingredients to the dry ingredients and mix just enough to moisten the dry ingredients. The mixture will be lumpy.

2. Spray a hot skillet or griddle with non-stick cooking spray. Spoon the batter, 1/4 cup at a time, onto the hot griddle. Cook until the top of each pancake is covered with tiny bubbles and the bottom is brown. Turn and brown the other side.

3. Place 2 pancakes on each plate and serve with Fitness Cheese and Fresh Apple Butter or Pineapple Peach Butter, if desired.

MAKES 8 PANCAKES

• EACH 2-PANCAKE SERVING CONTAINS APPROXIMATELY:

CALORIES: **262** | FAT: **8 g** | CHOLESTEROL: **54 mg** | SODIUM: **478 mg** | CARBOHYDRATES: **44 g** | PROTEIN: **6 g**

blueberry pancakes

Adding the blueberries while they are still frozen keeps them big and plump in the cooked pancakes. At Canyon Ranch we serve these pancakes with Blueberry Syrup.

1 egg

2 egg whites

1/2 cup non-fat milk

3/4 cup all-purpose flour

1/2 cup whole-wheat flour

2 1/4 teaspoons baking powder

1 1/2 teaspoons fructose

pinch salt

1/4 cup water

1 cup frozen blueberries, unthawed

fitness cheese (see page 361), optional

blueberry syrup (see page 364), optional

1. Combine the whole egg, egg whites, and milk in a bowl and beat with a wire whisk until blended.

2. In another bowl sift together all the flour, baking powder, fructose, and salt. Add the whisked liquid ingredients and the water and mix until the batter is smooth. If the batter is too thick, add a little more water to thin it out.

3. Heat a griddle or a large skillet and spray it with non-stick cooking spray. Spoon 1/4 cup of batter at a time onto the hot griddle. Sprinkle 2 tablespoons of blueberries onto the batter. Cook until the top of each pancake is covered with tiny bubbles and the bottom is golden brown. Turn and brown the other side.

4. To serve, place 2 pancakes on each plate and serve with fitness cheese and blueberry syrup, if desired.

MAKES 8 PANCAKES, OR 4 SERVINGS

• EACH SERVING CONTAINS APPROXIMATELY:

CALORIES: **190** | FAT: **2 g** | CHOLESTEROL: **80 mg** | SODIUM: **510 mg** | CARBOHYDRATES: **33 g** | PROTEIN: **8 g**

banana waffles with maple walnut syrup

These waffles are a great breakfast or brunch entree for parties. They can be made ahead of time and reheated just before serving. For an even prettier presentation, garnish each serving with a slice of grilled banana and a sprig of mint.

MAPLE WALNUT SYRUP:

2 tablespoons all-fruit cherry or berry jam

2 tablespoons maple syrup

3/4 teaspoon frozen orange juice concentrate, undiluted

WAFFLES:

2 medium ripe bananas, mashed

1 1/2 teaspoons corn oil

1/4 cup egg whites

3/4 cup low-fat (2 percent) milk

1 teaspoon vanilla extract

3/4 cup whole-wheat flour

1/4 cup all-purpose flour

1 teaspoon baking powder

1/4 teaspoon salt

4 teaspoons toasted and chopped walnuts

1. Combine all the ingredients for the syrup, mix well, and set aside.

2. Preheat a waffle iron.

3. Combine the bananas, corn oil, egg whites, milk, and vanilla in a bowl and beat until blended. Add the flours, baking powder, and salt and mix well.

4. Spray the hot waffle iron with non-stick cooking spray. Spoon 3/4 cup of the batter onto the center of the waffle iron. Cook until a golden brown, or until it stops steaming. Repeat with the remaining batter.

5. To serve, halve each waffle and top each half with 1 tablespoon of syrup and 1 teaspoon of toasted walnuts.

MAKES 2 WAFFLES, OR 4 SERVINGS

353

• EACH SERVING CONTAINS APPROXIMATELY:

CALORIES: 271 | FAT: 5 g | CHOLESTEROL: 3 mg | SODIUM: 279 mg | CARBOHYDRATES: 52 g | PROTEIN: 8 g

sweet potato waffles

At Canyon Ranch we serve these wonderful waffles with fresh fruit and pure Vermont maple syrup. They are also delicious served with Fresh Apple Butter (see page 359) and a dollop of Fitness Cheese (see page 361). If you're in a hurry, you can substitute 3/4 cup of canned pumpkin for the sweet potato in this recipe. You can also use this batter to make pancakes if you don't have a waffle iron.

1/2 pound sweet potatoes, peeled, cooked, and mashed (3/4 cup)

1 1/2 teaspoons melted corn oil margarine

1 medium egg white, lightly beaten

3/4 cup low-fat (2 percent) milk

1/2 cup whole-wheat flour

1 teaspoon baking powder

1/4 teaspoon salt

1. Preheat a waffle iron.
2. Combine the cooked sweet potatoes, margarine, egg white, and milk in a large bowl and beat until well blended. Add the flour, baking powder, and salt and mix until smooth.
3. Spray the hot waffle iron with non-stick cooking spray.
4. Spoon 3/4 cup of the batter onto the center of the waffle iron and bake until it stops steaming. Continue to make another waffle in the same manner with the remaining batter.

MAKES 2 WAFFLES, OR 4 SERVINGS

354

• EACH SERVING CONTAINS APPROXIMATELY:

CALORIES: **180** | FAT: **3 g** | CHOLESTEROL: **4 mg** | SODIUM: **255 mg** | CARBOHYDRATES: **33 g** | PROTEIN: **6 g**

granola

This granola is a favorite with hikers and bikers at Canyon Ranch. Not only is it a great snack, but it can be used as a topping for fruit, yogurt, and ice cream. Because it has no added fat it is much lower in calories than most commercial granola.

1¹/₂ cups rolled oats

¹/₄ cup finely chopped almonds

2 tablespoons fructose

2 tablespoons wheat germ

1¹/₂ tablespoons ground cinnamon

1. Preheat the oven to 350°F.
2. Combine all the ingredients in a medium bowl and mix well. Spread the mixture on a baking sheet or in a shallow pan.
3. Bake for 25 to 30 minutes, or until light brown, stirring frequently. Let cool completely and then store in an airtight container. It will keep in a cool place for at least a week.

MAKES 2 CUPS

• EACH ¹/₄-CUP SERVING CONTAINS APPROXIMATELY:

CALORIES: 104 | FAT: 3 g | CHOLESTEROL: 0 | SODIUM: 2 mg | CARBOHYDRATES: 16 g | PROTEIN: 4 g

breakfast bread pudding

This easy-to-make bread pudding freezes extremely well and therefore can be made ahead of time and popped in the microwave for a fast and healthy breakfast. It can also be made into muffins. Just mound the mixture into each of 12 sprayed muffin tins or custard cups and shorten the baking time by about 5 minutes.

1½ cups non-fat milk

2 tablespoons corn oil margarine, melted

4 egg whites

¼ cup sugar

1 tablespoon ground cinnamon

1 tablespoon vanilla extract

12 slices whole-wheat bread, diced into ½-inch cubes

⅔ cup dark raisins

1. Preheat the oven to 350°F.

2. Spray a 9 x 12-inch baking dish with non-stick cooking spray.

3. Combine all ingredients, except the bread and raisins, in a large bowl and mix well. Stir in the bread and raisins and allow to soak for 5 minutes.

4. Spoon the mixture into the prepared dish and bake in the preheated oven for about 30 to 35 minutes, or until firm and nicely browned. Cool on a wire rack for at least 10 minutes before cutting into squares 3 x 4 inches in size.

MAKES 12 SERVINGS

357

• EACH SERVING CONTAINS APPROXIMATELY:

CALORIES: 143 | FAT: 3 g | CHOLESTEROL: 1 mg | SODIUM: 195 mg | CARBOHYDRATES: 25 g | PROTEIN: 4 g

pasta power

For real pasta lovers this is the ultimate breakfast dish. Many guests like it topped with milk. It can also be served warm and topped with fat-free frozen yogurt for a healthy dessert.

½ cup fresh apple butter
(recipe follows)

2 teaspoons ground cinnamon

1 tablespoon vanilla extract

2 eggs, lightly beaten

4 cups whole-wheat fusilli pasta, or any spiral-cut pasta

½ cup raisins

4 cups non-fat or low-fat milk, optional

1. Preheat the oven to 350°F. Spray a 9 x 13-inch baking dish with non-stick cooking spray and set aside.

2. Combine the apple butter, cinnamon, and vanilla in a large bowl and mix well. Add the eggs and again mix well. Add the noodles and raisins and mix thoroughly.

3. Spoon the mixture into the prepared dish and bake, uncovered, in the preheated oven for 10 to 15 minutes, stirring occasionally, until warmed through.

4. Serve ½ cup of the pasta mixture in a cereal bowl. Top with ½ cup of milk, if desired.

MAKES 8 SERVINGS

358

• EACH ⅓-CUP SERVING WITHOUT MILK CONTAINS APPROXIMATELY:

CALORIES: **245** | FAT: **2 g** | CHOLESTEROL: **53 mg** | SODIUM: **21 mg** | CARBOHYDRATES: **48 g** | PROTEIN: **9 g**

fresh apple butter

Making your own apple butter is well worth the time and effort it takes. Even though there are many good brands available in the markets, homemade is tastier and much less expensive. This recipe is not the sterilized canning jar variety which will keep in the cupboard for months. However, it will keep for at least a week in the refrigerator. I prefer to use Golden Delicious apples in this recipe because they are so sweet, but many people prefer a variety of apple with more taste, such as Granny Smith, for apple butter.

8 cups peeled and thinly sliced apples

1/2 cup frozen unsweetened apple juice, undiluted

1 cup water

1 teaspoon ground cinnamon

1/2 teaspoon ground allspice

pinch ground cloves

1. Combine all the ingredients in a large saucepan and bring to a boil. Reduce the heat and simmer, uncovered, for 15 minutes, stirring occasionally. Remove from the heat and let cool slightly.

2. Spoon the mixture into a blender or food processor and blend until smooth.

3. Store, tightly covered, in the refrigerator.

MAKES 3 CUPS

359

• EACH 1/4-CUP SERVING CONTAINS APPROXIMATELY:

CALORIES: **39** | FAT: **negligible** | CHOLESTEROL: **0** | SODIUM: **11 mg** | CARBOHYDRATES: **10 g** | PROTEIN: **negligible**

pineapple peach butter

This fruit butter is a wonderful example of the advantages of using dried fruits for sauces and spreads. Their concentrated flavors make any additional sweetening unnecessary, and when reconstituted and blended, adding fat is not necessary for a smooth, creamy texture. This fruit butter is a delightful addition to toast, English muffins, bagels, pancakes, waffles, and French toast. It is also good used as a spread on sandwiches and is a great topping for yogurt and ice cream.

2 cups unsulfured dried peaches

1½ cups frozen pineapple juice concentrate, undiluted

1½ cups water

1 teaspoon ground cinnamon

unsulfured dried fruit
Dried fruit is sulfured to preserve its beautiful bright color, or in the case of apples, to keep them light in color. However, the darker, less colorful, unsulfured dried fruit are so much more flavorful than the brighter-colored, sulfured variety and they make infinitely better-quality fruit butters and sauces. You may have to go to a health food store to find unsulfured dried fruit, but it's well worth the trip.

1. Combine all the ingredients in a saucepan and bring to a boil.

2. Reduce the heat to low and simmer for 10 minutes, or until the peaches are tender.

3. Let cool slightly and blend in a blender or food processor until smooth. If stored, tightly covered, in the refrigerator, it will keep for at least 2 weeks.

MAKES 2 3/4 CUPS

• EACH 2-TABLESPOON SERVING CONTAINS APPROXIMATELY:

CALORIES: **70** | FAT: **negligible** | CHOLESTEROL: **0** | SODIUM: **2 mg** | CARBOHYDRATES: **18 g** | PROTEIN: **negligible**

fitness cheese

This low-fat spread tastes very much like crème fraîche. When possible, always make Fitness Cheese 24 hours before you plan to serve it. Both the taste and consistency will improve.

1 cup part-skim ricotta cheese

2 tablespoons plain non-fat yogurt

1. Combine the ingredients in a food processor and blend until satin smooth.

2. Store, tightly covered, in the refrigerator. It will keep for several days.

MAKES 1 CUP

crème fraîche

Crème fraîche is a thickened cream with a satin-smooth texture and a slightly tangy flavor. In France the cream is unpasteurized and therefore contains the bacteria to make it thicken naturally. In this country, where cream is pasteurized, the fermenting agents are obtained by adding either buttermilk or sour cream. The usual ratio is 2 tablespoons of buttermilk or sour cream to 1 cup of whipping cream. The mixture is then allowed to stand, covered, at room temperature from 8 to 24 hours, or until thickened. Crème fraîche is incredibly high in both calories and fat, and Fitness Cheese (see recipe above) is a good, healthier alternative.

361

• EACH 2-TABLESPOON SERVING CONTAINS APPROXIMATELY:

CALORIES: 44 | FAT: 2 g | CHOLESTEROL: 10 mg | SODIUM: 41 mg | CARBOHYDRATES: 2 g | PROTEIN: 4 g

apple and fig chutney

This chutney is a tasty accompaniment to any curried dish. It is also good stirred into curried salad dressing and certain sauces, such as Tofu Mayonnaise (see page 153) and Low-Fat White Sauce (see page 325). It is a wonderful low-fat replacement for butter or mayonnaise on many sandwiches, such as tuna and chicken.

4 cups chopped unsulfured dried apples

1 cup finely chopped dried figs

1 cup raisins, finely chopped

1 medium onion, finely chopped (1½ cups)

2 cups sugar

1¼ teaspoons ground ginger

¼ cup pickling spice, tied in a cheesecloth bag

2 cups water

2 cups apple cider vinegar

1. Combine all the ingredients in a large, non-aluminum saucepan and bring to a boil. Reduce the heat to low and simmer, uncovered, for 2 hours.

2. Let cool to room temperature. Remove and discard the cheesecloth bag containing the pickling spice. Store the chutney in a tightly covered container in the refrigerator where it will keep for months.

MAKES 43/4 CUPS

362

• EACH 2-TABLESPOON SERVING CONTAINS APPROXIMATELY:

CALORIES: 93 | FAT: negligible | CHOLESTEROL: 0 | SODIUM: 24 mg | CARBOHYDRATES: 24 g | PROTEIN: negligible

peanut butter delight

For peanut butter lovers, this is a marvelous way to enjoy the flavor with fewer calories and much less fat. Peanut butter has about 100 calories per tablespoon and almost all of those calories come from fat. Part-skim ricotta cheese has only 20 calories for the same amount and only half the calories come from fat. Therefore, when combined to create this rich-tasting sauce, they offer the best of both worlds.

1 cup part-skim ricotta cheese

1/4 cup unhomogenized smooth peanut butter (see page 329)

2 tablespoons skim milk

2 1/4 teaspoons vanilla extract

1/2 teaspoon ground cinnamon

2 tablespoons sugar

Combine all the ingredients in a food processor and blend until satin smooth. If stored, tightly covered, in the refrigerator, it will keep for about 1 week.

MAKES 1 1/4 CUPS

• EACH 2-TABLESPOON SERVING CONTAINS APPROXIMATELY:

CALORIES: 79 | FAT: 4 g | CHOLESTEROL: 8 mg | SODIUM: 32 mg | CARBOHYDRATES: 5 g | PROTEIN: 4 g

blueberry syrup

This syrup is perfect poured over Blueberry Pancakes (see page 352). It is also a good topping for fresh fruit, yogurt, and ice cream.

2 cups blueberries

6 tablespoons fructose

2 tablespoons fresh lemon juice

¼ teaspoon ground cinnamon

1 teaspoon cornstarch dissolved in
   1 teaspoon of water

Combine the blueberries, fructose, lemon juice, and cinnamon in a small saucepan and bring to a boil over medium-low heat. Stir in the dissolved cornstarch. Continue to cook the mixture until the blueberries begin to fall apart and the syrup thickens. Serve warm.

MAKES APPROXIMATELY 1 CUP

364

• EACH 1-TABLESPOON SERVING CONTAINS APPROXIMATELY:

CALORIES: 40 | FAT: negligible | CHOLESTEROL: 0 | SODIUM: 2 mg | CARBOHYDRATES: 10 g | PROTEIN: negligible

desserts

Many low-fat desserts are just as delicious and satisfying as their high-fat counterparts. However, when a favorite dessert simply cannot be lightened without appreciably changing its taste and texture, we firmly believe that a very small portion of something truly wonderful is a whole lot better than a plateful of some make-do dish. For this reason you will notice that the portion sizes vary considerably in this section of the book. Remember, one of the main points in the Canyon Ranch Nutrition Guidelines is our Mindful Eating philosophy which stresses the enjoyment of good food.

Another important Canyon Ranch meal-planning criterion is nourishing both body and spirit. When an enjoyable sweet is made from fresh, natural ingredients, the body benefits from the nutrition, and the experience of eating it does wonders for the spirit.

Fruits, with their natural sweetness, fabulous flavors, and vitamins, minerals, and fiber, are a perfect dessert. We not only offer fresh fruit plates after every meal but many Canyon Ranch desserts are fruit-based, using either fresh, canned, or dried fruit.

Dried fruit, shunned by many as being high in calories, is actually a wonderful food to use in desserts because of its intense flavor and natural sweetness. The Truly Fruity Cookie Bars recipe in this chapter is a perfect example of how rich and satisfying a small portion of dried fruit can be.

All of our cheesecakes make delicious party desserts, and your friends won't believe it when you tell them they're Canyon Ranch recipes. For your next holiday dinner serve our Sweet Potato Cream Cheese Pie or try our Pumpkin Crème Brûlée.

carrot cake

This carrot cake is an extremely popular dessert at Canyon Ranch, and many of our guests tell us that leftover cake is also their favorite breakfast bread. The reason for using a non-plastic bowl is that it is difficult to completely remove all fat residue from a plastic surface. Any fat, such as oil on the surface of the bowl, a tiny speck of the yolk, or any dairy fat like butter or cream, will make it impossible to beat egg whites. For this reason it is a good idea to separate the egg whites one at a time into a separate bowl before adding them to the other whites to be beaten. This will prevent ever getting even a speck of yolk in the whites, always a frustrating experience!

²/₃ cup chopped walnuts

2¹/₂ cups whole-wheat flour

¹/₄ cup fructose

1¹/₂ teaspoons baking soda

1¹/₂ teaspoons ground cinnamon

pinch salt

4 egg yolks

5 tablespoons canola oil

¹/₄ cup buttermilk

1¹/₂ teaspoons vanilla extract

4 medium carrots (1 pound), grated (2¹/₂ cups)

1³/₄ cups drained crushed canned pineapple

6 egg whites

GLAZE:

¹/₄ cup fructose

pinch baking soda

1¹/₂ teaspoons corn oil margarine

1¹/₂ teaspoons corn syrup

6 tablespoons buttermilk

1¹/₂ teaspoons vanilla extract

carrot curls and mint leaves for garnish, optional

368

1. Preheat the oven to 325°F.

2. Place the walnuts in a pan and bake in the preheated oven for about 8 to 10 minutes, or until golden brown. Watch them carefully because they burn easily. Set aside.

3. Spray a 9 x 13-inch baking pan with non-stick cooking spray. Set aside.

4. Sift the flour, fructose, baking soda, cinnamon, and salt into a large bowl.

5. In another bowl combine the egg yolks, oil, buttermilk, and vanilla and mix well. Add the liquid ingredients to the flour mixture and stir until completely moistened. Stir in the toasted walnuts, carrots, and pineapple.

6. Beat the egg whites in a clean, non-plastic bowl until they

how to make carrot curls

Using a Saladaka, the Japanese hand cutting tool that makes both hair-fine long shreds and spiral-cut curls, is the easiest way to make carrot curls. All you have to do is peel the carrot and cross-cut it into 3-inch-long segments. Press each carrot segment down on the spike and turn the handle to create a long, thin spiral of carrot. Remove the spiral from the bottom container and cut it into pieces the size of a flower. If you don't have a Saladaka, then use a peeler on the whole peeled carrot to make long strips. Curl each strip around your finger and drop it into a bowl of ice water. Saladakas are available in most Japanese markets and some cookware stores.

hold soft peaks. Fold them into the batter. Spoon the mixture into the prepared pan and bake in the preheated oven for 30 to 35 minutes, or until the cake springs back when touched gently in the center. Remove from the oven and allow to cool slightly.

7. Combine all the glaze ingredients, except the vanilla, in a small saucepan and bring to a boil. Reduce the heat to low and simmer for 5 minutes. Remove from the heat and stir in the vanilla.

8. Using the tines of a fork, poke holes all over the top of the cake. Pour the hot glaze evenly over the warm cake. Allow to cool to room temperature before cutting into 24 pieces, approximately 2 x 2 inches square. Garnish each serving with carrot curls and fresh mint leaves, if desired.

MAKES 24 SERVINGS

• EACH SERVING CONTAINS APPROXIMATELY:

CALORIES: 135 | FAT: 6 g | CHOLESTEROL: 49 mg | SODIUM: 132 mg | CARBOHYDRATES: 17 g | PROTEIN: 4 g

chocolate mint cake

This recipe is a good example of how the fat in baked goods can be replaced with applesauce and pureed prunes. The cellulose in apples and the pectin in prunes trap moisture in much the same way fat does and can be used to replace all, or at least half, of the fat in baked goods. There is also a product called Lighter Bake Butter and Oil Replacement made by Sunsweet, which combines both plums and apples and can be used as a total fat replacement in practically all baked goods. Another similar product is called WonderSlim Fat and Egg Substitute.

1 cup unbleached all-purpose flour

1/2 cup unsweetened cocoa powder

3/4 cup sugar

1 teaspoon baking powder

pinch salt

2 tablespoons unsweetened applesauce

1/2 cup low-fat (1 percent) milk

1 teaspoon vanilla extract

1 teaspoon mint extract

1 tablespoon instant coffee mixed with 2 tablespoons water

1/4 pound dried prunes, rehydrated and pureed

1/2 ounce semisweet chocolate, melted

2 egg whites

2 tablespoons non-fat chocolate fudge sauce

powdered sugar for garnish

370

To save time when making this cake, substitute 2 jars of baby food pureed prunes for the rehydrated and pureed dried prunes. Also, there are several brands of non-fat fudge topping available. They are usually found near the ice cream section in supermarkets.

1. Preheat the oven to 300°F.

2. Spray a 10-inch cake pan with non-stick cooking spray and lightly dust with flour.

3. Sift together all the dry ingredients into a large mixing bowl.

4. In a small bowl mix the applesauce, milk, vanilla and mint extracts, coffee, prunes, and chocolate. Add to the dry ingredients and mix well.

5. Beat the egg whites in a small, non-plastic bowl until stiff. Fold the beaten egg whites into the cake batter.

6. Spread the batter in the prepared pan. Bake in the

preheated oven for 35 to 40 minutes, or until a knife inserted in the middle of the cake comes out clean.

7. Remove the cake from the oven and cool on a rack. When the cake is cool, spread the top with the non-fat chocolate sauce. Sprinkle the top with powdered sugar just before serving. The easiest way to cut this cake into 12 equal servings is to first cut it into quarters. Cut each quarter of the cake into 3 equal wedges.

MAKES 12 SERVINGS

• EACH SERVING CONTAINS APPROXIMATELY:

CALORIES: **125** | FAT: **1 g** | CHOLESTEROL: **negligible** | SODIUM: **135 mg** | CARBOHYDRATES: **26 g** | PROTEIN: **3 g**

371

chocolate mocha cheesecake

It is always a delightful surprise for Canyon Ranch guests to experience this seemingly decadent dessert for the first time. For chocolate lovers it can easily become habit-forming!

CRUST:

1 tablespoon unsweetened applesauce

1¹/2 cups reduced-fat chocolate graham cracker crumbs (9 whole crackers)

FILLING:

6 ounces light cream cheese

6 ounces non-fat cream cheese

¹/3 cup non-fat sour cream

¹/3 cup fructose

2 teaspoons vanilla extract

10 egg whites (1 cup)

2 tablespoons strong brewed coffee

2 tablespoons non-fat chocolate sauce

372

1. Preheat the oven to 325°F.

2. To make the crust, combine the applesauce and graham cracker crumbs and press into the bottom of a 10-inch springform cake pan.

3. Combine the cream cheeses and sour cream in a bowl and mix until smooth. Add the fructose, vanilla, egg whites, and coffee and beat again until smooth. Pour the mixture into the prepared pan, reserving 1/4 cup.

4. Combine the reserved cheesecake mixture with the chocolate sauce and mix well. Pour over the top of the cake and swirl with the tip of a knife.

5. Bake in the preheated oven for 40 minutes. Turn off the heat, open the oven door slightly, and let the cheesecake cool in the oven for 30 minutes.

6. Remove from the oven and allow the cake to rest for at least 20 minutes before removing the sides of the pan.

MAKES 12 SERVINGS

• EACH SERVING CONTAINS APPROXIMATELY:

CALORIES: **150** | FAT: **5 g** | CHOLESTEROL: **10 mg** | SODIUM: **234 mg** | CARBOHYDRATES: **19 g** | PROTEIN: 6 g

peppermint patty cheesecake

The palate-pleasing flavor of peppermint makes just a small slice of this creamy, rich-tasting dessert a satisfying finale for many menus. Serving-size pieces can be successfully frozen in Ziploc bags and packed still frozen in sack lunches and picnic baskets.

CRUST:

3/4 cup chocolate graham cracker crumbs (4 1/2 whole crackers)

1 tablespoon water

FILLING:

3 cups fat-free cream cheese (24 ounces), at room temperature

1 egg

4 egg whites

3/4 cup plus 2 tablespoons fat-free sweetened condensed skimmed milk

1/4 cup unbleached all-purpose flour

2 tablespoons fructose

1 teaspoon peppermint extract

3 small peppermint candies, coarsely chopped

1. Preheat the oven to 300°F.

2. Spray a 9-inch springform cake pan with non-stick cooking spray.

3. Combine the graham cracker crumbs and water in a bowl, mix until moistened, and press into the bottom of the prepared pan.

4. Combine all the remaining ingredients, except the peppermint candies, in a bowl and beat with an electric mixer until smooth.

5. Spoon the batter into the pan on top of the graham cracker crust. Sprinkle the chopped candies around the edge of the cheesecake.

6. Bake in the preheated oven for 35 to 40 minutes, until the cake is firm but the center still moves slightly.

7. Cool completely on a wire rack. Refrigerate, tightly covered, for at least 4 hours or overnight before serving. To cut into 16 pieces, first cut the cake into quarters. Cut each quarter into 4 equal wedges.

MAKES 16 SERVINGS

373

• EACH SERVING CONTAINS APPROXIMATELY:

CALORIES: 135 | FAT: 2 g | CHOLESTEROL: 29 mg | SODIUM: 362 mg | CARBOHYDRATES: 19 g | PROTEIN: 12 g

lemon poppy seed cake

This luscious cake has the rich taste and dense texture usually associated with pound cake, which is amazing considering that it contains only a fraction of the fat found in "real" pound cake, made with a pound of butter, a pound of sugar, and a pound of flour.

3 tablespoons poppy seeds

1 tablespoon grated lemon zest

$1/2$ cup non-fat milk

$1/3$ cup canola oil

$1^1/4$ cups sugar, divided use

1 egg

2 teaspoons vanilla extract

$1^1/4$ teaspoons lemon extract

$1/3$ cup non-fat plain yogurt

$2/3$ cup unsweetened applesauce

$2^1/4$ cups all-purpose flour

$1^1/8$ teaspoons baking powder

$1/4$ teaspoon baking soda

$1/2$ teaspoon salt

4 egg whites

$1/8$ teaspoon cream of tartar

LEMON GLAZE:

1 cup confectioners' sugar

2 tablespoons fresh lemon juice

1 tablespoon grated lemon zest

1. Combine the poppy seeds, lemon zest, and milk in a saucepan and bring to a boil. Remove from the heat and allow to stand for at least 1 hour. If possible, cover and refrigerate overnight for flavors to marry more completely.

2. Preheat the oven to 350°F.

3. Spray a 9-inch bundt pan with non-stick cooking spray and set aside.

4. Combine the oil, 1 cup of the sugar, the egg, vanilla and lemon extracts, yogurt, applesauce, and poppy seed and milk mixture in a large bowl and mix well. In another bowl combine the flour, baking powder, baking soda, and salt and mix well. Slowly add the dry ingredients to the liquid ingredients and blend until smooth.

5. Combine the egg whites and cream of tartar in a clean, non-plastic bowl and beat with an electric mixer at high speed until the egg whites are foamy. Gradually add the remaining $1/4$ cup of sugar and continue to beat on high until the mixture is stiff but not dry. Fold the beaten egg whites into the batter, being careful not to overmix.

6. Spoon the batter into the prepared pan and bake in the

poppy seeds

The tiny dried seeds of the poppy plant measure only 1/16 inch in diameter. In fact, it takes about 900,000 of them to equal a pound. Poppy seeds are a bluish-gray color and have a crunchy texture and a nutty flavor. They are used in sauces, in salad dressings, in a variety of baked goods, and in cooked dishes of all types. Poppy seeds are particularly popular in Central Europe, the Middle East, and India. They can turn rancid if stored for too long at room temperature. They will keep, tightly covered, in the refrigerator for at least 6 months and in the freezer for a year.

preheated oven for 35 minutes, or until it springs back when touched gently in the center. Remove from the oven and place on a wire rack to cool.

7. Combine all ingredients for the lemon glaze in a small bowl and beat until smooth. Remove the cake from the bundt pan by first gently loosening it from the sides of the pan and then turning it upside down onto a plate. Drizzle the lemon glaze over the top. To cut into 24 pieces, first cut the cake into quarters. Cut each quarter into 6 equal servings.

MAKES 24 SERVINGS

• EACH SERVING CONTAINS APPROXIMATELY:

CALORIES: **150** | FAT: **4 g** | CHOLESTEROL: **9 mg** | SODIUM: **105 mg** | CARBOHYDRATES: **28 g** | PROTEIN: **2 g**

truly fruity cookie bars

This is an old Canyon Ranch recipe for sugar-free cookies. They provide a healthy treat for sack lunches and are wonderful as snacks for hiking and biking trips. For further convenience these cookie bars can be individually wrapped and frozen. Just pop a frozen cookie bar into your backpack and it will be ready to eat in less than an hour.

¼ cup chopped walnuts

1 cup raisins

½ cup chopped dried apricots

½ cup chopped pitted prunes

1 cup whole-wheat flour

3 tablespoons canola oil

1 tablespoon vanilla extract

¼ teaspoon salt

2 eggs

16 ounces canned unsweetened crushed pineapple, drained

1. Preheat the oven to 350°F.

2. Place the walnuts in a small baking pan and bake in the preheated oven for about 8 minutes, or until golden brown. Watch them carefully because they will burn easily.

3. Spray a standard-size (9 x 5-inch) loaf pan with non-stick cooking spray and set aside.

4. Combine the toasted walnuts, raisins, apricots, prunes, and flour in a large bowl and mix well.

5. In another bowl combine all the remaining ingredients and mix well. Add the liquid ingredients to the dry ingredients and again mix well. Spoon the mixture into the prepared pan and bake in the preheated oven for about 1 hour, or until a knife inserted in the center comes out clean.

6. Remove from the oven and cool on a rack. Turn out of the pan, wrap tightly, and refrigerate until cold. Cut the cold loaf down the center into halves. Then cut each half into 16 slices approximately $1/2$ x $2^1/2$ inches in size. Store the slices, tightly wrapped, in the refrigerator.

MAKES 32 COOKIE BARS

376

• EACH COOKIE BAR CONTAINS APPROXIMATELY:

CALORIES: **60** | FAT: **2 g** | CHOLESTEROL: **13 mg** | SODIUM: **22 mg** | CARBOHYDRATES: **10 g** | PROTEIN: **2 g**

pizzelle cups

Pizzelles are Italian cookies made in a pizzelle iron, which is like a small waffle iron. You can use the cups to hold sorbet, frozen yogurt, fruit, or whatever you might want to put into them. Pizzelle irons are available in most cookware stores and some Italian markets. If you don't have one, you can use a small waffle iron for this recipe.

2 egg whites

5 tablespoons plus 1 teaspoon unbleached all-purpose flour

2 tablespoons plus 2 teaspoons sugar

¼ teaspoon baking powder

4 teaspoons canola oil

¼ teaspoon vanilla extract

2 teaspoons water

1. Preheat the pizzelle iron.

2. Beat the egg whites in a non-plastic bowl until soft peaks form.

3. In another bowl combine the flour, sugar, and baking powder and mix well. Blend in the oil, vanilla, and water and then fold in the beaten egg whites.

4. Spray the hot pizzelle iron with non-stick cooking spray.

5. Spoon 2 tablespoons of the batter into the center of the grid and cook for 1 minute. Remove from the iron and immediately press it over the bottom of a ramekin or custard cup to cool and form into a cup shape. Repeat with the remaining batter.

MAKES 8 CUPS

377

• EACH CUP CONTAINS APPROXIMATELY:

CALORIES: 43 | FAT: 2 g | CHOLESTEROL: 0 | SODIUM: 25 mg | CARBOHYDRATES: 4 g | PROTEIN: 1 g

cherry streusel pie

This scrumptious pie is wonderful served with a dollop of light sour cream. Leftover pie can be mixed with yogurt and served as a special treat for breakfast.

CHERRY FILLING:

1/4 cup cornstarch

1/4 cup water

2 pounds frozen pitted sour cherries

1/2 cup fructose

pinch cinnamon

1/2 teaspoon almond extract

STREUSEL:

3 tablespoons brown sugar

6 tablespoons unbleached all-purpose flour

2 tablespoons butter

1 recipe for pâte brisée (recipe follows)

1. Preheat the oven to 350°F.

2. Mix the cornstarch and water in a small bowl and set aside.

3. To make the filling, combine the cherries, fructose, and cinnamon in a medium-size saucepan and place over medium heat. When the mixture begins to boil, add the dissolved cornstarch and cook, stirring frequently, for about 6 minutes, or until it thickens. Remove from the heat and stir in the almond extract.

4. To make the streusel, combine the brown sugar, flour, and butter in a small bowl. Mix by hand until the mixture resembles coarse crumbs.

5. Roll the pâte brisée into an 11-inch circle. Place in a 9-inch pie pan, crimping the edges to fit. Place the crust in the preheated oven and bake for 12 minutes, or until lightly browned. Fill with the cherry filling. Top with the crumb mixture.

6. Place the pie back in the preheated oven and bake for 40 more minutes, or until the top is lightly browned. Cool slightly on a rack before cutting. The easiest way to cut this pie into 12 equal servings is to first cut it into quarters. Cut each quarter of the pie into 3 equal wedges.

MAKES 12 SERVINGS

378

• EACH SERVING CONTAINS APPROXIMATELY:

CALORIES: **166** | FAT: **4 g** | CHOLESTEROL: **10 mg** | SODIUM: **77 mg** | CARBOHYDRATES: **31 g** | PROTEIN: **2 g**

pâte brisée

Pâte brisée (paht bree-ZAY) is a French term for a rich, flaky dough used for piecrusts in dishes such as pics, tarts, quiches, and the boat-shaped pastry shells called barquettes. In English it is often called short pastry, or just great piecrust! This recipe is a successful impostor used for making the short pastry in many of the pies and tarts served on Canyon Ranch menus. It has only a fraction of the fat and can be used for both sweet and savory dishes.

1 cup unbleached all-purpose flour

1/2 teaspoon salt

1/2 teaspoon fructose

2 tablespoons cold butter, diced

4 to 6 tablespoons ice water

1. Place all the ingredients, except the water, in a food processor. Pulse briefly to combine.

2. While the machine is running, slowly add enough water for the dough to form a ball. Pulse for 2 to 3 additional seconds. Do not overprocess.

3. Form the dough into a flat disk and wrap in plastic wrap. Refrigerate for 1 hour, or until ready to use. (You can do this a day ahead of time.)

379

MAKES 12 SERVINGS (1 SINGLE 10-INCH PIECRUST)

• EACH SERVING CONTAINS APPROXIMATELY:

CALORIES: 35 | FAT: 1 g | CHOLESTEROL: 4 mg | SODIUM: 70 mg | CARBOHYDRATES: 5 g | PROTEIN: negligible

honey plum pie

This delicious fresh fruit dessert can be made with other fruit such as apricots, nectarines, or peaches when plums are not available.

CRUST:

3/4 cup unbleached all-purpose flour

1/2 cup whole-wheat flour

1/4 cup light brown sugar

1 1/2 teaspoons baking powder

1/4 teaspoon salt

2 tablespoons unsalted butter, cold and cut into pieces

1 egg

1/4 cup skim milk

2 tablespoons applesauce

1 teaspoon vanilla extract

TOPPING/FILLING:

4 cups pitted fresh purple and red plums cut into 1/4-inch slices

1 tablespoon butter, for the topping

1/2 teaspoon ground cinnamon

1/3 cup honey

1. Preheat the oven to 375°F.

2. To make the crust, sift together the flours, sugar, baking powder, and salt in a bowl. Blend in the cold pieces of butter until the mixture has a crumblike texture.

3. In a separate small bowl beat the egg lightly and then beat in the milk, applesauce, and vanilla.

4. Add the egg mixture to the flour mixture and stir until the ingredients are moistened.

5. Lightly spray a 9 x 13-inch pan with non-stick cooking spray. Spoon the batter into the pan.

6. To make the topping, arrange the sliced plums in 4 rows lengthwise, overlapping each slice.

7. Melt the butter for the topping in a small saucepan. Remove from the heat, stir in the cinnamon and honey, and drizzle evenly over the plums.

8. Bake in the preheated oven for about 25 minutes, or until the plums are soft and the crust is golden. Remove from the oven and let cool to room temperature before cutting into 12 pieces, approximately 3 x 3 inches square.

MAKES 12 SERVINGS

• EACH SERVING CONTAINS APPROXIMATELY:

CALORIES: **155** | FAT: **4 g** | CHOLESTEROL: **26 mg** | SODIUM: **171 mg** | CARBOHYDRATES: **29 g** | PROTEIN: **3 g**

sweet potato cream cheese pie

This recipe was originally developed for Canyon Ranch holiday menus. However, it was so popular with the guests that we now serve it all year round. For an even more seasonal dessert, substitute mashed pumpkin for the sweet potatoes and serve Pumpkin Cream Cheese Pie for your next holiday party.

CRUST:

2 cups graham cracker crumbs

2 tablespoons unsweetened applesauce

FILLING:

1/2 cup low-fat cream cheese

5 tablespoons maple syrup

1 tablespoon honey

1/4 cup fresh orange juice

1 tablespoon ground cinnamon

1/4 teaspoon ground nutmeg

1/4 teaspoon ground cloves

1/4 teaspoon ground allspice

1/4 teaspoon ground ginger

2 tablespoons vanilla extract

2 medium sweet potatoes (1 pound), baked, peeled, and mashed (3 cups)

1 egg

2 egg whites

1. Preheat the oven to 350°F.

2. To make the crust, combine the graham cracker crumbs and applesauce in a food processor and pulse until the mixture is combined and holds together. Press it into a 9-inch pie pan. Set aside.

3. To make the filling, combine the cream cheese, maple syrup, honey, orange juice, spices, and vanilla in a food processor and blend until smooth. Add the sweet potato and again blend until smooth. Add the egg and egg whites one at a time and blend until smooth, creamy, and light.

4. Spoon the filling into the crust and smooth the top. Bake in the preheated oven for 45 to 55 minutes, or until the filling is set. Allow to cool on a rack and then refrigerate until cold before serving. To cut into 12 pieces, first cut into quarters. Then cut each quarter into 3 equal wedges.

MAKES 12 SERVINGS

381

• EACH SERVING CONTAINS APPROXIMATELY:

CALORIES: **160** | FAT: **4 g** | CHOLESTEROL: **23 mg** | SODIUM: **138 mg** | CARBOHYDRATES: **28 g** | PROTEIN: **4 g**

apple strudel

This delicious dessert is best served warm with a dollop of either Fitness Cheese (see page 361) or vanilla yogurt. Leftover strudel is also good for breakfast and a tasty treat in sack lunches.

3 tablespoons cornstarch

¼ cup water, divided use

1½ pounds apples, peeled and sliced

3 tablespoons fructose

¾ teaspoon ground cinnamon

½ cup raisins

1 recipe for pâte brisée (see page 379)

1 egg white, beaten

1 teaspoon sugar

382

1. Preheat the oven to 375°F.

2. Lightly spray a baking sheet with non-stick cooking spray and set aside.

3. Dissolve the cornstarch in 2 tablespoons of the water and set aside.

4. Spray a skillet with non-stick cooking spray and place over medium heat. When the pan is hot, add the apples, fructose, cinnamon, and the remaining 2 tablespoons of water. Cook, stirring frequently, until the apples are tender and then stir in the raisins.

5. Add the dissolved cornstarch to the apple mixture and cook until thickened. Remove from the heat and allow to cool.

6. Roll out the pâte brisée dough on a sheet of wax paper into an 8 x 14-inch rectangle. Spoon the apple mixture down the long edge of the dough. Roll up and seal the ends. Score the top of the strudel into 10 pieces.

7. Brush the top of the strudel with the beaten egg white. Sprinkle with sugar and transfer to the prepared baking sheet.

8. Bake in the preheated oven for 15 to 20 minutes, or until the top is lightly browned. Remove from the oven and trim any extra pastry off the ends. Cut into pieces approximately 1 inch wide and serve.

MAKES 10 SERVINGS

• EACH SERVING CONTAINS APPROXIMATELY:

CALORIES: **150** | FAT: **3 g** | CHOLESTEROL: **7 mg** | SODIUM: **101 mg** | CARBOHYDRATES: **31 g** | PROTEIN: **2 g**

banana turnovers

These sensational, fruity turnovers are the creation of Barry Correia, executive chef at Canyon Ranch in the Berkshires, and they are one of our most popular desserts. They are best served warm with a dollop of vanilla ice milk or frozen yogurt.

3 small bananas, thinly sliced (12 ounces)

2 teaspoons sugar

2 teaspoons butter

4 sheets phyllo pastry dough

phyllo dough

If you are not used to using phyllo, here are a few tips necessary for success with this uniquely different product. You will find it in the freezer section of your market. Carefully read the instructions for thawing it and then follow them exactly. Phyllo should thaw overnight in the refrigerator and come to room temperature prior to using it. If you try to rush these steps, the sheets will stick together and be difficult to manage. If you do follow the steps, it is easy to work with and lots of fun. Also, while you're working with each sheet of the phyllo, keep all the remaining phyllo covered with a sheet of wax paper or plastic wrap and a damp towel to prevent it from drying out. When using phyllo at Canyon Ranch, we spray it with non-stick cooking spray rather than brushing it with butter in order to reduce the fat.

1. Preheat the oven to 400°F.

2. Combine the bananas and sugar in a bowl and toss until well mixed.

3. Heat the butter in a sauté pan. Add the banana-sugar mixture and cook over medium-low heat for 10 minutes. Remove from the heat, put back in the bowl, and place in the refrigerator to chill.

4. Lay 1 sheet of the phyllo at a time on a flat work surface with the narrow end toward you. Spray with non-stick cooking spray and then fold into thirds lengthwise, spraying between each fold. Spoon 3 tablespoons of the banana filling about 2 inches from the bottom and slightly to the left-hand corner of the phyllo strip. Fold up the 2-inch flap over the filling. Fold the left-hand corner of the phyllo diagonally to the right-hand side of the phyllo to cover the filling. Continue folding in this flag-style fold until you reach the end of the sheet.

5. Lift the turnover onto a baking sheet and again spray with the non-stick cooking spray. Repeat with the remaining phyllo sheets and filling. Bake in the preheated oven for about 15 minutes, or until golden brown. Serve warm.

MAKES 4 SERVINGS

383

• EACH SERVING CONTAINS APPROXIMATELY:

CALORIES: 175 | FAT: 2 g | CHOLESTEROL: 5 mg | SODIUM: 145 mg | CARBOHYDRATES: 36 g | PROTEIN: 3 g

chocolate waffle cannoli

This recipe for cannoli varies from the classic Italian dessert in that the tube is baked in a waffle iron rather than being deep-fried. If you don't have a cannoli tube to shape the warm waffle, you can make a tube out of aluminum foil that is about $1^1/_2$ inches in diameter.

CANNOLI TUBES:

2 egg whites

2 tablespoons plus 2 teaspoons unbleached all-purpose flour

2 tablespoons plus 2 teaspoons whole-wheat flour

2 tablespoons plus 2 teaspoons dutch cocoa powder

$^1/_4$ teaspoon baking powder

2 tablespoons plus 2 teaspoons sugar

1 tablespoon plus 1 teaspoon canola oil

$^1/_4$ teaspoon vanilla extract

2 teaspoons water

CANNOLI FILLING:

$1^1/_4$ cups part-skim ricotta cheese

3 tablespoons mini semisweet chocolate pieces

$^1/_2$ teaspoon vanilla extract

12 tablespoons fat-free fudge sauce

1. To make the cannoli tubes, preheat a pizzelle or waffle iron.

2. Beat the egg whites in a non-plastic bowl with an electric mixer on high until they form soft peaks.

3. Combine all the dry ingredients in a bowl. Add the oil, vanilla, and water and mix well. Fold in the beaten egg whites.

4. Spray the pizzelle or waffle iron with non-stick cooking spray.

5. Spoon 1 tablespoon of batter in the center of the grid. Close and cook for 1 minute. Remove from the griddle and fold around a cannoli tube. Allow to cool on the tube.

6. To make the filling, combine all the ingredients and mix well.

7. Remove the cannoli from the molds and pipe 1 ounce (2 tablespoons) of the filling into each cannoli waffle tube. Top with 1 tablespoon of fudge sauce.

MAKES 12 SERVINGS

384

• EACH SERVING CONTAINS APPROXIMATELY:

CALORIES: **120** | FAT: **2 g** | CHOLESTEROL: **3 mg** | SODIUM: **30 mg** | CARBOHYDRATES: **11 g** | PROTEIN: **4 g**

pear in phyllo

This is both a sumptuous and beautiful dessert. If you prefer, use other sauces on the phyllo-wrapped pears. For chocolate lovers, the fat-free fudge sauce available in jars in supermarkets is a favorite.

4 cups water

1 tablespoon fresh lemon juice

1/4 teaspoon vanilla extract

1 tablespoon honey

2 large ripe bartlett pears, peeled, cored, and halved

2 tablespoons raisins

4 sheets phyllo pastry dough

1 egg white

1. Lightly spray a baking sheet with non-stick cooking spray and set aside.

2. Combine the water, lemon juice, vanilla, and honey in a saucepan and bring to a boil. Add the pear halves, reduce the heat to low, and simmer for 6 to 10 minutes, or until the pears can be pierced easily with the tines of a fork. Lift the pears out of the liquid and set aside. Add the raisins and continue to cook the liquid until reduced to about 1/2 cup. Remove from the heat, cover to keep warm, and set aside to serve as the sauce.

3. Preheat the oven to 325°F.

4. Lay 1 sheet of phyllo flat on a work surface and set 1 pear half in the center. Bring the sides straight up to form a purse or pouch. Using your fingertips, squeeze the sides together and twist slightly to seal. Repeat this process with the remaining phyllo and pears. Carefully transfer them to the prepared baking sheet.

5. Whip the egg white with a whisk or a fork until foamy. Brush each pear bundle with the egg white and bake in the preheated oven for 8 to 10 minutes, or until golden brown.

6. To serve, spoon 2 tablespoons of the raisin sauce on each serving plate and set the phyllo-wrapped pear in the center of the plate.

MAKES 4 SERVINGS

385

• EACH PHYLLO-WRAPPED PEAR HALF CONTAINS APPROXIMATELY:

CALORIES: 130 | FAT: negligible | CHOLESTEROL: 0 | SODIUM: 97 mg | CARBOHYDRATES: 32 g | PROTEIN: 3 g

spa baklava

This is a recipe that I developed for Canyon Ranch many years ago for our first Greek menu. It is still my favorite dessert following a Greek or Middle Eastern meal. For a few pointers on working with phyllo dough, see page 383.

$1/2$ cup walnuts

$1/4$ cup corn oil margarine

$1/2$ cup honey, divided use

1 teaspoon ground cinnamon

pinch ground cloves

$1/2$ teaspoon vanilla extract

$1/2$ pound phyllo pastry dough

1. Preheat the oven to 250°F.

2. Using a food processor with a metal blade, grind the walnuts to the consistency of fine gravel and set aside.

3. Combine the margarine and $1/4$ cup of honey in a saucepan and cook over low heat until the margarine is completely melted. Add the cinnamon, cloves, and vanilla and mix thoroughly.

4. Spray a 10 x 14-inch baking sheet with non-stick cooking spray. On a slightly damp towel, place 1 layer of phyllo dough. Using a pastry brush, lightly brush the entire surface with the honey mixture. Add another layer of phyllo and repeat. Sprinkle the second layer with $1^1/4$ tablespoons of the ground walnuts, leaving a bare edge along one end.

5. Using the towel to help roll the phyllo, roll up (as you would a jelly roll) toward the bare edge and close neatly. Place the roll on the baking sheet. Brush it with another light layer of the honey mixture. Repeat the procedure two more times. Bake in the preheated oven for about 40 minutes, or until golden brown. Watch very closely after 30 minutes because the rolls will brown suddenly. Cool on a wire rack.

6. When the baklava is cool, warm the remaining $1/4$ cup of honey and paint the honey on each roll with a pastry brush. Cut each roll diagonally into about 9 triangular-shaped pieces.

MAKES 3 ROLLS, OR 27 PIECES

• EACH PIECE CONTAINS APPROXIMATELY:

CALORIES: 77 | FAT: 3 g | CHOLESTEROL: 0 | SODIUM: 41 mg | CARBOHYDRATES: 10 g | PROTEIN: 1 g

strawberry-rhubarb crisps

When fresh rhubarb is not available, fresh frozen rhubarb works well in this recipe, or you can omit it completely and double the amount of the strawberries. When using the frozen product, it is not necessary to steam it because it has already been slightly cooked before packaging. Also, you can use the topping in this recipe for fruit crisps of all types.

TOPPING:

1/2 cup packed brown sugar

2 cups unbleached all-purpose flour

1 cup rolled oats

2 tablespoons melted unsalted butter

1 cup frozen apple juice concentrate, undiluted

1 1/2 teaspoons baking powder

1 1/2 teaspoons baking soda

3/4 teaspoon salt

FILLING:

2 cups rhubarb cut in 1-inch pieces

2 cups hulled and quartered strawberries

1 cup light brown sugar

1. Preheat the oven to 375°F.

2. Combine all the topping ingredients in a bowl and mix well.

3. To make the filling, steam the rhubarb for 5 minutes, or until tender but not mushy. Combine the steamed rhubarb, strawberries, and sugar and mix well.

4. Spray eight 1/2-cup ramekins with non-stick cooking spray. Place 1 teaspoon of the topping mixture in the bottom of each cup. Fill with 1/4 cup of the strawberry-rhubarb mixture. Top with 1 tablespoon of the topping mixture.

5. Bake, uncovered, in the preheated oven for 12 to 15 minutes, or until browned and crisp. Serve warm.

MAKES 8 SERVINGS

387

• EACH 1/4-CUP SERVING CONTAINS APPROXIMATELY:

CALORIES: 355 | FAT: 4 g | CHOLESTEROL: 8 mg | SODIUM: 478 mg | CARBOHYDRATES: 76 g | PROTEIN: 5 g

blackberry-orange cobbler

You can cut this recipe in half; however, leftovers can easily be reheated for future meals, and cold cobbler is wonderful for picnics and sack lunches.

3 cups blackberries (12 ounces)

1/2 teaspoon grated or finely chopped orange zest

1/4 cup fructose, divided use

1 tablespoon water

1 tablespoon frozen orange juice concentrate, undiluted

1 egg

3 tablespoons non-fat milk

1 tablespoon unsalted butter, melted

2 tablespoons non-fat sour cream

1/4 teaspoon vanilla extract

1/2 cup unbleached all-purpose flour

1/2 teaspoon baking powder

pinch salt

1. Preheat the oven to 350°F.

2. Mix the blackberries with the orange zest, 2 tablespoons of the fructose, water, and orange juice concentrate. Divide the berries among 6 ramekins, 1/2 cup each. Set aside.

3. Combine the egg, milk, butter, sour cream, vanilla, and the remaining 2 tablespoons of fructose in a bowl. Mix well and set aside.

4. In another bowl combine the flour, baking powder, and salt. Add the dry ingredients to the wet ingredients. Mix to combine just until all the ingredients are moistened. Do not overmix.

5. Spoon 1 1/2 tablespoons of batter on top of the berry mixture in each ramekin. Place the ramekins on a baking sheet and bake in the preheated oven for 15 to 20 minutes, or until the tops are lightly browned.

MAKES 6 SERVINGS

388

• EACH 1/2-CUP SERVING CONTAINS APPROXIMATELY:

CALORIES: **140** | FAT: **3 g** | CHOLESTEROL: **42 mg** | SODIUM: **140 mg** | CARBOHYDRATES: **26 g** | PROTEIN: **3 g**

peach crumble

A crumble, originally an English dessert, can be made from any fresh fruit and topped with a variety of crumbled toppings, such as uncooked cereals or bread or cake crumbs. When fresh peaches are not available, thawed frozen peaches work well in this recipe. For easier handling, place the custard cups on a baking sheet before putting them in the oven. It is difficult to remove the individual cups from the oven without either spilling the contents or burning your hands.

PEACH FILLING:

2 3/4 cups peeled and sliced fresh peaches

pinch ground cinnamon

pinch nutmeg

2 tablespoons fructose

2 teaspoons cornstarch

CRUMBLE TOPPING:

3 tablespoons quick-cooking oats

pinch ground cinnamon

1/4 cup unbleached all-purpose flour

1 tablespoon whole-wheat flour

1 tablespoon plus 1 teaspoon packed brown sugar

2 teaspoons apple juice

1 tablespoon unsalted butter, softened

1. Preheat the oven to 300°F.

2. Lightly spray 6 custard cups with non-stick cooking spray.

3. To prepare the filling, combine the peaches, cinnamon, nutmeg, fructose, and cornstarch in a bowl and mix well. Spoon the mixture into the prepared custard cups.

4. Bake in the preheated oven for 10 to 15 minutes, or until the liquid begins to bubble and thicken.

5. While the peaches are baking, prepare the topping: Combine the oats, cinnamon, flours, and brown sugar in a small bowl and mix well. Stir in the apple juice and butter.

6. Remove the custard cups from the oven and sprinkle the topping over the peaches. Return them to the oven and continue to bake for 10 more minutes, or until lightly browned.

MAKES 6 SERVINGS

• EACH SERVING CONTAINS APPROXIMATELY:

CALORIES: **111** | FAT: **2 g** | CHOLESTEROL: **5 mg** | SODIUM: **1 mg** | CARBOHYDRATES: **22 g** | PROTEIN: **2 g**

lemon panna cotta

Panna cotta is a smooth-textured Italian pudding that is like a custard without the eggs. The name actually means "cooked cream." However, this low-fat version offers a quick, easy, and satisfying spa alternative. It is delicious served with fresh fruit as a breakfast treat or as a healthy dessert. You can vary the taste range in this recipe just by using different extracts, such as almond, coconut, maple, or rum.

2 envelopes unflavored gelatin

¼ cup cool water

4 cups low-fat (1 percent) milk

¼ cup sugar

1 teaspoon vanilla extract

1½ teaspoons pure lemon extract

2 cups diced fresh fruit, optional

4 sprigs fresh mint for garnish, optional

picture-perfect unmolding
You can also unmold any jelled dish by inverting it onto the serving dish and then using a hair dryer to blow hot air on the bottom. This is the method used by many food stylists for photography because it avoids the seepage around the mold caused by dipping it in hot water.

391

1. Soften the gelatin in the cool water and set aside. Combine the milk and sugar in a saucepan and cook over medium heat, stirring frequently, until it comes to a simmer. Remove from the heat, add the dissolved gelatin, and stir until it is completely dissolved. Stir in the vanilla and lemon extracts and divide evenly into 4 molds or custard cups. Refrigerate for at least 4 hours or overnight before unmolding.

2. To serve, dip the molds into hot water and then loosen with a knife if necessary. Unmold each panna cotta on a large plate and arrange ½ cup of the fresh fruit in a circle around it, if desired. Garnish with a mint sprig, if desired.

MAKES 4 SERVINGS

• EACH SERVING CONTAINS APPROXIMATELY:

CALORIES: 168 | FAT: 2 g | CHOLESTEROL: 10 mg | SODIUM: 122 mg | CARBOHYDRATES: 24 g | PROTEIN: 8 g

pumpkin crème brûlée

When making this dessert it is important to place the cooked custards on a baking sheet after removing them from the water bath so that they can all be placed easily and safely under the broiler at the same time.

2 eggs

2 egg whites

1 cup canned pumpkin

¹/₃ cup fructose

¹/₄ teaspoon salt

1 teaspoon ground cinnamon

1 cup canned evaporated skim milk

³/₄ cup (2 percent) milk

1¹/₂ teaspoons vanilla extract

8 teaspoons sugar

392

1. Preheat the oven to 300°F.

2. Spray eight 3-inch ramekins or custard cups with non-stick cooking spray and set aside.

3. Combine the eggs and egg whites in a bowl and lightly whisk them together. Stir in the pumpkin, fructose, salt, and cinnamon. Add the milks and vanilla and mix well.

4. Fill each prepared ramekin with ¹/₂ cup of the mixture.

5. Place the ramekins in a baking dish and add enough boiling water to come up to level of the filling in the cups.

6. Bake in the preheated oven for 40 minutes, or until a knife inserted in the center comes out clean.

7. Remove from the oven, carefully lift out of the water bath, and place on a baking sheet. Preheat the broiler.

8. Evenly spread 1 teaspoon of the sugar on top of each custard. Place the custards under the broiler until the sugar liquefies and turns a dark caramel color. Serve at once.

MAKES 8 SERVINGS

• EACH ¹/₂-CUP SERVING CONTAINS APPROXIMATELY:

CALORIES: **140** | FAT: **2 g** | CHOLESTEROL: **58 mg** | SODIUM: **160 mg** | CARBOHYDRATES: **25 g** | PROTEIN: **6 g**

caramelized custard

This dessert is called flan in Spain, crème caramel in France, and crema caramella in Italy. It is a custard that has been baked in a caramel-coated mold and then chilled. When it's turned upside down onto a plate, it is automatically sauced with the caramel in the mold. In this lower-fat, Canyon Ranch version, the sauce is made separately and then served over the custard to better control the exact amount of sauce on each serving.

CUSTARD:

2 eggs

4 egg whites

1/4 teaspoon salt

1/4 teaspoon fructose

1 1/4 teaspoons vanilla extract

2 cups low-fat (2 percent) milk

CARAMEL SAUCE:

1/2 cup sugar

2 tablespoons water

1/2 teaspoon lemon juice

3 tablespoons water, boiling

ground nutmeg for garnish, optional

1. Preheat the oven to 325°F.

2. Combine all the ingredients for the custard in a bowl and blend with a wire whisk until smooth.

3. Spray 6 ovenproof custard cups with non-stick cooking spray. Spoon 1/2 cup of the custard mixture into each.

4. Bake in a water bath (see box following recipe) in the preheated oven for 35 to 40 minutes, or until firm. A knife inserted in the middle should come out clean. Remove from the oven and cool. Refrigerate until cold.

5. To make the caramel sauce, combine the sugar, 2 tablespoons of water, and lemon juice in a small saucepan. Bring to a boil over high heat to dissolve the sugar. Continue to boil the mixture until the sugar begins to change color slightly. Reduce the heat and simmer about 3 to 4 more minutes, until the mixture becomes a golden color.

water bath

A water bath is a technique used to cook fragile dishes such as custards and sauces without curdling or breaking them. It consists of placing the container of food to be cooked in a larger container of warm water, which then surrounds it with an even, more gentle heat. The French call this technique *bain marie*. It can also be used to keep foods warm.

6. Remove from the heat and cool for 5 minutes.

7. After 5 minutes add boiling water, 1 tablespoon at a time, to the caramel sauce until the desired consistency is achieved.

8. Invert each custard cup onto a dessert plate to unmold. Sprinkle with nutmeg if desired and drizzle 1 teaspoon of caramel sauce over each.

MAKES 6 SERVINGS

• EACH SERVING CONTAINS APPROXIMATELY:

CALORIES: 120 | FAT: 3 g | CHOLESTEROL: 53 mg | SODIUM: 184 mg | CARBOHYDRATES: 18 g | PROTEIN: 6 g

panettone bread pudding

Panettone is a sweet Italian bread that can be served as bread, coffee cake, or dessert. It also makes a sensational bread pudding, and because the bread already has so much taste and texture of its own, it doesn't require the addition of many other ingredients. It is wonderful served warm with a dollop of vanilla frozen yogurt or ice milk. Panettone is available in some supermarkets and all Italian markets.

1 can (12 ounces) evaporated skim milk

4 egg whites

¼ cup sugar

1 teaspoon vanilla extract

2 tablespoons melted butter or corn oil margarine

1 pound panettone, cut into ½-inch cubes (8 cups)

panettone
Panettone is a sweet Italian bread made with raisins, citron, pine nuts, and anise. Originating in Milan, it is usually baked in a cylindrical shape and served for holiday gatherings and celebrations such as Christmas and weddings.

1. Preheat the oven to 350°F.

2. Combine all the ingredients except the cubed bread in a large bowl and mix well. Stir in the bread and allow to soak for 5 minutes.

3. Spray an 8 x 8-inch pan with non-stick cooking spray. Spoon the mixture into the prepared pan and bake in the preheated oven for about 35 minutes, or until firm. Cool on a rack for at least 10 minutes before cutting into 12 pieces.

MAKES 12 SERVINGS

• EACH SERVING CONTAINS APPROXIMATELY:

CALORIES: **181** | FAT: **5 g** | CHOLESTEROL: **33 mg** | SODIUM: **205 mg** | CARBOHYDRATES: **28 g** | PROTEIN: **6 g**

peanut butter pudding

Everyone who knows me knows how much I love peanut butter and that I am always working on new and unusual ways to use it. This easy-to-make pudding is one of my favorites. I have purposely used a little more liquid with the 1 envelope of gelatin than is called for on the package. The reason for this is that I wanted a creamy, custardlike texture rather than a firmly jelled pudding. For an even creamier texture, use a cream-style peanut butter rather than the chunky style called for in this recipe. You can also make this recipe in a pie pan, on either a regular or a graham cracker crust, and call it Peanut Butter Pie.

3 tablespoons water

1 envelope unflavored gelatin

1¹/2 cups canned evaporated skim milk (12 ounces)

1 cup non-fat milk

¹/3 cup chunky unhomogenized peanut butter (see page 329)

3/4 cup packed dark brown sugar

1 tablespoon vanilla extract

1. Add the water to the gelatin and allow to soften.

2. Combine the canned evaporated milk, non-fat milk, peanut butter, and brown sugar in a saucepan and cook over medium heat, stirring constantly with a wire whisk. Just before the mixture comes to a boil, remove from the heat. (If allowed to boil, the mixture will separate and have a grainy texture. This does not ruin the taste, but it does detract from the appearance.) Add the vanilla and gelatin and mix well. Allow to cool to room temperature.

3. Pour ¹/2 cup in each of 6 ramekins or custard cups. Refrigerate for at least 4 hours before serving. If you do not have small ramekins, pour the mixture into 1 larger dish.

MAKES 6 SERVINGS

397

• EACH ¹/2-CUP SERVING CONTAINS APPROXIMATELY:

CALORIES: **261** | FAT: **7 g** | CHOLESTEROL: **3 mg** | SODIUM: **191 mg** | CARBOHYDRATES: **29 g** | PROTEIN: **21 g**

raspberry cream parfait

If you don't have parfait glasses, then use a juice glass or any clear container for this dessert. It is pretty garnished with a couple of fresh raspberries and a sprig of mint.

8 cups fresh raspberries, divided use

1/3 cup fructose

2 tablespoons unbleached all-purpose flour

1 1/2 cups (9 whole crackers) reduced-fat chocolate graham cracker crumbs

2 tablespoons unsweetened applesauce

1 tablespoon warm water

1 cup fat-free cream cheese, at room temperature

1. Set aside 2 cups of the raspberries. Combine the remaining 6 cups of raspberries, fructose, and flour in a saucepan and cook over low heat until the raspberries break apart and the mixture thickens, about 10 minutes. Remove from the heat and allow to cool to room temperature. Cover tightly and refrigerate until cold.

2. Combine the graham cracker crumbs, applesauce, and water in a bowl and mix well. Press 3 tablespoons of the mixture into the bottom of each of 8 parfait glasses. Top the crumbs in each glass with 1/4 cup of the reserved fresh raspberries.

3. Combine the chilled raspberry mixture and cream cheese in a blender or food processor and blend until smooth. Top each serving with about 1/2 cup of the blended mixture. Refrigerate for at least 2 hours before serving.

MAKES 8 SERVINGS

• EACH 3/4-CUP SERVING WITH CRUST CONTAINS APPROXIMATELY:

CALORIES: **212** | FAT: **3 g** | CHOLESTEROL: **0** | SODIUM: **189 mg** | CARBOHYDRATES: **44 g** | PROTEIN: **5 g**

spiced guava-strawberry sorbet

This gorgeous and unusual dessert is a favorite at Canyon Ranch. If you don't want to take the time to make the pizzelle cups, just serve it in sherbet glasses garnished with fanned strawberries.

1½ cups peeled and chopped
   fresh guava

1 cup chopped fresh strawberries

½ cup plus 2 tablespoons water

1 teaspoon ground allspice

3 tablespoons sugar

1½ teaspoons fresh lime juice

8 pizzelle cups (see page 377),
   optional

1. Combine all the ingredients, except the pizzelle cups if you are using them, in a bowl and mix well. Transfer the mixture to a sorbet or ice cream maker and run for 20 minutes, or until the desired firmness is reached. Freeze until ready to serve.

2. To serve, scoop ⅓ cup of sorbet into a pizzelle cup or sherbet glass.

MAKES 8 SERVINGS

399

• EACH ⅓-CUP SERVING IN A PIZZELLE CUP CONTAINS APPROXIMATELY:

CALORIES: 40 | FAT: negligible | CHOLESTEROL: 0 | SODIUM: 1 mg | CARBOHYDRATES: 10 g | PROTEIN: negligible

beverages

Everyone who has ever been to a Canyon Ranch resort knows the importance we place on water. When you check in you are given your own water bottle to make it easier for you to drink at least 8 glasses of water each day. Water is by far the healthiest beverage in the world, and we are delighted that it has finally come into its own as a status drink. You can now buy bottled water from almost every place in the world, plain or sparkling, flavored or natural, and with price tags ranging from nominal to outrageous. For anyone on a low-sodium diet, there are now many low-sodium soda waters available, as well as bottled distilled water, which is completely sodium-free.

There was a time when your guests would have been rather surprised, if not shocked, to have been offered water at a cocktail party. Now that it is the beverage of choice among many fitness-oriented young urban professionals, it is considered chic in many circles to serve a variety of waters at parties. For a still more sophisticated water beverage offer your guests a Canyon Ranch Cocktail. We have been serving this counterfeit cocktail before dinner at Canyon Ranch since the day we opened in December 1979 and the recipe for it starts this chapter.

Also included here are our delicious Lemonade, our truly special Strawberry Daiquiri, and many of our most popular fruit shakes.

canyon ranch cocktail

This "cocktail" has a decided advantage over most non-alcoholic drinks in that it is not sweet, the calories are negligible, and it is low in sodium. You can serve this pretty pink drink in a stemmed wineglass, a highball glass, or a beer mug. Most bars and cocktail lounges have all the ingredients so you can order it when dining out as well as preparing it at home. When combining sparkling water and Angostura bitters, always pour the water in the glass and then add the bitters to it. If you put the bitters in first, then add the sparkling water, it will foam up so vigorously that it will overflow the glass.

sparkling water

angostura bitters

fresh lime or lemon juice, optional

a word about bitters
The story of how Angostura aromatic bitters were originally developed by the young and dashing Dr. J. G. B. Siegert reads like a romance novel. Dr. Siegert was a German army surgeon who had achieved distinction in the Napoleonic Wars. In 1820, he joined the great General Simón Bolívar in the fight for South American independence. Seeking to develop a cure for the stomach disorders that were a constant problem among the troops, he experimented tirelessly with herbs and spices from all over the world. After four years of research, he perfected the formula for Angostura aromatic bitters, named for the city in which he lived. His formula quickly became famous throughout the world as an aid to digestion, a pick-me-up, and an essential ingredient in many mixed drinks.

1. Fill the glass with sparkling water.

2. Add a couple of dashes of the bitters, or enough to make the drink a pretty pink color.

3. Add lime or lemon juice to taste, if desired.

402

• EACH SERVING CONTAINS APPROXIMATELY:

CALORIES: **negligible** | FAT: **negligible** | CHOLESTEROL: **negligible** | SODIUM: **negligible** | CARBOHYDRATES: **negligible** | PROTEIN: **negligible**

carob cooler

This delightful impostor can be served cold or hot in place of either cocoa or cappuccino. If serving it hot, omit the ice when blending and heat the blended mixture before serving.

⅓ cup low-fat (2 percent) milk

1½ teaspoons carob powder

2 tablespoons non-fat milk powder

¾ teaspoon fructose

¾ teaspoon vanilla extract

⅔ cup crushed ice

Combine all the ingredients in a blender and blend until smooth.

MAKES 1 CUP, OR 1 SERVING

carob
Carob comes from the pod of the tropical carob tree. It has a sweet edible pulp, which after drying is roasted and ground into powder. The powder both looks and tastes a bit like chocolate and is often used as a substitute for chocolate in health food products.

403

• EACH SERVING CONTAINS APPROXIMATELY:

CALORIES: **103** | FAT: **4 g** | CHOLESTEROL: **7 mg** | SODIUM: **68 mg** | CARBOHYDRATES: **12 g** | PROTEIN: **5 g**

strawberry daiquiri

This beautiful and refreshing drink is a perfect substitute for a fancy alcoholic beverage at cocktail parties.

1 quart frozen strawberries

4 teaspoons rum extract

3 tablespoons fructose

4 teaspoons fresh lemon juice

2/3 cup fresh orange juice

1 cup crushed ice

1. Combine all the ingredients in a blender and blend until smooth.

2. Serve immediately in a stemmed cocktail glass.

MAKES 6 CUPS, OR 8 (3/4-CUP) SERVINGS

• EACH SERVING CONTAINS APPROXIMATELY:

CALORIES: 48 | FAT: negligible | CHOLESTEROL: 0 | SODIUM: 1 mg | CARBOHYDRATES: 11 g | PROTEIN: negligible

404

lemonade

For a sparkling lemonade, use a sparkling water in place of the plain water in this recipe. To keep from diluting the lemonade with ice cubes, make the ice cubes out of lemonade to chill the drink. For Limeade, use fresh lime juice instead of lemon juice.

3/4 cup fresh lemon juice

1/4 cup fructose

3 cups water

1. Combine the lemon juice and fructose in a pitcher and stir until the fructose is completely dissolved. Add the water and mix well.

2. Refrigerate until cold before serving or serve over ice cubes.

MAKES 1 QUART, OR 4 (1-CUP) SERVINGS

• EACH SERVING CONTAINS APPROXIMATELY:

CALORIES: 47 | FAT: 0 | CHOLESTEROL: 0 | SODIUM: 7 mg | CARBOHYDRATES: 13 g | PROTEIN: negligible

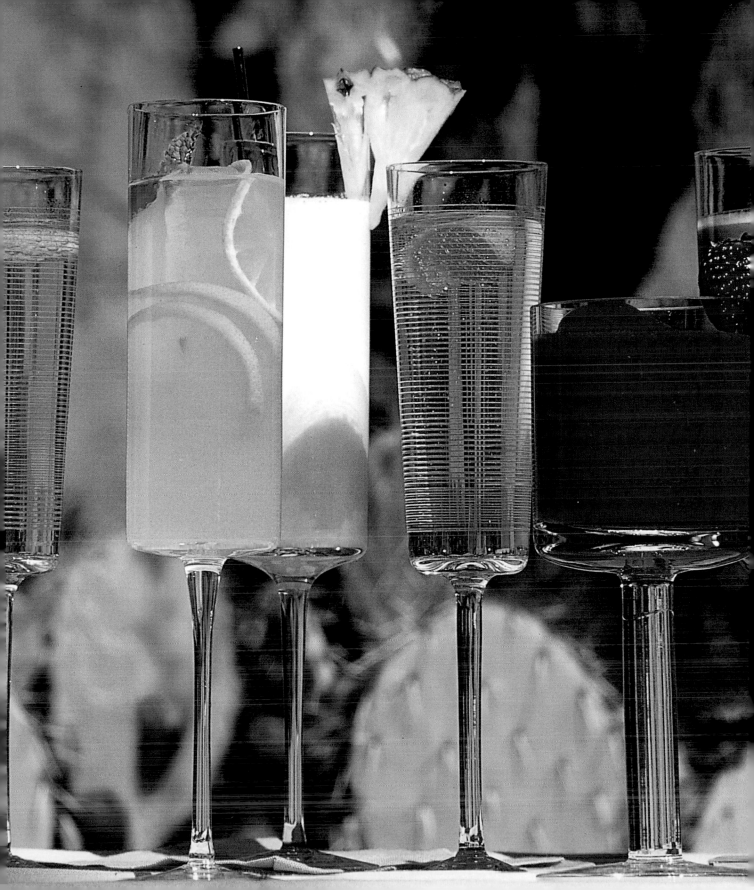

banana peanut butter punch

For peanut butter lovers, this is the ultimate way to take a healthy milk break. The frozen banana gives the punch a thick, creamy texture and so much sweetness that you don't need any sugar. It also adds a lot of both potassium and vitamin C. In fact, this nutritious drink is literally a meal in itself and is often served at Canyon Ranch as our shake of the day.

1 cup non-fat milk

1/2 cup frozen banana slices

1 1/2 tablespoons unhomogenized peanut butter (see page 329)

1/4 teaspoon ground cinnamon

1/2 teaspoon vanilla extract

ground cinnamon or nutmeg for garnish, optional

Combine all the ingredients, except the garnish, in a blender and blend until smooth and creamy. Pour into a tall glass and garnish with a sprinkle of ground cinnamon or nutmeg, if desired.

MAKES ABOUT 13/4 CUPS, OR 1 SERVING

about frozen bananas
All blended banana drinks are better made with frozen bananas. It gives them a thicker, creamier consistency. Peel and slice ripe bananas and store them in airtight Ziploc plastic bags in the freezer.

• EACH SERVING CONTAINS APPROXIMATELY:

CALORIES: **334** | FAT: **13 g** | CHOLESTEROL: **4 mg** | SODIUM: **243 mg** | CARBOHYDRATES: **44 g** | PROTEIN: **15 g**

paradise punch

This refreshing tropical drink is great for breakfast or as a pick-me-up snack any time of the day.

1/2 cup non-fat milk

1/2 cup unsweetened pineapple juice

2 tablespoons non-fat cottage cheese

1/2 teaspoon sugar

1/4 teaspoon vanilla extract

1/4 teaspoon coconut extract

2 ice cubes, crushed

1. Combine all the ingredients in a blender and blend until smooth.

2. Serve in a chilled glass.

MAKES ABOUT 1 1/2 CUPS, OR 1 SERVING

• EACH SERVING CONTAINS APPROXIMATELY:

CALORIES: 143 | FAT: negligible | CHOLESTEROL: 5 mg | SODIUM: 157 mg | CARBOHYDRATES: 26 g | PROTEIN: 8 g

blueberry shake

This shake is great for breakfast or as a calcium-rich snack any time of the day. Any frozen fruit can be substituted for the blueberries in this shake; when using raspberries, strain the shake before serving.

1/2 cup frozen blueberries, unthawed

2 teaspoons fructose

2/3 cup non-fat milk

1 tablespoon non-fat milk powder

Combine all the ingredients in a blender and blend until smooth.

MAKES 1 1/4 CUPS, OR 1 SERVING

the reasons behind frozen fruit
Never thaw the fruit before making a fruit drink or it won't be as thick and rich-tasting. In fact, when using fresh fruit it is better to freeze it before using it to make shakes. When frozen fruit is not available, crushed ice will also serve to both chill and thicken the drink, but it dilutes it as well.

• EACH SERVING CONTAINS APPROXIMATELY:

CALORIES: **126** | FAT: **negligible** | CHOLESTEROL: **3 mg** | SODIUM: **94 mg** | CARBOHYDRATES: **25 g** | PROTEIN: **6 g**

orange shake

This tasty beverage is reminiscent of the famous frothy orange drink, named for a Roman emperor, so frequently found in shopping malls.

¹/3 cup low-fat (2 percent) milk

1 tablespoon non-fat milk powder

2¹/2 teaspoons fructose

2¹/2 teaspoons frozen orange juice concentrate, undiluted

3/4 teaspoon vanilla extract

¹/2 cup crushed ice

Combine all the ingredients in a blender and blend until smooth.

MAKES 1 CUP, OR 1 SERVING

• EACH SERVING CONTAINS APPROXIMATELY:

CALORIES: 85 | FAT: 1 g | CHOLESTEROL: 6 mg | SODIUM: 50 mg | CARBOHYDRATES: 14 g | PROTEIN: 3 g

peanut butter shake

For a higher-protein vegetarian breakfast, omit the ice in this recipe and pour the peanut butter shake mixture over your favorite cereal.

4 teaspoons unhomogenized peanut butter (see page 329)

¹/2 cup non-fat milk

3 tablespoons non-fat milk powder

1 teaspoon fructose

1 teaspoon vanilla extract

²/3 cup crushed ice

Combine all the ingredients in a blender and blend until smooth.

MAKES 1 CUP, OR 1 SERVING

• EACH SERVING CONTAINS APPROXIMATELY:

CALORIES: 286 | FAT: 11 g | CHOLESTEROL: 7 mg | SODIUM: 271 mg | CARBOHYDRATES: 26 g | PROTEIN: 18 g

soy shake

This rich, creamy, and nutritious non-dairy beverage is a tasty addition to any breakfast. It's also a great way to take a healthy drink break at any time. You can make it in minutes if you already have frozen banana slices in your freezer. If you don't, peel and slice a couple of ripe bananas, put the slices in a Ziploc plastic bag, and place them in the freezer until frozen solid. For variety you can substitute other fruit juices, such as orange, pineapple, or prune, for the apple juice called for in this recipe.

10½ ounces lite tofu (see page 35)

1¼ cups unsweetened apple juice

1½ cups frozen banana slices

3/4 cup water

Combine all the ingredients in a blender and blend until smooth.

MAKES ABOUT 6 CUPS, OR 3 (2-CUP) SERVINGS

Keeping frozen banana slices in your freezer at all times is a wonderful quick tip. They add both taste and a creamy texture to many beverages and can also be used to make instant sorbet just by pureeing them in a juicer or a food processor.

• EACH SERVING CONTAINS APPROXIMATELY:

CALORIES: 134 | FAT: 1 g | CHOLESTEROL: 0 | SODIUM: 89 mg | CARBOHYDRATES: 26 g | PROTEIN: 7 g

banana yogurt smoothie

Not only is this a delicious drink, but it is also a superb topping for cereal of all types.

3/4 cup fruit-flavored non-fat yogurt

1 teaspoon honey

1 small banana

1/2 cup non-fat milk

pinch ground cinnamon, optional

1. Combine all the ingredients, except the cinnamon, in a blender and blend until smooth.

2. Serve in an attractive glass, garnishing the top with a dusting of cinnamon, if desired.

MAKES ABOUT 14 OUNCES, OR 2 (SCANT 1-CUP) SERVINGS

411

• EACH SERVING CONTAINS APPROXIMATELY:

CALORIES: 115 | FAT: negligible | CHOLESTEROL: negligible | SODIUM: 58 mg | CARBOHYDRATES: 25 g | PROTEIN: 4 g

canyon ranch menus

Most people are well aware of the importance of good nutrition and try to eat in a healthy manner most of the time—except when they're entertaining. Then all the stops are pulled because they wrongly think that they can't please or impress their company with anything but traditional high-fat menus. When planning your next party, pretend you are going to be the guest. In other words, design a Canyon Ranch menu that you would like to be served if you were someone else's company. You will be amazed at the difference it will make in your menu planning and how appreciative your guests will be.

The following 6 menus of varying types are designed to help you get started. You can either follow them exactly or simply use them as guidelines to create your own. Ultimately, your personal touch is what makes your parties special.

Brunch
Vegetarian Luncheon
Southwestern Fiesta
Asian Medley
Middle Eastern Picnic
Holiday Feast

BRUNCH

The word brunch, a contraction of the words breakfast and lunch, is generally used to describe a meal served later than breakfast but earlier than lunch. Traditionally, brunch is more popular as a meal shared by family and friends on Sunday than on any other day of the week. However, this Canyon Ranch menu can also be used for a luncheon or a light supper.

Mixed Melon Soup
Individual Vegetable Frittatas
Hazelnut Bread

VEGETARIAN LUNCHEON

When hosting a luncheon, especially for a special occasion such as a birthday party, graduation, bridal shower, or watching a football game, this make-ahead vegetarian menu will allow you the time to enjoy your own party and serve your guests a memorable meal. We serve the salad as a vegetarian entree at Canyon Ranch; however, it is also good with water-packed tuna or diced cooked poultry or meat added to it. This menu also adapts well for buffet service.

Zucchini Bisque
Wild Rice Salad
Sweet Potato Cream Cheese Pie

SOUTHWESTERN FIESTA

The robust tastes and spicy aromas of Southwestern cuisine have become popular all over the world. At Canyon Ranch in Tucson, the center of the Southwest, this unique and flavorful cuisine is extremely popular with our guests. For your next fiesta, decorate your garden or patio with colorful piñatas and serve your guests authentic Canyon Ranch Southwestern dishes.

Ecuadorian Shrimp Ceviche
Corn Chowder with Chipotle Peppers
Chicken Fajitas
Caramelized Custard

ASIAN MEDLEY

At Canyon Ranch we serve a variety of Asian cuisines. Their cooking places great importance on the color, fragrance, taste, form, and nutritional benefits of the dishes served. This menu is comprised of our most popular Asian dishes. Start your party by giving all of your guests chopsticks to eat with—you can always have forks handy for backup.

Miso Soup
Asian Scallop Stir-Fry
Asian Pasta
Spiced Guava-Strawberry Sorbet

MIDDLE EASTERN PICNIC

This picnic menu is ideal for a portable meal of any kind. It can be prepared ahead of time and transported safely without refrigeration. For a glamorous Middle Eastern picnic, spread Persian rugs out on the beach or in a park and pack colorful plates and napkins in your basket to complete the exotic theme. Instead of volleyball, why not try belly dancing? It's great exercise and perfect for burning calories!

Hummus with Roasted Red Pepper Sauce
Whole-Wheat Pita Bread
Tabbouleh
Grilled Vegetable Sandwich on Lavash Bread
Spa Baklava
Fresh Seasonal Fruit

HOLIDAY FEAST

At Canyon Ranch we serve our holiday meals in courses, just as we serve all our other meals. However, traditionally at home, most holiday meals are served family style, with all the serving dishes on the table. This manner of serving makes the meal more relaxed and informal, and it doesn't matter if the food isn't piping hot. In fact, food historians tell us that in colonial times all food was served closer to room temperature. With this in mind, cooking and serving this holiday meal should be easy and lots of fun. Also, every dish on this menu can be prepared a day or two ahead of time to prevent any last-minute stress for the host or hostess. Another remarkable fact about this meal is that if you eat a serving of everything on the entire menu, the total adds up to only 758 calories, with just 7 grams of fat. That means that one of your special gifts for your family and friends is a sumptuous holiday feast with less than 5 percent of the calories coming from fat!

Sweet Potato Soup
Cold Pea Salad
Turkey with Mushroom Apple Gravy
Cranberry Concassé
Mashed Potato and Shallot Casserole
Herbed Vegetable Medley
Cherry Streusel Pie

planning your canyon ranch weekend at home

Most of us want to stay in good shape and everyone loves to be pampered. What better way to do this than create a Canyon Ranch Weekend in your own home with a few of your friends. An even number works best for many of the partner stretches and exercises you might want to do, so it's best to invite an uneven number of other people to join you for the weekend.

Planning is an essential part of a successful spa weekend and allows you to have everything you need at hand, creating a more enjoyable time for you as well as for your guests. From the time people arrive through the entire weekend, you should have as enjoyable and relaxing a weekend experience as your guests.

Your guests will probably arrive at your home Friday evening following a stress-filled day at work or a hectic day at home dealing with spouses, children, and pets, so the first thing on the agenda is for everyone to completely unwind and relax. The sound of ocean waves or falling rain in the background is very soothing, and both are available on tapes and CDs. Having a written schedule of planned activities available for each participant will help set the scene for the weekend and add to everyone's anticipation.

Meals for the weekend should follow the same nutritional guidelines we use in meal planning at Canyon Ranch. This means paying attention to your feelings of hunger and how they are satisfied, as well as truly enjoying your food and being aware of its many nutritional qualities. It also means slowing down to allow sufficient time for not only enjoying your meals more but also allowing time for the brain to respond and let you know when you are no longer hungry. This is the time when you should stop eating, not when you feel full. Indulge your preferences for flavors and textures, plan exciting and delicious as well as healthy meals for the weekend, and savor the sensory experience that eating should be. You should never feel deprived, even when you are trying to lose weight.

Plan sinless parties for your guests, complete with non-alcoholic cocktails, like the Canyon Ranch Cocktail (see page 402), Strawberry Daiquiri(see page 404), or maybe just a tall glass of Lemonade (see page 404). Serve spa hors d'oeuvres such as Garbanzo Nuts or Eggplant Caviar (see pages 44 and 41). Have fun planning creative Canyon Ranch menus for every breakfast, lunch, and dinner using the recipes in this book. Let your imagination run wild!

Decorations, table settings, spa activities, and all accessories needed for your weekend should be purchased well in advance. Even additional sleeping accommodations can be handled easily and efficiently. Whatever you need can be either rented or purchased at local sporting goods stores, department stores, and even some grocery stores. For example, if you need more beds, air mattresses may be purchased at sporting goods stores for about $35, or roll-away beds can be rented for the weekend for as little as $25. If you are adventurous and pool your costs with your friends, for approximately $200 you can rent a canopy with sides and sleep outdoors in the fresh air on your rented beds or air mattresses. Summer is an ideal time for a spa weekend because so many of the activities can be done outdoors, including your morning walks, swimming, and doing stretching, exercising, or yoga on a grassy area. Even just relaxing and taking a nap in a hammock in between activities is rejuvenating. However, indoor activities also work well if you designate one room in the house to be the gym or workout room. Have a television with a VCR available for yoga, stretching, strengthening, and aerobic tapes. Furniture can be removed and replaced with exercise mats, a few workout benches, dumbbells, and several mirrors propped against the walls. If possible, a stationary exercise bike and treadmill would be great pieces of equipment for your gym as well.

On their arrival, you might want to give your guests their own water bottles, which they can keep as both a memento of the weekend and as a reminder of the importance of continuing to drink at least 8 glasses of water a day when the weekend is over.

Plan your first evening meal so that everything can be prepared in advance and all you have to do is preheat the oven for the entree, toss the salad, and serve the dessert. Since the Greeks are credited with first telling us about the importance of physical fitness and started the Olympic Games, why not start off your fitness weekend with a Greek meal. An ideal make-ahead menu could include Greek Salad (see page 107), Pastitsio (see page 290), and Spa Baklava (see page 386), with fresh fruit for dessert.

While the meal is cooking, the appetizing aromas from the kitchen will further add to the ambiance, and you and your friends can relax out on the patio or in front of a crackling fire with your Canyon Ranch Cocktails (see page 402) and begin the unwinding process. At some point you can either quietly excuse yourself to finish preparing the evening meal or invite your guests into the kitchen to help you get everything ready to serve. You can serve dinner on trays or buffet style and let your guests help themselves. If you want to create a more formal setting, have your table set for a sit-down dinner. After dinner your guests may want to talk, read, listen to music, or watch an old movie. Or maybe just get to bed early.

A Saturday morning walk is a wonderful way to start the day and get you warmed up for some stretching exercises. If you're close to the beach, it's a great place for an early morning walk. However, walks on the trails in local parks and hills can also be very enjoyable. In fact, any variety of locations around your neighborhood can work well for group walks and be lots of fun. Just do a little homework and plan the walking course ahead of time. A pair of comfortable walking shoes and a bottle of water are the only essential parts of your walking uniform, unless, of course, you want to go a step further and have sweat shirts or T-shirts made with your "spa" logo on them for your weekend. Also, if you're walking in the sun, protect your skin with sunscreen and wear a hat to shade your face.

A breakfast shake, such as a Banana Yogurt Smoothie (see page 411) or an Orange or Blueberry Shake (see pages 409 and 408), is a perfect light morning snack before your walk, and it can be prepared in just minutes. When you return you can have the rest of your breakfast all ready by setting up a bagel or muffin buffet with Fitness Cheese (see page 361) and Fresh Apple Butter (see page 359) for toppings and a selection of colorful fresh fruits. It's easy to prepare and a snap to clean up. Following breakfast you're ready to get started on the activities planned for the rest of the day.

If a swimming pool is available, a swim and exercises in the shallow end of the pool are very refreshing after a walk. Midmorning is a good time to swim because the sun's rays are not as strong and the chance of burning is not as much of a problem. If a pool is not available, you can start the morning in your gym with a stretching tape on the VCR, followed by an aerobic workout led by a member of the group or the person on your favorite exercise tape. (Remember, you'll burn $1^1/2$ calories per minute while you're sitting, 5 per minute during a brisk walk, and serious aerobic exercise increases that number to 15 calories per minute.)

Lunch can be served at home, either in or out-of-doors buffet style, or packed as a picnic to enjoy on the beach or at a nearby park. There are a number of easy-to-pack salads and sandwiches in this book. One of my favorites is the Grilled Vegetable Sandwich on Lavash Bread (see page 178), or you can prepare the entire Middle Eastern Picnic in the Canyon Ranch Menus chapter (see page 412).

After lunch, the warm herbal baths can begin. In case only one bathtub is available, a schedule would be a good idea to allow everyone a turn to luxuriate in the warm scented water. While guests are waiting for their turns in the herbal bath, they can exercise, either alone or as a group.

You might even want to acquire tapes on massage techniques. Then, with massage oils available, your guests can decide whether they would like to learn how to give each other massages. The rest of the afternoon could be left open to let everyone do whatever he or she likes best: relax, swim, or work out with weights or exercise tapes.

A theme party for dinner on Saturday night can be lots of fun. For example, you could have a Mexican fiesta, an Asian feast, or a Texas barbecue and tell your friends in advance what the theme is going to be so that they can bring appropriate attire. And, of course, you would want to plan the menu to match the theme of the evening. For a Mexican fiesta serve baked chips with Tomato Salsa and Canyon Ranch Guacamole (see pages 324 and 36), Gazpacho (see page 58), Fish Tacos or Cheese Enchiladas (see pages 209 and 164) and Caramelized Custard (see page 394) with fresh fruit for dessert. For an Asian Feast, serve Hot and Sour Soup (see page 76), Cucumber Raita (see page 40) with mini rice cakes, Asian Scallop Stir-Fry or Vegetable Tofu Stir-Fry (see pages 230 and 193), and Spiced Guava-Strawberry Sorbet (see page 399) for dessert. For a Texas Barbecue, serve baked chips with Tofu Guacamole (see page 35), Coleslaw (see page 99), Barbecued Chicken with Oven Fries (see pages 239 and 301) or Vegetarian Chili with Jalapeño Corn Bread (see page 195 and 340), and Peach Crumble (see page 390) for dessert.

Sunday morning should mark the end of a happy and healthy weekend. After a walk and a workout, your guests will be ready for a memorable Canyon Ranch brunch. You might want to have cooking stations where they can prepare their own omelets, pancakes, or waffles. If possible, have them gather around one table for their last meal together before reentering the outside world. Who knows, it may even lead to a discussion about when and where the next Canyon Ranch Weekend at Home is going to take place!

IN GRATEFUL ACKNOWLEDGMENT

Barry Correia, Executive Chef, Canyon Ranch in the Berkshires
John Luzader, Executive Chef, Canyon Ranch in Tucson

index

422

423

429

433

435

436